ET   29456

Deinstitutionalization
and Institutional Reform

Deinstitutionalization
and Institutional Reform

By

R. C. SCHEERENBERGER, Ph.D.

*Superintendent, Central Wisconsin
Colony and Training School
Madison, Wisconsin
Past President, National Association of
Superintendents of Public Residential
Facilities for the Mentally Retarded*

CHARLES C THOMAS • PUBLISHER
Springfield • Illinois • U.S.A.

Published and Distributed Throughout the World by
CHARLES C THOMAS ● PUBLISHER
Bannerstone House
301-327 East Lawrence Avenue, Springfield, Illinois, U.S.A.

© *1976, by* CHARLES C THOMAS ● PUBLISHER
ISBN 0-398-03552-0
Library of Congress Catalog Card Number: 75-45404

With THOMAS BOOKS *careful attention is given to all details of
manufacturing and design. It is the Publisher's desire to present books that are
satisfactory as to their physical qualities and artistic possibilities and
appropriate for their particular use.* THOMAS BOOKS *will be true to those
laws of quality that assure a good name and good will.*

Printed in the United States of America
R-1

Library of Congress Cataloging in Publication Data
Scheerenberger, R C
  Deinstitutionalization and institutional reform.

  Bibliography: p.
  Includes indexes.
    1. Mentally handicapped.   2. Mental retardation
facilities.   8. Mental retardation services.
I. Title. [DNLM: 1. Mental retardation.   2. Mental
retardation--Legislation.   3. Residential facilities.
4. Residential facilities--Legislation.
WM300 S315d.
HV3004.S337   344'.73'0323   75-45404
ISBN 0-398-03552-0

to Emilie, Dana and Matt

PREFACE

THE current emphasis on both deinstitutionalization and institutional reform is based on a heightened sense of responsibility for the recognition of the rights of the mentally retarded and other developmentally disabled citizens. This heightened sense of responsibility is reflected in a growing concern that each retarded person in need of services receives them in the least restrictive environment possible, preferably in his home and/or community. If residential programming is required, that program must be individually designed and offered in an atmosphere which fosters total development and independence.

For purposes of this text, a residential facility (or institution) is defined as "an organizational entity that has physical identity and administrative integrity and conducts a program of services directed primarily to enhancing the health, welfare, and development of individuals classified as mentally retarded. The primary purpose of a residential facility is to protect and nurture the dignity, health, and development of each individual requiring 24-hour programming services"* (Joint Commission on Accreditation of Hospitals, 1971). While this definition covers a wide variety of residential facilities, the major concern of the discussions to follow is with the large state-operated residential facility.

Inasmuch as these dual, interrelated topics of deinstitutionalization and institutional reform are of interest to many people with widely diverse backgrounds, an effort has been made to place both subjects in some perspective. For this reason the discussions of deinstitutionalization and institutional reform are preceded by several chapters on mental retardation, residential living, the current status of residential programs and litigation.

The entire field of mental retardation is in transition; many

---

*Joint Commission on Accreditation of Hospitals, *Standards for Residential Facilities for the Mentally Retarded.* (Chicago, Joint Commission on Accreditation of Hospitals, 1971.)

changes have occurred, are occurring and will continue to occur throughout the foreseeable future. Both community services and the residential components will be affected. Thus, the discussions to follow represent a state-of-the-art analysis rather than a final report. Nevertheless, the contents should assist in expediting an understanding of current philosophies, trends and problems as they relate to deinstitutionalization and, at the same time, provide a basis upon which to interpret future developments. In this way it is hoped that the book will be of value to parents, interested lay persons, students and professionals.

ACKNOWLEDGMENTS

I WISH to express my gratitude to Stephen Jones, Ph.D., and Robert St. John, M.S.W., for reading the original manuscript and for offering many pertinent observations and suggestions. I am most appreciative of the efforts of Lois Murray, Kathy Reiner, Jan Erickson and Pam Kilen in preparing the manuscript for publication. Many thanks also to Shirley Thompson for photographing the tables and figures.

R.C.S.

CONTENTS

Deinstitutionalization
and Institutional Reform

Chapter 1

MENTAL RETARDATION

T HE underlying philosophy of this text is that deinstitutionalization is a highly desirable goal for all but a relatively small number of retarded persons. For the latter, institutional reform is critical. In order to place these statements in perspective, it is necessary to start by reviewing briefly some of the more salient aspects of mental retardation as they relate to deinstitutionalization and institutional reform. Since this discussion will be very limited, persons interested in a more comprehensive overview of mental retardation are referred to such basic texts as Robinson and Robinson (1965), Smith (1971), Baroff (1974), and Kauffman and Payne (1975).

MENTAL RETARDATION DEFINED

Mental retardation is a generic term which identifies a relatively large group of persons whose intellectual functioning and related behaviors, for any one of several hundred known reasons, are significantly below those of the population in general. As defined by the original President's Panel on Mental Retardation (1962) mental retardation "is a simple designation for a group of complex phenomena stemming from many different causes but one key common characteristic found in all cases is inadequately developed intelligence."

Mental retardation, regardless of its cause or form, is determined primarily on the basis of the sociocultural standards of the given society. Kanner (1949) aptly illustrates the relativity of mental retardation,

> In less complex, less intellectually centered societies, the mentally retarded would have no trouble in obtaining and retaining a quality of realizable ambitions. Some might even be capable of gaining superiority by virtue of assets other than those mea-

3

sured by the intelligence test. They could make successful peas-
ants, hunters, fishermen, tribal dancers. They can, in our own
society, achieve proficiency as farm hands, factory workers,
miners, waitresses...Their principle shortcoming is a greater
or lesser degree of inability to comply with the intellectual requirements of their society. In other respects, they may be as
mature or immature, stable or unstable, secure or insecure,
placid or moody, aggressive or submissive, as any other member
of the human species. Their "deficiency" is an *ethnologically
determined phenomena* relative to the local standards and even
within those standards, relative to the educational postulates,
vocational ambitions, and family expectancies. They are "sub-
cultural" in our society but may not be even that in a different,
less sophisticated setting.

Thus, in a society which places little emphasis on intellectual
pursuits, a person's intelligence, especially its verbal dimensions,
may be of little or no significance, and that person may never be
identified as possessing any peculiar characteristics. This is not,
however, the situation in the United States. At some time during
their lives, most retarded individuals become visible and require
special assistance.

The most commonly accepted definition of mental retardation
is that promulgated by the American Association on Mental
Deficiency (Grossman, 1973), **"Mental retardation refers to significantly subaverage general intellectual functioning existing concurrently with deficits in adaptive behavior, and manifested
during the developmental period."**

In order to comprehend the implications of this concept it is
necessary to consider its three prime components — (1) significantly subaverage general intellectual functioning, (2) existing
concurrently with deficits in adaptive behavior, and (3) manifested during the developmental period.

Significantly subaverage general intellectual functioning "refers to a performance which is more than two standard deviations
from the mean or average of a standardized individual test of
intelligence" (Grossman, 1973). In other words, the connotation
of significantly subaverage general intellectual functioning with
respect to commonly employed statistical indices of measured

intelligence is applied to those individuals whose assessed ability on a standardized individual test of intelligence falls below the point of minus two standard deviations (i.e. 2.01 to 5.01). The concomitant range of intelligence quotients (IQ's) as exemplified by scores attainable on the *Stanford-Binet Intelligence Scale* is 67 to 19.

Though a standardized individual test of intelligence administered by a well-trained, competent psychologist can yield very usable data, no known technique exists for *directly* assessing intelligence or intellectual potential. We cannot, for example, count an individual's neurons and conclude that he is retarded, normal or gifted. Rather, we must rely on evaluation devices which sample behavior considered indicative of intellectual functioning. Subsequently, an individual's capacity is *inferred* on the basis of his performance on such tests as the *Stanford-Binet Intelligence Scale*.

Numerous factors may influence a child's performance on any test of intelligence, many of which have no direct bearing on innate intellectual capacity. For example, there are a large number of youngsters in various parts of the country who come from bilingual homes. This may influence their performance. Sociocultural value systems also may play a significant role in the child's motivation to learn and perform within certain educational settings. Kvaraceus and Miller (1958) sequestrated middle and lower-class values based on systems of behavior reflective of value sets. In brief, middle-class values were defined as those consistent with Christian-Judeo traditions, e.g. a strong interest in education, ambition and setting goals ahead of time. In contrast, lower-class systems, which are not indigenous to a poverty setting, stress (1) staying out of trouble; (2) immediate gratification; (3) "toughness," or the physical rather than mental abilities in achievements; (4) excitement; (5) luck and fate rather than planning and foresight; (6) masculinity, e.g. the con artist is a hero, an educator is effeminate; and (7) autonomy as opposed to a need for equalized, cooperative group status. Though, as stated, such value systems are not indigenous to any sociocultural group, they are relatively prevalent in poverty areas. Youngsters with little interest in academic training may not perform well on standardized tests of intelligence which reflect more traditional values.

Other sociocultural influences which may adversely affect both learning and testing behavior include reduced communication and language between mother and child, a different approach to problem solving, e.g. mother tells child the answer rather than having him propose solutions, and the absence of the hidden curriculum. The *hidden curriculum* refers to the experiences offered by middle-class parents in preparing their children for school. Such training is not evident in the management-oriented home frequently found in poverty situations.

In addition, the cognitive aspects of learning among children in poverty areas have been well documented by Reisman and Metfessel (Black, 1966). Collectively, research studies would indicate that youngsters from poverty areas (1) are slow at cognition tests, but not stupid; (2) appear to learn through physical, concrete approaches; (3) are pragmatic rather than theoretical; (4) show deficiencies in auditory attention and interpretation skills; (5) possess a different vocabulary and use fewer words to express themselves; (6) learn less from what they hear than middle-class children; (7) use inductive rather than deductive reasoning; (8) have little insight; (9) are symbolically deprived; (10) need to see immediate application of what is learned; (11) have poor attention spans; and (12) have significant gaps in knowledge and learning. Each of these characteristics may have an impact on a child's test performance. This is particularly true of those individuals whose measured intelligence falls within the mild range of retardation. Thus, it is imperative that intelligence test results be assessed or interpreted against a broader picture of the child's development and adaptive behavior.

The necessity for impairment in adaptive behavior constitutes the unique feature of the definition of mental retardation promulgated by the American Association on Mental Deficiency (AAMD). Adaptive behavior, as conceived by Heber in an earlier version of the AAMD definition (1961), involved (1) maturation, or the rate at which an individual develops his basic motor and self-care skills; (2) learning, or the ability with which an individual gains knowledge from his experiences; and/or (3) social adjustment, or the ability with which the individual is capable of independently sustaining himself in a manner consistent with the standards and requirements of the society. Grossman (1973) defined adaptive behavior as the "effectiveness or degree with which the individual meets the standards of personal independence and social responsibility expected of his age and cultural group." Expectancies associated with adaptive behavior vary with age. Thus, during infancy and early childhood, dimensions of adaptive behavior emphasize sensory-motor skill development, communication skills, self-help skills and socialization. During childhood and early adolescence, adaptive behavior is reflected primarily in the application of basic academic skills and the utilization of appropriate reasoning and judgment in the mastery of the individual's environment. Social skills, such as participating in group activities, and interpersonal relationships are also of consequence. Adaptive behavior during late adolescence and adulthood emphasizes the combination of vocational and social responsibilities and performances.

Regrettably, there are very few examinations today which will provide a precise, valid measure of adaptive behavior beyond infancy and early childhood. Nevertheless, one would not classify a person as mentally retarded if his measured intelligence were normal or above, regardless of his adaptive behavior. Nor should an individual with an IQ below 80 be classified as mentally retarded unless he demonstrates significant deficiencies in adaptive behavior.

The third dimension of the definition being considered involves the developmental period. According to Grossman, the developmental period ranges from birth through eighteen years of age.

This brief discussion of a definition of mental retardation accompanied by the inherent limitations of individual tests of intelligence plus the absence of precise scales of adaptive behavior was intended to emphasize two points. First, great caution must be exercised when classifying a person as mentally retarded; secondly, it is extremely difficult to obtain definitive, valid information upon which to render such a judgment, especially among the mildly affected.

The preceding comments have concentrated upon certain commonalties of persons considered to be mentally retarded. This does not, however in any way imply that the retarded are a homogenous group of individuals. In fact, they are extremely heterogeneous in terms of their actual skills, social abilities, physical development, interests and affective behavior. As a group, they are more different than alike.

CLASSIFICATIONS OF MENTAL RETARDATION

Mental retardation is subject to an interminable number of classifications, formal and informal, intended to satisfy the needs of a discipline, service or area of investigation. For purposes of the present discussion, attention will be limited to a description of three interrelated systems based on (1) degree of retardation, (2) adaptive behavior and (3) educability. These systems, singularly or in combination, are frequently utilized in the study and reporting of mental retardation.

The degree-of-retardation nomenclature assumes that general intelligence can be plotted quantitively along a continuum, ranging from profound retardation to giftedness. The AAMD classification of measured intelligence, designed to augment the combination subaverage general intellectual functioning-impaired adaptive behavior definition, is divided into four categories — mild, moderate, severe and profound. The corresponding IQ ranges or boundaries for the various levels on standard deviations of the *Stanford-Binet Intelligence Scale* are presented in Table I.

TABLE I
DEGREE OF RETARDATION, EDUCATIONAL CLASSIFICATION,
AND COMMONLY ESTIMATED PERCENTAGES

Degree of retardation	Educational classification	I.Q. (Stanford-Binet)	Percent of total population	Percent[*] of retarded population
Mild	Educable	52-67	2.67	89.0
Moderate	Trainable	36-51	.18	6.0
Severe	{ Totally Dependent	20-35	.10	3.5
Profound		< 19	.05	1.5
Total	--	--	3.00	100.0

[*] From: President's Committee on Mental Retardation (1972)

While degree-of-retardation nomenclatures based on intelligence scores are of value, especially with respect to demography and generic discussions of programming, they are extremely limited when applied for purposes of identifying and planning for the individual mentally retarded person. The IQ, or equivalent mental age (MA), is of minimal value in understanding the child's interests, cultural experiences, motivation, motor skills, personality characteristics, and potentialities for social and vocational adequacy. Individuals with identical chronological ages (CA's) and IQ's do not possess identical learning or adjustment characteristics.

As indicated previously, in order to compensate for the deficiencies associated with statistically-oriented nomenclatures, there has been a growing interest in developing a classification based on adaptive behavior or those abilities, skills and responses essential to an individual's adjustment to his environment. Grossman (1973) developed a rather extensive listing of adaptive behaviors distributed by chronological age and level of retardation. He took into consideration such aspects as degree of independency, physical skills, communication, social adaptability, economic activity, occupational adequacy and self-direction. A sampling of anticipated abilities of retarded persons according to level of retardation at chronological age fifteen and above is presented in Table II.

Though this classification is divided into levels, the behavior of many retarded persons will vacillate across boundaries, depending upon the particular area of ability being considered. For example, a mildly retarded adolescent may be functioning very well with regard to anticipated academic achievement, but a physical or emotional problem may reduce his degree of independence to the level of partial self-support.

While adaptive behavior is dependent on such variables as physical abilities, emotional stability and social experiences, intelligence does retain an important role with respect to both general level of behavior and degree of variation. The profoundly retarded will require substantial care and supervision and usually will not demonstrate behavior associated with higher levels

TABLE II

ILLUSTRATIONS OF ADAPTIVE BEHAVIOR BY LEVEL OF
RETARDATION AT 15 YEARS OF AGE AND OLDER

Level of Retardation	Adaptive Behaviors
Mild	Exercises care for personal grooming, feeding, bathing, and toilet. Goes about home town with ease; communicates complex verbal concepts and understands them; carries on everyday conversation, but cannot discuss abstract or philosophical concepts; interacts cooperatively or competitively with others and initiates some group activities, primarily for social or recreational programs; can be sent to several shops to make purchases; can make change correctly; may earn living but has difficulty handling large amounts of money without guidance; can cook simple foods, prepare simple meals; as an adult, can engage in semi-skilled or simple skilled jobs; initiates most of his own activities; conscientious about work and assumes much responsibility but needs guidance for tasks with responsibility for such major tasks as health care, care of others, and a complicated occupational activity.
Moderate	Feeds, bathes, dresses self; may prepare easy foods; may wash and/or iron and store own clothes; good body control; good gross and fine motor coordination; may carry out simple conversation; uses complex sentences; recognizes words; may interact cooperatively and/or competitively with others; may be sent on shopping errands for several items without notes; may make minor purchases; adds coins to dollar with fair accuracy; may do simple routine household chores.
Severe	Feeds self adequately with spoon and fork; can put on clothes; may tie shoes; bathes self with supervision; is toilet trained; can run, skip, hop, dance; may communicate in complex sentences; recognizes signs, words, but does not read with comprehension prose material; may participate in group activities spontaneously; may be sent on simple errands and make simple purchases; may prepare simple foods; can help with simple household tasks; makes efforts to be dependable and carry out responsibilities.
Profound	Feeds self with spoon or fork; tries to bathe self but needs help; partially toilet trained; may hop or skip; may have speaking vocabulary of over 300 words and use grammatically correct sentences; may use gestures to communicate needs; understands simple verbal communication; participates in group activities and simple group games; interacts with others in simple play and expressive activities.

Adapted from: Grossman (1973)

of functioning. In contrast, the mildly retarded may reveal markedly variable behavioral patterns. Both the level and variability of adaptive behavior will increase with increased intelligence. Some estimate of intelligence, furthermore, is necessary to the interpretation of adaptive behavior, e.g. there is a significant difference between mildly and severely retarded persons who cannot read.

At present, our lack of knowledge concerning the essential components of adaptive behavior (other than categorically) and the precise sequence of their development prevents the formulation of behavioral classifications capable of rendering reliable, sophisticated information. Behavioral scientists, however, are continually investigating this problem, and it is anticipated that over the next few years more definitive developmental norms will be available. A combination of these norms with other systems of classification and objective tests for assigning levels of functioning will constitute a major step in providing for accurate diagnosis and extended planning.

The third common nomenclature divides mental retardation into three broad educational categories — educable mentally retarded (EMR), trainable mentally retarded (TMR) and uneducable or totally dependent (SMR/PMR). Kirk (1973) defined the educable mentally retarded child as

> one who, because of subnormal mental development, is unable to profit sufficiently from the program of the regular elementary school, but who is considered to have potentialities for development in three areas: (1) educability in academic subjects of the school at a minimum level, (2) educability in social adjustment to a point where he can get along independently in the community, and (3) minimal occupational adequacies to such a degree that he can later support himself partially or totally at the adult level.

The trainable retarded child was defined as

> one who is not educable in the sense of academic achievement, ultimate independent social adjustment in the community, or independent occupational adjustment at the adult level. This is what differentiates the trainable mentally retarded from an educable mentally retarded. The trainable mentally retarded

child, however, has potentialities for learning: (1) self-help skills, (2) social adjustment in the family and in the neighborhood, and (3) economic usefulness in the home, in a residential school, or in a sheltered workshop.

Finally, Kirk (1973) classified the severely and profoundly retarded in the broad category of the "totally dependent or custodial" mentally retarded child, which he defined as "one who, because of very severe mental retardation, is unable to be trained in total self-care, socialization, or economic usefulness and who needs continued help in taking care of his personal needs. Such a child requires almost complete care and supervision throughout his life, since he is unable to survive without help."

Again, caution must be exercised in interpreting the training characteristics or potential of even the more seriously affected retarded. Over the past ten years, new approaches and techniques have been developed and applied most successfully with the severely and profoundly retarded, many of whom have revealed startling degrees of skill acquisition. Though the severely and profoundly retarded will not, in all probability, ever attain a proficiency level associated with the borderline trainable or educable retarded, many, with proper training, will and are performing at a level very close to that associated with the trainable child. In fact, many youngsters who, prior to training, were considered to be severely retarded have revealed sufficient gains in both measured intelligence and adaptive behavior to be reclassified as trainable.

INCIDENCE OF MENTAL RETARDATION

Similar to and associated with some of the difficulties which have been discussed with regard to defining and assessing mental retardation, it is impossible to posit a highly reliable estimate of the incidence of mental retardation, either in its totality or by its various subcategories. The most frequently quoted estimate, as shown in Table I, is that approximately 3 percent of the total population will, *at some time during their lives*, be considered mentally retarded. Also, as shown in Table I, of the total retarded population, 89 percent is estimated to be mildly retarded, 6 percent to be moderately retarded, and approximately 5 percent to be severely or profoundly retarded.

Actual prevalence studies have yielded significantly different results. Definition, tests used, size of sample, sampling technique and geographic distribution are just a few of the variables which influence demographical estimates. A comparison of the Onondaga census (New York Department of Mental Hygiene, 1955) with the study conducted by Weiner in 1958 will demonstrate clearly how definitional differences will influence the final results.

Mental retardation, according to the Onondaga census, included "all children under 18 years of age, and residents of Onondaga County on March 1, 1953, identified as definitely mentally retarded, or suspected of mental retardation on the basis of developmental history, poor academic performance, IQ score or social adaptation when contrasted with their age peers" (New York Department of Mental Hygiene, 1955). This broad definition readily encompassed problems involving subaverage intellectual functioning, educational retardation and sociopersonal inadequacy. In 1958, Weiner (Kirk and Batemen, 1964) estimated the incidence of mental retardation in Hawaii; however, she employed more specific criteria. When group test data were available, students with an IQ less than 65 were considered mentally retarded; if group test data were not available, retardation was estimated on the basis of academic performance. For example, students in the third grade and above were considered mentally retarded only if they were three or more years below grade in reading and arithmetic; in Grades 1 and 2, the retarded were considered as those who could not read a preprimer nor do arithmetic computations with sums below 10. The results of these surveys, which have been plotted in Figure 1, show that the relatively indiscriminating concept of mental retardation employed in the Onondaga study consistently produced a higher prevalence of retardation. The discrepancies between the two studies are especially pronounced within the chronological age range of ten to sixteen years.

It is interesting to note that, in spite of the statistical differences between the two studies, there is a similar pattern with respect to

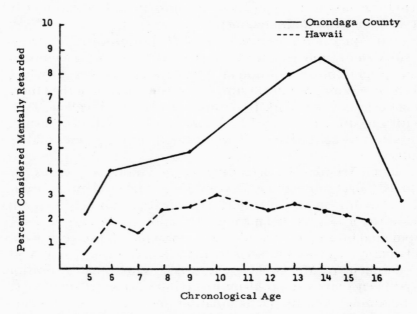

Figure 1: Incidence of Mental Retardation: Comparison of Onondaga County and Hawaii Study. From: Scheerenberger (1964).

the distribution of incidence as related to chronological age. The lowest prevalence of retardation occurred at the extreme ends of the distribution, i.e. CA five and sixteen to seventeen; the highest prevalence was encountered between the ages of eight and sixteen. This same pattern was apparent in the Lewis (1929) study conducted in England; the greatest frequency of retardation was evident during late childhood and early adolescence — age group five through nine (15.5 per thousand or 1.6 percent); ten through fourteen (25.6 per thousand or 2.6 percent) and fifteen through nineteen (10.8 per thousand or 1.1 percent).

These patterns have been reconfirmed in a number of subsequent studies. According to Scheerenberger (1964), three primary reasons account for this unequal distribution:

1. During infancy and early childhood mild retardation usually is not apparent. The demands of preschool life apparently are

within the adaptive capabilities of nearly all children. Subsequently, diagnosed retardation among children from birth to six years of age normally involves the occurrence of moderate, severe and profound degrees of subaverage intellectual functioning. The combination of marked developmental lags, observable physical stigma and multiple handicapping conditions tends to isolate the more severely retarded.

2. As consistently reported in the literature, the highest prevalence of retardation occurs during the school years. This is when most mildly retarded persons are identified. This is natural in view of the heavy emphasis placed on the acquisition of abstract academic skills. At no time is mental retardation quite as obvious as when a retarded youngster attempts to comprehend a complex verbal concept.

3. Following the termination of formal education, the prevalence of retardation tends to subside. Once again many mildly retarded persons are capable of unobtrusively satisfying the less verbal demands of adult society. The prevalence of retardation during adulthood is reduced further by the relatively high preadult mortality rate among the more severely and profoundly retarded.

One other very important factor relating to the incidence and prevalence of mental retardation requires mention. A disproportionately large number of persons diagnosed as mentally retarded emanate from poverty areas. According to the President's Committee on Mental Retardation (1968), the rate of selective service rejection for intellectual underachievement is 23 percent nationally but 60 percent among groups in low income areas. Also, "three-fourths (75%) of the Nation's mentally retarded are to be found in isolated and impoverished urban and rural areas; and a child in a low-income rural or urban family is 15 times more likely to be diagnosed retarded than is a child from a higher-income family" (President's Committee on Mental Retardation, 1968). This inflated occurrence of retardation in poverty areas involves primarily the mildly retarded.

While there is no question that there are remarkable variances in the prevalence of mental retardation as affected by sociocultural experiences and situations as well as chronological age, the overall 3 percent estimate is inappropriate for planning purposes. A more reasonable estimate in terms of how many retarded persons require services at any one time was advanced by Tarjan and his associates in 1973. They purported that only 1 percent of the total population should be considered mentally retarded for purposes of programming. This estimate takes into consideration the three factors affecting prevalence studies previously mentioned. A comparison of the 1 percent estimate as opposed to the 3 percent estimate is shown in Table III. These data are based on a prototype population of 100,000 persons and include reference to both degree of retardation and chronological age.

TABLE III
ESTIMATED PREVALENCE OF MENTAL RETARDATION
IN A PROTOTYPE COMMUNITY OF 100,000

I. Q.	Age (in years)				Total
	0-5	6-19	20-24	25+	
A. Overall prevalence: 3%					
0-19	12	24	8	56	100
20-49	48	96	32	224	400
50+	300	600	200	1400	2500
Total	360	720	240	1680	3000
B. Overall prevalence: 1%					
0-19	8	18	4	20	50
20-49	36	70	20	74	200
50+	25	600	25	100	750
Total	69	688	49	194	1000

With courtesy of: Tarjan, et. al., (1973)

This brief discussion has highlighted several key factors related to deinstitutionalization and institutional reform. First, it is most difficult in many cases to determine accurately whether or not mental retardation actually exists, let alone making the further determination that residential programming is required. Secondly, the mentally retarded constitute a very heterogeneous group of persons. Thirdly, based on adaptive behavior, most mildly and moderately retarded persons can live in the community quite successfully if sufficient programming and support are available. In contrast, many of the more severely and profoundly retarded who present serious multiply handicapping conditions will require at least some degree of extended residential care, treatment and training. Finally, as demonstrated, it is most difficult to arrive at a reliable estimate of the total incidence of mental retardation which is important to projecting future residential needs and institutional reform.

One final point, only a few retarded persons are or have ever been admitted to a residential facility for extended programming. Reports for fiscal years 1943 to 1944 (Penrose, 1949), 1953 to 1954 and 1963 to 1964 (Heber, 1970) and 1973 to 1974 (Scheerenberger, 1975) all indicate that during that year less than one mentally retarded person per 10,000 people was being served in a residential facility (.63, .88, .95 and .83, respectively). It is generally estimated that no more than 3 percent of the total mentally retarded population has, at any time during their life, received extended care in a residential facility.

SUMMARY

Mental retardation is a complex, multifaceted problem. The definition of mental retardation used as a basis of this text included reference to measured intelligence, adaptive behavior and age of onset. Levels of retardation include mild (educable), moderate (trainable), and severe and profound (totally dependent). The exact number of mentally retarded persons is unknown. The most commonly cited estimate is that 3 percent of the population probably will be classified as mentally retarded sometime during their life. This estimate, however, is influenced by a number of variables, and its application to programming is quite limited. Of particular concern to deinstitutionalization and institutional reform is the fact that very few mentally retarded persons have ever required extended residential services.

REFERENCES

Baroff, G. S.: *Mental Retardation: Nature, Cause, and Management.* New York, Wiley, 1974.

18   *Deinstitutionalization and Institutional Reform*

Black, M.: Characteristics of the culturally disadvantaged child. In Frost, J., and Hawkes, G. (Ed): *The Disadvantaged Child.* New York, Houghton-Mifflin, 1966.

Goldstein, H.: Population trends in U.S. public institutions for the mentally deficient. *Am J Ment Defic, 63*:599-604, 1959.

Grossman, H. (Ed.): *Manual on Terminology and Classification in Mental Retardation.* Washington, American Association on Mental Deficiency, 1973, p. 5, 11.

Heber, R.: *A Manual on Terminology and Classification in Mental Retardation.* Washington, American Association of Deficiency, 1961.

Heber, R.: *Epidemiology of Mental Retardation.* Springfield, Thomas, 1970.

Kanner, L.: *A Miniature Textbook of Feeblemindedness.* New York, Child Care Publications, 1949, p. 8.

Kauffman, J., and Payne, J.: *Mental Retardation.* Columbus. Merrill, 1975.

Kirk, S.: *Educating Exceptional Children.* New York. Houghton-Mifflin, 1973, pp. 164, 166.

Kirk, S., and Bateman, B.: *Ten Years of Research at the Institute for Research on Exceptional Children.* Urbana, U of Ill Pr, 1964.

Kvaraceus, W., and Miller, W.: *Delinquent Behavior.* Washington, National Education Association, 1959.

Lewis, E.: *Report on the Investigation into the Incidence of Mental Defects in Six Areas.* Report of the Mental Deficiency Committee, Part IV. London, H.M.SO., 1929.

National Institute of Mental Health, Office of Biometry. *Patients in Mental Institutions (Part 1):1964.* Washington, Superintendent of Documents, 1966.

New York Department of Mental Hygiene: *Technical Report of the Mental Health Unit.* Syracuse, Syracuse U Pr, 1955.

Penrose, L.: *The Biology of Mental Defect.* London, Sidgwick and Jackson, 1949.

President's Committee on Mental Retardation: *MR 68: The Edge of Change.* Washington, U.S. Government Printing Office, 1968, p. 19.

President's Panel on Mental Retardation: *A Proposed Program for National Action to Combat Mental Retardation.* Washington, U.S. Government Printing Office, 1962, p. 4.

Robinson, H., and Robinson, N.: *The Mentally Retarded Child.* New York, McGraw, 1965.

Scheerenberger, R.: Mental Retardation: Definition, classification, and prevalence. *Ment Retard Abstr, 1*:432-441, 1964, p. 10.

Smith, R. M.: *An Introduction to Mental Retardation.* New York, McGraw, 1971.

Tarjan, G., Wright, S., Eyman, R., and Keeran, C.: Natural history of mental retardation: Some aspects of epidemiology. *Am J Ment Defic, 77*:369-379, 1973, p. 370.

Chapter 2

EFFECTS OF RESIDENTIAL LIVING

RESIDENTIAL facilities for the mentally retarded, especially those under state auspices, are undergoing severe criticism and condemnation. Many persons have come to believe that all residential facilities are "bad" and deleterious to the development of those individuals they intend to serve. Let us examine these allegations by reviewing the research literature relevant to (1) separation from parents, (2) developmental aspects, (3) variance between and within residential facilities, (4) success of intervention efforts and (5) the physical environment.

SEPARATION FROM PARENTS

The single most powerful factor in the personality development of the child is the happiness and stability of the home in which he spends his early years. We do not mean by such a home that it need be characterized by a high level of education, a high standard of living, or even a high degree of success in meeting its problems, important and desirable as these may be. We mean a happy and stable home, one in which there is affection and consideration among the members for each other; one in which the individual members are emotionally secure and in mental health (Dewey and Humber, 1951).

Few persons would deny the importance of the home or the position advanced by Dewey and Humber.

Research with normal infants and children has demonstrated unequivocally that parental attachments are formed very early in life and are of extreme import. Schaffer and Emerson (1964), for example, conducted a cross-sectional study of the social attachment among sixty infants from birth to twenty-four months of age. Their results indicated that discriminate attachment becomes apparent at approximately eighteen weeks of age and remains evident at twenty-four months of age. Though youngsters

19

will cry and accept the attention of anyone under normal or usual circumstances, they definitely seek a particular person (mother and/or mother and father as a joint object) when tired or ill. During the first year of life an infant develops a hierarchy of preferences with the mother and father being the most important. Others (e.g. grandparents, siblings or neighbors) are important, but they cannot satisfy basic affectional and security needs. The two most important variables with regard to the intensity of maternal-child relationship, as discovered in this study, were the degree of maternal responsiveness and the amount of maternal interaction. In other words, a close relationship between mother and child requires involvement and interaction. *Simple maternal availability, i.e. the amount of time which the mother spends together with her child, without interaction did not influence the degree of closeness.* A mother's constant presence apparently does not guarantee that the infant will develop a very close attachment to her.

The advantages of a secure parental relationship were succinctly summarized by Jersild (1968),

> A child who has been reared in a climate of acceptance has many advantages. While still helpless and weak, the child can count on protection...In an atmosphere of affection a child has an opportunity to acquire an attitude of confidence and trust in those who reared him. As he grows older, he will be in a better position to develop his own capacity for affection for others. In a climate of affection and understanding he will have a kind of freedom — freedom to grow, to venture, to try and fail and then to try again....

Regrettably, research with both normal and retarded children has indicated that early parental separation adversely affects these critical areas of development.

Robertson of the Tavistock Children's Research Unit in London wrote a classic primer on what happens to children requiring prolonged hospitalization for an illness. Following the observation that tending of young infants by several persons is disadvantageous for reasons of attachment, he identified three stages of "settling in" — (1) protest, (2) despair and (3) denial. Protest is manifested in the child's screaming, crying and other similar forms of behavior at being left or separated from his parents. Despair is characterized by parental visits which involve clinging behavior and upset when parents leave. The final stage, denial, is reflected in the child's positive reaction to parental visits but with no demonstrated need for intimacy. Robertson (1958) described the behavior of one young girl in the denial stage, "During the week her behavior in the ward was increasingly bright and cheerful, and she stopped crying or — as far as anyone noticed — mentioning her parents. But though superficially amiable she was attached to no one." Upon her return home after eighteen months of hospitalization, the girl was difficult to manage, hyperactive, willful and destructive. She shrugged off any attempted caresses by her parents. This behavior was still evident a year later. As concluded, "For most children under 4 years it is our observation that no amount of love and understanding will make up for the absence of the mother" (Robertson, 1958). One final observation concerning this report — the transition from initial protest to denial occurs over a matter of weeks, not years.

The effects of early residential placement on "normal" infants has been investigated on numerous occasions. Let us examine several of these studies. If the findings of the Schaffer and Emerson (1964) study previously described can be generalized, then placement into a sterile residential setting should result in reduced responsiveness to adults and a depressed level of activity.

In 1961, Provence and Ritvo studied the effects of maternal deprivation on institutionalized normal infants and children employing a clinical approach, i.e. frequent, prolonged observations; varied testing; and other studies. The results revealed that delays in motor development and vocalization were the first observable characteristics to be adversely affected. Also, the youngsters' personal relationships became distorted; they demonstrated poor ability to use toys and other play materials, and they showed little spontaneity and curiosity. At one year of age, their general appearances and external responses were lacking vigor and energy.

In 1962, Provence and Lipton published an expanded report on seventy-five infants and children, four months to six years of age, living in a residential facility. The description of the nursery-type facility was quite similar to many residential facilities serving the retarded — neat, clean, brightly colored, some toys and a set routine. Beyond meeting the very minimal care needs of the infants, there was little interaction between personnel and residents, except for a few "favorites". Perhaps the following observation offers an adequate summary of the children's responses: "The quietness and orderliness of these groups disappeared as soon as the children saw the investigators; a large part of the group would cluster around us, with uplifted arms, and the children who had been most recently admitted to the institution would call, 'Mommy,' a cry often taken up by others" (Provence and Lipton, 1962). Such behavior represents the hallmark of personal deprivation. Other findings included delay in differential response to attendants as opposed to strangers, tenuous emotional ties, absence of playful activity with others, and impoverishment of affective behavior. The youngsters were amiable but bland, failed to turn to adults for help or to solve a problem, and had difficulty in initiating social contact.

Highlights from one reported case history about Teddy illustrate the characteristic pattern of reduced functional behavior and affectiveness. At twenty-six weeks of age, Teddy was doing very well when compared with the other infants, however his behavior changed substantially over a period of eighteen weeks. At forty-four weeks of age, his appearance, mood and reactions to people had altered significantly —

> He was solemn-faced, unsmiling, and miserable looking . . . He could sit, pull to a stand, and could creep a few steps on all fours. He did little creeping, however, and did more rocking than creeping in this position . . . He made no effort to recover a hidden toy . . . The interest he showed in the toys was mainly for holding, inspecting, and rarely mouthing. When he was unhappy, he now had a cry that sounded neither demanding nor angry — just miserable — and it was usually accompanied by his beginning to rock . . . Outstanding were his soberness, his forlorn appearance, and lack of animation. (Provence and Lipton, 1962)

Though Teddy's behavior as described is similar to that of many retarded youngsters in residential facilities, his measured intelligence remained within the normal range of expectancy.

Another study with similar results was reported by Gewirtz (1965), who investigated the course of infant smiling in four child-rearing environments in Israel — town family, kibbutz, residential institution and day nursery. While all subjects tended to show a common pattern in the development of smiling behavior, by eighteen months of age, smiling behavior in the residential institution and day nursery had decreased in frequency by approximately 50 percent as compared with children in the kibbutz and family setting. As concluded by Gewirtz (1965),

> Infants for whom the appearance and behaviors of persons are not discriminative for reinforcement... should exhibit fewer smiles and other responses. Thus, we might expect fewer smiles to persons by Ss in environments characterized by low child-caretaker ratios and high personnel turnover; and it is on the basis of this limited responsiveness to persons displayed by those Ss that such environments might be evaluated as inadequate.

Moss (1966), in his review of the literature and discussion of how children feel about being placed away from home recorded,

> Children... have ambivalent reactions to the idea of discussing their feelings about past separations. On the one hand, they thirst for more understanding of the past — particularly of how and why they came into placement. They want to fill in the unknown facts and feelings of their past to know more about themselves and what they want to become. On the other hand, they do not feel strong enough to bear the pain of exploring their feelings... Often children who resist discussing their parents in the hope that they will change are those whose parents are most inconsistent and rejecting. These are the parents who talk about taking the child home but never make any plans, who promise to visit the child and do not, who rarely write to him, who forget his birthday, and who care little about the child and his needs. Such children suffer deeply since they are constantly confused about what to expect from their parents... Such children may transfer their conflicting feelings about their parents to the institution itself. Although they wish to trust their parents to meet their emotional needs, they are not sure they can, and this ambivalence is repeatedly acted out inerratic

behavior in the institution. A child may also hide his feelings about separation behind a pseudo-mature objectivity. Outwardly, he is like an adult; inwardly, he is the child torn with yearning for his unmet dependency needs to be met.

Though Moss was not addressing himself to the experiences of the mentally retarded in residential facilities, a series of case studies reported by Braginsky and Braginsky (1971) clearly illustrate his points. When mildly retarded subjects were asked why they had been placed in the residential facility, most referred to their parents,

> Mr. K.W. (CA 20; age at admission: 10 year). "Busted up, that's why I came here . . . like when I came here I wasn't retarded and I'm not a retardate. I came from a broken home . . . my mother was on welfare. She didn't use it right, so they put the kids away."

> Mr. I.D. (CA 20; age at admission: 15 years). "I'm homesick. I've been here almost five years. I have suffered angry from being here. I can't sleep at night . . . I take off from here every six months. I run home to my parents."

> Mr. M.D. (CA 20; age at admission: 9 years). "My mother told me I wasn't put here as mental retardation. I was put here because I was a juvenile delinquent when I was small . . . My mother, she didn't really put me here, but at the time she didn't have no way of taking care of me either. So this is where she stuck me."

> Mr. R.P. (Age 13; age at admission: 5 years). "Because my father he wasn't working . . . He had no money or nothing and he can't support me or nothing, so he put me here . . . My father is going to take me out in June for good."

Results of several dream studies involving retarded residents, including adolescents and adults, revealed that being reunited with one's family was a very predominant theme (De Martino, 1954, and Sternlicht, 1966). Anyone working in a residential facility with mildly retarded persons fully realizes the anguish and pain these residents suffer as a consequence of parental separation.

Little is known about the degree of attachment between the severely or profoundly retarded child and his mother. Some persons assume that this relationship does not really develop among these youngsters. Yet, a recent case history reported by Perry and Friedman (1973) refutes such an assumption. *T* was born out of wedlock and his clinical diagnosis was chronic malnutrition and failure to thrive secondary to maternal neglect. The boy first came to the attention of medical authorities when he was approximately seven months old, at which time his appearance was that of a wizened little old man. He displayed almost no spontaneous movements. While he was able to raise both his head and legs, he could not move. At ten months of age he was unable to sit unsupported and did not reach for a bottle when hungry. Yet, he cried and clung to his mother when the examiners tried to pick him up. At one year, four months, he was still unable to sit unsupported or crawl. He did, however, respond to his mother by smiling and cooing whenever she touched or talked to him. He followed her movements with his eyes and seemed upset when she was very far from him. At one year, five months, he cried when the examiners blocked his view of his mother. At this same age he was still unable to sit unsupported, could not support his body when held in a standing position, nor was he capable of horizontal locomotion. Thus, while *T* certainly gave many signs of severe retardation, there was little question that he had formed a definite attachment to his mother. (*T* died at 23 months of age.)

It is impossible to ascertain with any degree of surety how a severely or profoundly retarded child reacts to family separation. Most persons working with the severely and profoundly retarded in a residential setting are cognizant of the fact that only a few of them do not respond to their parents. Usually such residents are either very young and severely or profoundly retarded or, if older, very profoundly retarded. Many profoundly retarded adults, however, who have been fortunate enough to have retained parental contact through the years do recognize their parents and respond enthusiastically and affectionately to their appearance.

The mildly retarded are able to express their familial needs, the more severely retarded are not. Though it is probable that the effects of separation are dependent upon age at the time of separation and the degree of attachment, one should never underestimate the traumatic personal experiences associated with this separation even though the individual may be substantially retarded. As illustrated by the examples provided by Braginsky and Braginsky (1971), most residents were from very poor homes by middle class standards, e.g. poverty-ridden, with child abuse and neglect, alcoholism and little actual parental attention. Nevertheless, the effects of separation were still overwhelming and persistent.

DEVELOPMENTAL ASPECTS

The preceding discussion focused on the potential impact of parental separation. Let us now turn our attention to the broader effects of residential living. Though many aspects of resident behavior have been investigated, the following brief review of the literature will be limited to intelligence and related functioning, personality development, language and speech, educational achievement and labeling.

Intelligence and Related Functioning

One of the early classic studies involving the effects of institutionalization was conducted by Goldfarb in 1945. He studied the intellectual development of children first committed to an orphanage and later placed in a foster home. Fifteen experimental subjects and fifteen controls were monitored. The average age at time of the evaluation was approximately twelve years; the average age of admission to the residential facility was 4.5 months. The orphanage was described as one of extreme deprivation, e.g. no individual attention, lack of personal possessions and minimal stimulation. A comparison of the intelligence scores of the children placed in the foster home with those who remained in the orphanage revealed the latter to be mildly retarded and significantly behind in language development.

In 1947, Goldfarb studied adolescents who had spent their early years in an institution prior to placement in a foster family. Those adolescents who were well adjusted when placed in a foster home were well adjusted as teenagers; those who were not well adjusted when first placed with a foster family were not well adjusted in their teens. On the basis of these results, Goldfarb concluded, "Increasingly, the weight of evidence would bolster the conclusion that most of the variation in community adjustment of children, whose first years were spent in an institution is to be explained by the primary privation experienced in the institution." Environmental deprivation was defined as (1) a lack of warm, affectionate and continued contact between a child and a specific adult; (2) superficial human relationships; (3) limited stimulation and ordinary cultural and language experiences; and (4) substitution of external institutional control for the individual development of internal controls.

Stedman and Eichorn (1965) studied ten matched pairs of Down's syndrome children living at home and in a residential setting. The former were significantly advanced in terms of walking, weight and mental and social maturity.

Similar results were obtained several years later by Stimpson *et al.* (1968). In this instance, forty Down's syndrome children (CA 6 to 12) who had been admitted to a large state residential facility during their first year of life were studied. The control group included twenty-five Down's syndrome children living at home. No significant differences were observed with regard to height or weight. Walking, talking, self-feeding and toilet training, however, were all significantly depressed among the residential sample. Mean IQs and social quotients (SQs) were lower among the residential population than among the community controls — IQ 18 and 36, respectively; SQ 29 and 54, respectively.

Sternlicht and Siegel (1946) found that residential living had a profound adverse effect on the residents' intellectual functioning. This was particularly true with regard to younger residents and moderately retarded males.

Francis (1970) studied the behavior of 112 Down's syndrome persons with mental ages of less than two years and found that with increasing age, object-oriented behaviors decreased while self-oriented behaviors, rocking, diffuse movements and postures increased. Attention to visual stimuli, watching others and general levels of activity also diminished. Reduced functioning was attributed to a lack of stimulation and interest in the residential environment as opposed to aging per se.

Clarke and Clarke (1958) reported on an investigation concerning the fluctuation of measured intelligence among subjects fourteen to fifty years of age following residential placement. Results of this study, which was conducted in 1954, revealed an average gain of 6.5 IQ points following twenty-seven months of residential programming. The range in fluctuation was -5 points to +25 points. Greatest gains (i.e. 25 points) were made by subjects with initially lower intelligence scores and those who originally came from "bad" homes. Clarke, Clarke and Redman (Clarke and Clarke, 1958) later reported that intelligence quotients continued to rise for all subjects. Again, those residents from inadequate homes revealed the most significant gains.

In contrast to the results of these studies which indicated that intelligence quotients dropped or increased, Holowinsky (1962) found no significant changes over three decades. He studied the data from records of fifty-seven mentally retarded adults who had lived in a private residential facility for an average of thirty-two years. The mean age at the time of admission was thirteen years, six months, and the mean IQ was 47. Over a period of thirty years the average IQ remained relatively constant, i.e. no statistically significant differences were observed. He reported that 67 percent of the residents showed no change; 14 percent had some increase; and 29 percent had some decrease. Decrements were noted primarily among the more severely retarded and those residents admitted prior to sixteen years of age.

The results of these studies demonstrate that a residential environment *may* influence measured intelligence and related behavior favorably or negatively. Most of the reports indicated that the younger, more retarded resident is particularly susceptible to adverse residential influences as measured by a standardized test of intelligence. When most of these studies were conducted, however, extensive programming was not available for the moderately or more seriously retarded. In contrast, educational programs and vocational training experiences were reasonably well established for the mildly retarded and borderline individual.

Personality Development

A substantial number of investigations have been concerned

with the effects of residential living on the personal development of retarded persons. In an extended and impressive series of studies Zigler explored the effects of institutionalization on the personality development and motivation of the retarded. In 1961 he summarized the results of his studies with the following conclusions:

1. Institutional retarded children tend to have been relatively deprived of adult contact and approval, and hence have a higher motivation to secure such contact and approval than do normal children.
2. While retarded children have the higher positive-reaction tendency than normal children due to a higher motivation to interaction with an approving adult, they also have a higher negative-reaction tendency. This higher negative-reaction tendency is the result of a wariness which stems from retarded children's more frequent negative encounters with adults.
3. Institutionalized retarded children have learned to expect and settle for lower degrees of success than have normal children.
4. An inter- versus outer-directed cognitive dimension may be employed to describe differences in the characteristic mode of attacking environmentally presented problems (Zigler, 1966).

In essence, retarded individuals in a residential environment are in need of, and therefore highly responsive to, social reinforcement from an approving adult, yet they are wary of approaching an adult, have lower expectancy levels and are more prone to seek environmental cues and advice of others rather than rely on their own judgment. Zigler reconfirmed these conclusions and his basic position in 1975.

A recent study by Balla *et al.* (1974), which will be reviewed in more detail in a later discussion, supported Zigler's finding that many residents tend to be wary of adults. Gardner and Forehand (1974) also supported Zigler's contention concerning the outer-directiveness of residents. In this study, mildly retarded males living in a residential setting tended to imitate significantly more on a word-modeling task than did subjects living in the community. The implication was that residential facilities foster imitative behavior and reliance on others rather than encouraging independence.

A number of studies have been concerned with the self-concept of persons in a residential facility and have produced equivocal results. Guthrie, Butler and Gorlow (1963), for example, found that educable girls in a residential setting had more negative self-attitudes than educable girls attending a community special class. In contrast, Lambeth (1967) and Lawrence and Winschel (1973) found no differences between the self-concept of adolescent male residents when compared with teenage mentally retarded students in a public special educational program.

Rosen *et al.* (1971) conducted a study to explore the effects of residential living on goal setting and self-confidence among residential retarded adolescents as compared with adolescent retarded individuals in the community and a normal control group matched on the basis of chronological age. Though retarded persons in the residential setting tended to reveal a lower level of expectancy, the authors concluded, "Institutionalized and non-institutionalized retardates showed more striking similarities than differences and both groups differed significantly from normals of the same chronological age."

Heber (1964) reviewed a number of studies conducted prior to 1961 concerning personality disorders among residents and found a reported range of 16 to 56 percent of the total resident population was considered disturbed. He observed, "It would be remarkable were this not so in view of the fact that behavior disorders are acknowledged as being a major precipitant of institutionalization in this group."

A study by Hobbs (1964) reported a higher prevalence of antisocial and/or unsocial behavior among adolescent and adult residents as compared with nonresidential retarded persons of similar ages and intelligence. Undesirable behavior included theft, physical violence, unmanageable behavior and sexual misconduct. She concluded that "the institutionalized group was strikingly less socially competent than the group seen in the community. The most likely explanation is that socially inadequate individuals tend to be institutionalized and that institutionalization contributes further to their social inadequacy." Whether or not one wishes to accept Hobb's explanation, there is little doubt that there is a higher incidence of emotionally disturbed and socially maladjusted persons in residential facilities, and such behavior is a primary factor leading to institutionalization.

In a slightly different approach to the study of behavior, Kay and McKinney (1967) studied the fluctuation in friendships among eighty-nine retarded adolescents in residential settings as compared with 223 normal teenagers. The retarded demonstrated greater fluctuation in friendships which, to the investigators, raised the question of personal stability.

Floor and Rosen (1975) studied "helplessness" among twenty retarded adolescent and adult residents, twenty adolescent and adult retarded persons living at home, and sixteen college students, predominantly psychology majors. Helplessness was defined as a personality variable reflecting an inability to take effective action in a problem situation. Though both groups of retarded persons were considerably more helpless than the college students, there were no statistically significant differences between their respective performances.

Research into the personality characteristics and self-concepts of retarded persons in residential facilities tends to indicate that such environments are not conducive to desirable development, especially among the younger and more seriously affected. Yet, there also is evidence to indicate that this need not be true in all instances.*

Speech and Language Development

Many studies have reported that the development of language and communication skills among the retarded in residential facilities is delayed. Lyle (1959) attempted to determine whether moderately retarded children in a large residential facility were also retarded in verbal intelligence as compared to a group of trainable

---

*Readers interested in an expanded discussion of personal-social characteristics of the mentally retarded are referred to Sternlicht and Deutsch (1972) and Balthazar and Stevens (1975).

youngsters living at home and attending a day school. The verbal intelligence of subjects in the residential setting was retarded by twelve months for mongoloid children and six months for non-mongoloid youngsters when compared with the performance of the control group.

Schlanger (1954) found retarded persons in the residential setting to be slower than expected with regard to sentence length and average number of words used per minute. Sievers and Essa (1961) also reported that retarded residents had lower scores than similar subjects living in the community on the *Developmental Language Facilities Test.*

In another comparative study, Spradlin (1963) ascertained that retarded persons in the residential environment had a higher incidence of speech defects. Stuttering is also relatively common (Schlanger, 1953, and Chapman and Cooper, 1973).

Unlike those studies concerned with measured intelligence and personality development, there seems to be almost universal agreement that the development of language and communication skills is significantly repressed in a residential setting. Whether this reflects the absence of a stable adult with whom to communicate or whether the environment and its population reduces the need or motivation to communicate has not been clearly identified in the literature. Undoubtedly, all factors are influential.

Yet, there again is evidence to indicate that language development need not be delayed or repressed when a child is in a residential facility. Tizard *et al.* (1974) observed the language development of eighty-five children two to five years of age in thirteen residential nursery groups. These youngsters, who were not mentally retarded, did not reveal any signs of *institutional retardation.* Their mean test scores on both verbal and nonverbal tests were average. As concluded by the authors,

> Our evidence strongly suggests that intellectual retardation is not a necessary consequence of institutional placement; even in our 'worst' nurseries, the mean test scores were average, while in the 'best' nurseries the children's language comprehension scores were considerably above average. Since many of the children were of lower-working-class parentage, it seems likely that

intellectually they have in fact benefited from their institutional upbringing.

The researchers attributed the results to two primary reasons. First, none of the children had unusual birth histories, and none had suffered from early neglect or frequent environmental shifts often associated with a child's life prior to residential placement. Secondly, the nursery facilities provided adequate physical care, ample books and play equipment, and were characterized by small groups of residents with a high staff ratio. There also was a substantial amount of adult conversation with the children, and daily reading lessons were introduced for the specific purpose of promoting language development.

Educational Achievement

Several studies were located which compared the results of both trainable and educable youngsters in a formal training setting with those of retarded persons receiving similar educational op-portunities in the community. Peck and Sexton (1961) compared the progress of three groups of trainable mentally retarded young-sters receiving training in a public school, a parent-sponsored day center, and a state residential facility. Their results indicated no statistically significant differences with regard to social adjust-ment, self-care, language development, physical development of gross and small muscles, arts and crafts, economic usefulness and music. Bensberg (1953) also reported no significant differences of equivalent subjects matched on mental age in academic perfor-mance of either moderately or mildly retarded individuals, re-gardless of where they were receiving their formal training.

The implication of such studies is that, given adequate educa-tional and training programs, retarded persons in residential facilities will perform as well as those in a community setting.

Labeling

The potential labeling effect of residential placement also needs to be examined briefly. The entire question of labeling children mentally retarded or developmentally disabled or delinquent is of marked current interest as witnessed by the recently-published three-volume series by Hobbs (1975a, 1975b). According to Hobbs (1975a), major problems associated with labeling include:

> Children who are categorized and labeled as different may be permanently stigmatized, rejected by adults and other children, and excluded from opportunities essential for their full and healthy development.

> Children may be assigned to inferior educational programs for years, deprived of their liberty through commitment to an institution, or even sterilized on the basis of inadequate diagnostic procedures, with little or no consideration of due process.

> A number of members of minority-group children — Chicanos, Puerto Ricans, Blacks, Appalachian Whites — have been inaccurately classified as mentally retarded on the basis of inappropriate intelligence tests, placed in special classes or programs where stimulation and learning opportunities are inadequate and stigmatized.

> Classification of a child can lead to his commitment to an institution that defines and confines him as a delinquent, blind, retarded, or emotionally disturbed. The institution may evoke behavior appropriate to his label, thus making him more inclined to crime, less reliant than he could be on residual vision, less bright than his talents, more disturbed than he would be in a normal setting.

The controversy over the effects of labeling the mentally retarded as well as the absence of any scientific verification of such effects are thoroughly reviewed and analyzed by MacMillian *et al.* (1974) with responses by Guskin (1974) and Rowitz (1974). In essence, while many persons contend that labeling and categorization are detrimental to a child's self-perception as well as to the expectancies of others, it has been difficult to isolate the labeling factor in order to draw any definitive conclusions. Nonetheless, there is evidence to indicate that at least the mildly retarded view their residential placement as humiliating.

Many former residents devote considerable energy to hiding or denying the fact that they have been in an institution for the retarded. This is well illustrated by the experiences and feelings expressed by mildly retarded adults discharged from a large residential facility in California,

> (A woman) When I got out of that place it was horrible. I knew everyone was looking at me and thinking that it was true what they thought I was. I couldn't stand for people to think that about me. That's a terrible thing for people to think.

> (A man) When I was in the colony I was always worried. I'll admit it. You know, I was worried did they really think I was like them others. The ones that couldn't do nothing or learn nothing.

> (A woman) I don't even want to think about the colony. Some of the people there was so odd, I don't know why... The worst thing is always trying to hide it from everybody. I just don't want nobody to know I was in that mental State hospital. I'm ashamed of it . . . I pray that nobody will ever find out about me (Edgerton, 1967).

There is little question that the individuals interviewed above felt stigmatized and were anxious over their placement history. It is difficult to ascertain whether this reaction is related to residential placement per se or whether such a placement gave high visibility to and evidence of their label of retardation. Regardless, the consequences were severe.

The testimony of these adults also identifies a problem which is not given enough consideration in the field of mental retardation and residential programming. Placement of mildly retarded persons with the severely and profoundly retarded may be, and probably is, perceived as degrading. An unequivocal fear expressed by the former residents was analogous to guilt by association, e.g. "I was worried did they really think I was like them others. The ones that couldn't do nothing or learn nothing."

Two major problems associated with comparative studies such as those reviewed involves both the retarded population sampled and the possibility of interacting effects between preadmission and residential experiences. As observed by Jersild (1968),

> Children placed in an institution by reason of necessity... are children of misfortune. Due to bad luck, or poor heredity, or a combination of both, they are outcasts. Their parents either could not or would not care for them, or placed them with

solicitous relatives. Thus a selective process has been at work before they are placed in an institution and, in many instances, it continues after they are there.

Retarded persons in residential facilities are frequently atypical of the retarded population in general. Though the reasons underlying residential placement will be examined in a later section, it should be recognized that many residents present multiple handicapping conditions; many have proven difficult to manage in the community; many are emotionally disturbed; many come from broken or otherwise inadequate homes; and many are illegitimate and have never known a warm, close family relationship. Retarded persons are not committed to a residential facility simply because they are retarded.

Recognition of the potential effect of preadmission experiences upon subsequent development in a residential facility has long been recognized by most researchers. For example, Zigler (1966) wrote,

> The motive structure of the institutionalized retardate is influenced by an interaction between pre-institutional social history and the effects of institutionalization. This effect is complicated by the fact that institutionalization does not constitute a homogeneous psychological variable. Instead, institutions differ and underlying psychological features of the particular institution must be considered before predictions can be made concerning the effects of institutionalization of any particular child.

Several studies have included reference to preresidential experiences. The investigation by Clarke and Clarke previously cited referred to inadequate or "bad" homes.

Another example is offered by Balla, Butterfield and Zigler (1974). These investigators studied the behavior of residents from four residential facilities. A total of 103 mentally retarded children were evaluated initially on measures of MA, IQ, responsiveness to social reinforcement, verbal dependency, wariness of adults, imitativeness and behavior variability. To determine deprivation scores as they related to preresidential experiences, the social histories of all subjects were assessed on the *Social Deprivation Scale* developed previously by Zigler, Butterfield and Goff. This scale provides an estimate of preadmission experiences along four dimensions — (1) continuity of residency; (2) parental attitudes toward institutionalizing the child; (3) familial richness, or the intellectual and economic level of the parents; and (4) familial harmony, or the degree of parental rejection or neglect of the child. In addition, two overall estimates of preresidential deprivation were provided by the experimenters. It should be noted that all judgments were based on records; parents were neither contacted nor interviewed. A follow-up study was conducted 2.5 years later. A summary of the results included:

> Mental ages increased slightly from a mean of 7.15 to 7.57. The gain, however, was less than anticipated on the basis of initial IQ scores. No relation was found to preadmission history.
>
> Overall IQ's remained relatively constant. In one facility, low deprived familially retarded children had higher IQs over the 2.5-year period; in another, highly deprived familially retarded children had higher IQ's.
>
> In three facilities, highly deprived subjects were less wary; in one facility the less deprived were less wary.
>
> All individuals appeared less imitative at the time of the second testing; no interaction effects involving deprivation were observed.
>
> In one residential facility low deprived residents were less verbally dependent over the 2.5-year period while in another facility, highly deprived subjects were less dependent. No differences were observed between the two remaining facilities.
>
> Highly deprived individuals revealed no change in behavioral variability; low deprived were less variable in terms of their behavior.

It was concluded that there was much less variability between residential facilities as a consequence of social deprivation as measured than anticipated. The authors also reflected that since subjects at only one institution revealed a high degree of social reinforcement value, perhaps residential facilities were providing better adult contacts than previously assumed.

In another study, attempting to relate preadmission experiences with residential behavior, Kershner (1970) studied forty-two mentally retarded children, mean age of nine years at the time of admission, and one year later on measures of SQ and IQ as well as their families' pre and post interview results to estimate the adequacy of family functioning. A group of twenty-seven retarded children living in the community served as controls. The parental interview process involved the development of a protocol from which ratings could be made for family functioning, including home and household practices, social activities, health practices, care and training of children, family relationships and family unity, individual behavior and adjustment. Both groups of retarded youngsters revealed a decrease in IQ over the one-year period. IQ decreases among youngsters remaining in the community were related to family functioning, i.e. decrements were greatest among those individuals in homes with a poor family rating. The mean SQ for community youngsters increased. IQ losses for retarded persons in a residential facility, however, were not considered to be related to family functioning.

Kershner also noted that removal of the retarded child from the home resulted in increased family unity. In contrast, retaining the child at home placed increased stress on the family with a resultant decrease in effective family relationships.

These studies represent an inchoate effort to clarify a very complex phenomenon, the interrelationship of child, home and residential experiences. It is doubtful, however, that research studies will ever yield more than a very general impression of this interrelationship. The potential variables are interminable. First, there is the infant or child with his own complement of biological, psychological and sociopersonal attributes and proclivities; secondly, there is the family with its quality of interrelationships, social status and aspirations, beliefs and values, as well as reactions to the retarded child; thirdly, there is the neighborhood and community with its values and beliefs (individual or collective) and its acceptance of the retarded; fourthly, there is the residential facility with its philosophy, attitudes and offerings. Any one of these variables could be further refined. For example, the mother's relation to the child has been investigated under various models and assumptions, including intelligence (Heber and Garber, 1972), age (Ehlers, 1966), degree of acceptance (Grossman, 1972), attitudes (Klebanoff, 1959) and preconceptual feelings of guilt (Hamilton, as cited by Jersild, 1968). Even these variables are relatively all-encompassing. What about the more subtle aspects of maternal response, such as the fact that mothers of premature infants interact less frequently with their child than do mothers of full-term siblings (Leiderman *et al.*, 1973)? As indicated by Eisenberg (1964),

> The dependence of the brain damaged upon his environment is nowhere more clear than in his family relations. His defect, if it is obvious at birth, may alter parental attitudes towards him. What is the impact on the development of maternal feelings of having a child who does not respond as he should, who is a source of frustration rather than pride? Parental behavior may be so skewed as to induce in the child the very patterns of disturbance we would have recognized as psychogenic had the presence of brain damage not pre-empted our attention.

While it is obvious that the element of maternal behavior must affect a seriously retarded child, rarely will one ever know with certainty as to how he perceives and interprets such behavior.

Variances Between and Within Residential Facilities

Prior to considering the effectiveness of intervention programs, it is important to recognize that significant differences exist not only between but also within residential facilities. These differences have been amply documented in several studies.

In 1968, King and Raynes compared the living patterns of moderately retarded persons in three different settings — (1) an institution with a resident population of 300, (2) a voluntary home with seventy-six residents, and (3) a hostel with sixteen children. Most of the subjects (n = 18, 22 and 16, respectively) ranged in chronological age from seven to twelve. Residents in the hostel were consistently more advanced than those in the other two types of facilities. For example, 94 percent of the residents in the hostel used a knife and fork as compared to only 11 percent in the institution. Also, 56 percent of the residents in the hostel spoke in sentences; only 17 percent performed similarly in the larger residential facility. The authors concluded, however, that size of the facility was not a significant variable. Rather, they proposed that the discrepancies in performances, all of which favored the hostel, reflected a higher degree of autonomy, a greater emphasis on individualized patterns of care, more variable working hours with house parents readily available when residents were at home, absence of regimentation and active engagement with the community.

Tizard (1970), in collaboration with King and Raynes, reported another study involving two residential facilities with resident populations of 300 to 400, a hostel with sixteen residents, and a voluntary home with fifty residents. The *Scale of Child Management Practices* was used to gather data on such items as variations in bedtime; the use of the garden, dormitory and courtyard by ambulant children; mealtime and bathing practices; personal clothing and other possessions; and accessibility to other areas within the facility. A high score implied rigidity, block treatment, few opportunities for individual expression, and a wide social distance between staff and children. The two large residential facilities scored high, i.e. sixteen to twenty-three points, which led to the impression that they were institutional rather than child-oriented. The two smaller facilities scored below seven points. It was contended that the results did not reflect on the number of residents, size of child care groups, or staff/resident ratios. Rather, it was proposed that the large facilities did not foster close interpersonal relations and interaction between staff and residents. Other problems mentioned included the number of staff surrounding a child, frequent transferring of residents to different areas, centralized versus decentralized administration, and infrequent use of community facilities.

Variances in attitudes of residential personnel towards the retarded and the role of residential services also have been observed. Barrett (1971), for example, reported a study of two wards which reflected distinctly different philosophies. One ward showed considerable concern for the development and training of residents while the other, serving a similar population, did not. Both philosophies proved self-fulfilling.

Studies by Butterfield *et al.* (1968) and Klaber (1969) revealed similar results, i.e. differences among aide personnel with regard to the retarded and programming in general. There was, however, a significant difference. These studies involved several residential facilities, and while there were intradifferences between aide personnel, there were also significant interdifferences. In other words, there was a tendency for aide attitudes to vary between residential facilities, presumedly as a function of each facility's general programmatic philosophy.

Variances in philosophy and attitudes are by no means limited to aide personnel; they are also evident among first-line administrators. For example, Overbeck (1971) utilized the Efron and Efron *Scale of Attitudes Toward the Mentally Retarded* with forty-one charge attendants in a large southwestern residential facility and found a statistically significant relationship between authoritarian factors and segregation vs. institutionalization of the mentally retarded. Charge attendants with authoritarian leanings tended to support the notion of protecting society from the mentally retarded by isolating them in residential facilities. Also, a recent study by Amble *et al.* (1971) indicated that charge personnel may actively discourage close interaction between aides and residents. The authors concluded, after examining the intelligence and personality preference patterns of thirty-one child care aides who had been rated previously by charge personnel as to effectiveness, that the latter tended to reject the brighter aide whose attitudes "would be considered more favorable to rehabilitating the mentally retarded, i.e. tended to be less strict, encourage communication and verbalization, foster less dependency, avoid work conflict, be less irritable and less concerned with aggressive behavior, be less reclusive and tolerate more privacy."

These studies demonstrate rather clearly that the results of any given investigation into the behavior of residents based solely on *institutionalization* have very limited generality. Again, residential living per se is not a variable.

EFFECTS OF INTERVENTION PROGRAMS

Many efforts have been made to provide programs intended to intervene or disrupt any adverse influences associated with a sterile environment. The intervention technique employed depends upon the age and ability of the child. As will be seen, however, special programming has been successful with nearly all residents, regardless of chronological age.

With regard to infants, Rheingold (1956) substituted a "mother" for multiple "mothers" in a residential facility. The purpose of this experiment was to answer the question, "What effect will an increase in social responsiveness to one person, the 'mother' have upon responsiveness to other persons?" In this instance, each mother worked with four babies who lived in one room. The experimenter was responsible for feeding, bathing, diapering, soothing, holding, talking to and playing with these four babies for seven and one half hours a day, from 7:30 A.M. to 3:00 P.M., five days a week for eight weeks (a total of 300 hours). During these hours, no one else cared for the babies. The outstanding result of this study was that the youngsters developed a tremendous social responsiveness. There was, however, no significant difference in intellectual development, nor did the subjects seem to discriminate between the experimenters and other strangers. As indicated, however, the babies were extremely responsive to all adults.

In another study, Sayegh and Dennis (1965) were interested in the effects of supplementary experiences upon the behavioral development of infants in institutions. In this case, youngsters four to twelve months old resided in an orphanage in Beirut, Lebanon. The enrichment program offered involved one-hour supplementary experiences for fifteen days. Activities included accustoming infants to sit upright, encouraging interest in objects and developing skills related to object manipulation. In one month, the developmental age increased four times that of the pre-experimental pattern. When enrichment ceased, only two of the five subjects revealed subsequent gains during the second month. It was contended that the gains realized reflected learning rather than any form of parental attachment.

McKenney and Keele (1963) also found that increased mothering caused significant changes in two young institutionalized retarded subjects. The youngsters' verbal behavior improved, it became purposeful and goal-oriented, and there was a marked reduction in asocial reactions. Interestingly, the increased mothering program was provided by twelve mildly retarded surrogates who spent at least four hours a day with the two severely retarded boys, five days a week for a total period of five weeks.

Nursery school programs have proven particularly successful with the young child. The study most commonly cited in this area was reported by Kirk in 1958. In this project, eighty-one mentally retarded children between the ages of three and six were studied for a period of three to five years. Of the eighty-one subjects, twenty-eight participated in a community preschool program and fifteen were enrolled in an institutional program. The remaining thirty-eight subjects served in appropriate contrast groups. The preferred training experiences resulted in improved functioning among most subjects. Of the forty-three subjects participating in a preschool program, thirty (70 percent) made and maintained significant gains with respect to both measured intelligence and social performance. Greatest gains were enjoyed by those children residing in inadequate psychosocial environments. Retarded youngsters living in a residential facility who were enrolled in the preschool program had an average IQ gain of 10.1 points in one year. In contrast, nonparticipating residents in a residential setting had an average IQ loss of 6.5 points. Retarded subjects in the community also realized significant IQ gains — +11.8 points for those enrolled in a preschool program and +6.9 points for those who remained at home. Other findings indicated that retarded persons with organic involvement and those from adequate homes received minimal benefits from preschool training.

In 1970, Mitchell and Smeriglio introduced an activity therapy program for a group of moderately and severely retarded children in a residential setting to facilitate the development of social competence. All subjects were three to twelve years of age. After three years, subjects enrolled in the program maintained their preadmission rate of social development; the SQ of control subjects, i.e. those without the program, declined approximately ten points. The program was particularly effective among those residents who were moderately retarded.

Vogel *et al.* (1967) reported similar findings to those just presented with regard to providing an educational program for moderately retarded youngsters. In this instance, subjects were re-evaluated 3.8 years following the establishment of the program. Moderately retarded persons enrolled in the formal training program gained approximately 1.4 IQ points which was not considered significant; however, the control group revealed an overall loss of 9.65 points. It was also discovered that youngsters not enrolled in the program who occasionally went home lost only 6.3 points as compared with 12.6 points for those who never went home. Also, youngsters who were organically involved tended to lose more than those of familial origin.

Specially-designed intensive training programs have also resulted in facilitating significant gain in self-help skills. This has been demonstrated in several studies, e.g. Eyman *et al.* (1970) and Cortazzo *et al.* (1973).

Finally, intervention efforts introduced during adolescence can have a marked effect on improving the self-concept of retarded persons in a residential setting. Ghannad (1969) found that a planned program of interaction with men had enhanced the self-concepts of institutionalized adolescents. Corder (1970) reported similar findings with retarded girls as a result of physical fitness training.

Thus, there is evidence to indicate that intervention in an appropriate form at almost any age can have a very definite, positive effect upon the resident's feelings of self-worth performance and studies cited in this discussion as well as those mentioned previously also indicate that, with proper programming, retarded persons in a residential facility will do as well as those in the community at least with regard to academic performance, acquisition of self-help skills, and social development as measured by the *Vineland Social Maturity Scale*.

THE PHYSICAL ENVIRONMENT

Every aspect of residential living possesses the potential to influence (positively or negatively) the development and behavior of each resident. One very critical dimension of residential living is the physical environment. Yet, it frequently is considered only in terms of health and safety, maintenance, traffic patterns and maximal utilization of space at minimal cost. While these are very important administrative considerations, when they are viewed independently of residents' needs and programs or when final decisions are based solely or primarily on such factors, the resultant physical facility usually proves to be wholly inadequate in terms of human development.

According to the President's Committee on Mental Retardation (1970) a residential facility

> should provide a warm, stimulating social setting, devoid of any form of dehumanizing conditions. The retarded should be helped to live as normal a life as possible in safety. Small groupings designed to promote maximal social and emotional growth appropriate to the retarded persons should be effected. The living quarters should provide maximal opportunity for privacy, with closets, lockers, etc., for personal possessions. Living quarters should be consistent with cultural norms, with due regard to health, safety, and conformity to the accepted community standards... Existing facilities as well as proposed facilities should attempt to establish a total environment — physical, psychological, and social — that will provide effective programming for small groups of individuals in a highly personalized atmosphere.

This position reflects a responsibility which makes it incumbent upon each residential facility to provide that environment which is most appropriate for human growth and development. Certainly, no sanction is given to the warehousing phenomenon which still typifies some of today's facilities.

One of the most common and totally inappropriate characteristics of the physical environment involves the confinement of a large number of residents to a limited, relatively impersonal area, i.e. fifteen or more residents living together, sharing a common dormitory and day room. Grunewald (1971), in his monograph on the dynamics of residential living as influenced by the environment, placed considerable emphasis on "the principle of the small group,"

> Many workers have observed the positive effect on a severely retarded individual when he was removed from a large ward of 20-30 persons to a small group of 10 or less (5 to 8 would be preferable). Suddenly the retardate's reaction becomes predictable and one sees that he can recognize and grasp reality . . .

> From these observations we deduced that an influence for favorable development is to be found partly in the small number of interpersonal relations forced upon the retarded thus making them potentially stimulating rather than frustrating, and partly in the home-like atmosphere and equipment of the room and of the unit to which the room is connected.

A variety of research with small groups of normal persons in confinement have identified a number of characteristics which also typify the behavior of retarded persons living in many of our residential facilities. Smith (1969), for example, did an extensive review of the research literature dealing with small groups in confinement, including controlled isolated-group experiments, military service in isolated duty stations, submarine-service habitability, aerospace assessments and reports of expeditions and explorations. The results based on normal adult human subjects consistently revealed an inability of such persons to tolerate confinement. Within a relatively short period of time (usually 10 to 15 days), subjects became hostile, rude, uncooperative, passive, irritable, depressed, compulsive and lethargic. They defied rules and regulations, adopted a survival of the fittest attitude, and developed a tremendous territorial need. Conditions of confinement were further aggravated by heat, noise and bad odors. In essence, while normal adults cannot tolerate close and continuous confinement with other persons, retarded individuals are placed in such environments every day with the full expectation and knowledge that they will remain in that setting for an extended period of time.

Need for Territory

Territorial needs of the retarded have been well identified. According to Paluck and Esser (1971a), "territorial behavior results in more order in the environment through the establishment of consistent spatial patterning between individuals . . . It is also possible that territoriality has an additional functional role among confined groups in that it serves to reduce the constant stress of interpersonal contact by isolating the individual from the groups for period of time."

These two researchers (1971a, 1971b) conducted a series of studies examining the territorial behavior of moderately and severely retarded males in a residential facility. In the first study, subjects quickly established their own territories in the playroom. Further, the nature of the territoriality and the manner in which it was staked out reflected the subject's position in the social or dominance hierarchy. Twenty months later the subjects' territorial behavior was re-evaluated. Interestingly, residents recalled and reclaimed the same territory as they had done nearly two years previously.

Hereford *et al.* (1973) also examined the question of territory. In this study it was found that bedwetting and soiling among nine profoundly retarded adults decreased as the territory surrounding their beds was increased and visual boundaries established.

There is no question that even the severely and profoundly retarded need to have a place (as well as possessions) of their own. Ownership and privacy are vital. Regrettably, opportunities for both are all too rare in many residential facilities. The situation most commonly found was described by Cleland and Dingman (1970),

> The restrooms, beds, and night stands represent a few of the more common areas ordinarily reserved for patient use, but none, ordinarily, are inviolable private areas. In practice, patients at any level of retardation seek out areas of relative privacy. For the profoundly retarded whose capacity for mobility through space is limited, one finds a not infrequent positioning in spots of relative privacy, i.e., under their beds, in the same chair or corner day after day, or similar unoccupied spots where 'squatter's rights' are open.

Sensory-Perceptual Deprivation

The literature is redundant with animal studies concerning the adverse effects of sensory-perceptual deprivation. Reviews of such research by Beach and Jayne (1954), Hebb (1958) and Bronfenbrenner (1968) all demonstrated that animal subjects in deprived settings showed a reduced level of learning performance, grossly affected problem solving behavior, an inability to use visual and

auditory cues appropriately, radically reduced normal explora-
tory behavior, and abnormal behavior and posturing.

In addition, many authorities believe that there are definite
developmental periods when certain experiences are critical.
Speman (Beach and Jayne, 1954), for example, advances the
"Theory of Induction" which in essence states that there are
"brief periods in the behavioral development of animals during
which the future of certain aspects of behavior is so strongly
affected by contemporary environmental influences that have no
such effect at other points along the life span."

In contrast to deprivation-oriented studies, other animal experiments have been concerned with the effects of an enriched environment. These studies, all of which used rat and mice subjects,
indicated that enriched early environmental experiences e.g.
playing with "toys" and environmentally-supported explora-
tion, resulted in (1) increased weight of the cerebral cortex, including the visual and somosthetic areas; (2) greater depth of the
cerebral cortex; (3) an increased enzymatic activity (AChE); and
(4) increased problem solving ability (Rosenzweig *et al.*, 1968,
1972, and Henderson, 1970).

Though the results of animal studies cannot be translated directly to either the residential environment or the mentally retarded as learners, one cannot ignore their implications. There is
sufficient evidence among studies concerning institutionalized
retardates to lend credence to the fact that reduced functional
ability is a consequence of environmental deprivation. According
to Yarrow (1970),

> The importance of adequate sensory stimulation to the develop-
> ment of cognitive abilities in young children has been well
> documented. Data from experimental studies on animals in-
> volving restriction in stimulation can be integrated meaning-
> fully with data on infants and young children in institutions.
> The findings of developmental retardation in children who
> have been exposed to institutional environments are paralleled
> by findings of sensory impairment in animals deprived of
> stimulation.

Casler (1968), in his excellent review of the literature, also contends that environmental deprivation will account for such rhythmically-oriented stereotype behavior as head banging, rocking and whirling among retardates in a residential facility. Also, brain-damaged children suffer especially from isolation and environmental deprivation.

The physical environment and its stimulus properties must be considered and studied for even the infant resident. Research by Fantz, e.g. 1965, and others have demonstrated unequivocally that the newborn are sensitive to visual stimuli and will respond differentially. For example, Friedman *et al.* (1970) studied the response patterns of newly born infants (24 to 90 hours old) and found that they attended visual stimuli and revealed both habilitation and a definite tendency to respond to novel stimuli when introduced.

This sort of behavior has been demonstrated among the mentally retarded. Miranda (1970), for example, studied the performances of sixteen Down's syndrome infants (mean CA 33.6 weeks, SD 2.8 weeks) and twenty normal infants (mean CA 31.6 weeks, SD 1.4 weeks). She found that both groups attended visual patterns and both groups revealed recognition memory for patterns displayed.

The environment, however, must also exercise control over the nature and degree of stimulation. Too much stimulation can have the same effect as too little. Studies by Brackbill have shown that excessive stimulation will reduce the arousal level of infants. In one project (1970) she and her associates studied twenty-four normal infants with a median age of twenty-seven days. The infants were bombarded with continual stimulation involving four different modalities — auditory, visual, proprioceptive-tactile and temperature. The net effect was that infants cannot tolerate high levels of stimulation. Infants spent an average of one out of every twenty minutes in quiet sleep under condition of no stimulation, but over nine minutes under continual stimulation. Increasing the number of stimuli resulted in an increase in quiet sleep accompanied by decreases in crying, heart rate, irregularity of respiratory rate and motor activity. The authors concluded that "it appears that the change in arousal level produced by continuous stimulation is not an adjunct of some cognitive, cortically mediated function . . . but is instead the product of a primitive, subcortical mechanism" (1970). Similar results were reported by Brackbill and her colleagues in an earlier study (1970), Birns *et al.* (1965) and Irwin (1941).

The retarded appear to be similarly affected even though the research evidence is very limited. Brackbill (1970) replicated her study with an anencephalitic infant, ninety days of age, with the same results as reported previously. Cromwell and his associates (1963) conducted a series of studies which indicated that visual stimulation or the absence thereof markedly affects the behavior of retarded subjects. The fact that both auditory and visual stimulators produced decreased general activity among severely retarded residents was recently demonstrated by Forehand and Baumeister (1970).

It is not uncommon in residential facilities to find that the day room for young retarded children has a noise level so high that it increases hyperactivity among certain residents while forcing others to withdraw into themselves.

Modifying the residential environment can produce positive results. Kreger (1971), for example, reported on a compensatory environment program which was developed for behaviorally disturbed, severely and profoundly retarded residents. Space was rearranged to reduce congestion and overcrowding and to increase utilization, availability and variety of sensory stimulation. Though statistical data were not presented, staff "found the residents happier, more content, more interested in the world around them, less withdrawn, less disturbed, and above all more comfortable than they had ever been . . . Self-abusive and stereotypic behavior also diminished."

Staff Effectiveness

No research could be located concerning the effects of the physical environment upon the interrelationships of staff and residents. Warren and Mondy, however, reported on a study involving fifteen attending adults observing more than 800 samples of behavior of forty-nine ambulatory institutionalized retardates with a mean CA of 106.3 months and a mean SA of 22.2

months. Their results revealed that attending adults "failed to respond at all to either appropriate or inappropriate behavior. The result of such failure to respond, of course, was to allow behavior patterns to develop in a non-systematic fashion" (Warren and Mondy, 1971).

Undesirable adult attending behavior of this nature is rather common in residential facilities in spite of the quality of personnel or their training. It is most difficult, if not impossible, for two or three cottage personnel faced with twenty children in a noisy day room to develop a close interrelationship with individual residents and be in an effective position to implement proper reinforcement procedures. If it is desired that staff respond to youngsters in the same manner as they would in their own homes, it would appear that changing the physical environment to meet such requirements is essential.

In addition, it is not uncommon in many residential facilities for a resident to be removed from his living area to receive some form of individualized instruction or special therapy. During that brief interval in the child's daily activities he frequently performs at a most adequate level. Most of the benefits accrued in specialized training, however, are lost when the child returns to his living area. If the resident's living area, in terms of its physical and psychological environment, does not support individualized treatment and training efforts, the effects of these efforts are seriously vitiated. In brief, the resident's unit or living area in his home, and it must function as such in the best sense of the term.

SUMMARY

The effects of residential living were explored from several perspectives, including separation from parents, specific developmental areas, labeling, variances between and within residential facilities, intervention programs and the physical environment. Separation from parents, regardless of the quality of the home situation, creates anxiety among most moderately and mildly retarded persons. While it is assumed that even the severely and profoundly retarded suffer from such an experience, their limited ability to communicate precludes any specific determination as to its subsequent effect on behavior.

Review of the research literature with regard to such developmental areas as intelligence and related functioning, personality, speech and language as well as education produced equivocal results. In many instances, retarded residents did not perform as well as their peers in the community. To what extent such repressed performances reflected preadmission experiences, individual characteristics of the subjects, or the effects of residential life remain relatively unclear. There is evidence, however, to indicate that the degree of personal interaction between staff and residents, the availability of specially designed programs, the existence of a supportive physical environment, and a commonly-held positive developmental philosophy by all residential personnel definitely influences resident behavior and growth.

In general, it can be concluded while resident living need not repress human functioning and can be of great assistance, the required quality of residential life and programming is not evident in many of our residential facilities. Facilities which are insufficiently staffed with well-trained personnel to design and implement individualized programs and which can only provide conditions of mass living are not in a position to foster maximum human development. Thus, it is the quality of residential services rather than institutionalization per se which must be examined.

REFERENCES

Amble, B., Bellamy, E., Gideon, C., Parks, B., and Shaffer, A.: Child care aides: Intellectual, personality, and preference patterns to job performance. *Ment Retard*, 9(5):6-10, 1971.

Balla, D., Butterfield, E., and Zigler, E.: Effects of institutionalization on retarded children: A longitudinal cross-institutional investigation. *Am J Ment Defic*, 78(5):530-549, 1974.

Balthazar, E., and Stevens, H: *The Emotionally Disturbed, Mentally Retarded.* Englewood Cliffs, P-H, 1975.

Barrett, B.: Behavioral differences among an institution's backward residents. *Ment Retard*, 9(1):4-9, 1971.

Beach, J., and Jayne, J.: Effects of early experience upon the behavior of animals. *Psychol Bull*, 51:239-248, 1954.

Bensberg, G.: The relation of academic achievement of mental defectives to mental ages, sex, institutionalization, and etiology. *Am J Ment Defic*,

53:327-330, 1953.

Birns, B., Blank, M., Bridger, W., and Escalona, S.: Behavioral inhibition in neonates produced by auditory stimuli. *Child Devel, 36*:639-645, 1965.

Brackbill, Y.: Continuous stimulation and arousal level in infants: Additive effects. *Proceedings, 78th Annual Convention, American Psychological Association,* 1970, 271-272.

Brackbill, Y., Adams, G., Crowell, D., and Gray, M.: Arousal level in neonates and preschool children under continuous auditory stimulation. *J Exp Child Psychol, 4*:178-188, 1966.

Braginsky, D., and Braginsky, B.: *Hansels and Gretels: Studies of Children in Institutions for the Mentally Retarded.* New York, HR&W, 1971.

Bronfenbrenner, U.: Early deprivation in mammals: A cross-species analysis. In Newton, G., and Levine, S.: *Early Experience and Behavior: The Psychobiology of Development.* Springfield, Thomas, 1968, pp. 627-764.

Butterfield, E., Barrett, C., and Bensberg, G.: A measure of attitude which differentiates attendants from separate institutions. *Am J Ment Defic, 72*:890-899, 1968.

Casler, L.: Perceptual deprivation in institutionalized settings. In Newton, G., and Levine, S. (Eds.): *Early Experience and Behavior.* Springfield, Thomas, 1968, pp. 573-626.

Chapman, A., and Cooper, E.: Nature of stuttering in a mentally retarded population. *Am J Ment Defic, 78*:153-157, 1973.

Clarke A., and Clarke, A.: *Mental Deficiency.* Glencoe, Free Pr, 1958.

Cleland, C., and Dingman, H.: Dimensions of institutional life: Social organization, possessions, time and space. In Baumeister, A., and Butterfield, E. (Ed.): *Residential Facilities for the Mentally Retarded.* Chicago, Aldine, 1970, pp. 138-162.

Corder, W.: Effects of physical education on the psychophysical development of educable mentally retarded girls. *Dissertation Abstr, 30*:3776, 1970.

Cortazzo, A., Schwartz, B., and Allen, R.: *Divisional Concept — A Model for Progress.* Opa Locka, South Florida Foundation for Retarded Children, 1973.

Cromwell, R., Baumeister, A., and Hawkins, W.: Research in activity level. In Ellis, N. (Ed.): *Handbook of Mental Deficiency.* New York, McGraw, 1963, pp. 632-663.

De Martino, M.: Some characteristics of the manifest dream content of mental defectives. *J Clin Psychol, 10*:175-178, 1954.

Dewey, R., and Humber, W.: *The Development of Human Behavior.* New York, Macmillan, 1951, p. 261.

Edgerton, R.: *The Cloak of Competence.* Berkeley, U of Cal Pr, 1967, p. 206.

Ehlers, W.: *Mothers of Retarded Children.* Springfield, Thomas, 1966.

Eisenberg, L.: Behavior manifestations of cerebral damage. In Birch, H. (Ed.): *Brain Damage in Children: The Biological and Social Aspects.* Baltimore, Williams & Wilkins, 1964, pp. 61-76.

Eyman, R., Tarjan, G., and Cassidy, M.: Natural history of acquisition of basic skills by hospitalized retarded patients. *Am J Ment Defic, 75*:120-129, 1970.

Fantz, R.: Visual perception from birth as shown by pattern selectivity. *Annuals NY Acad Sci, 1*:793-814, 1965.

Floor, L., and Rosen, M.: Investigating the phenomenon of helplessness in mentally retarded adults. *Am J Ment Defic, 79*:565-572, 1975.

Forehand, R., and Baumeister, A.: Effects of variations in auditory-visual stimulation on activity levels of severe mental retardates. *Am J Ment Defic, 74*:470-474, 1970.

Francis, S.: Behavior of low-grade institutionalized mongoloids: Changes with age. *Am J Ment Defic, 75*:92-101, 1970.

Friedman, S., Carpenter, G., and Nagy, A.: Decrement and recovery of response to visual stimuli in the newborn human. *Proceedings, 78th Annual Convention, American Psychological Association*, 1970, pp. 273-274.

Gardner, H., and Forehand, R.: Effects of institutionalization upon word modeling responses of retarded subjects. *Am J Ment Defic, 78*:759-761, 1974.

Gewirtz, J.: The course of infant smiling in four child-rearing environments in Israel. In Foss, B. (Ed.): *Determinants of Infant Behavior*. New York, Wiley, 1965, pp. 205-260.

Ghannad, R.: The effects of planned interaction of adult males with institutionalized mentally retarded boys upon their sex-role identification and self concepts. *Dissertation Abstr, 20*:3001, 1969.

Goldfarb, W.: Effects of psychological deprivation in infancy and subsequent stimulation. *Am J Psychiatry, 102*:18-33, 1945.

Goldfarb, W.: Variations in adolescent adjustment of institutionally-reared children. *Am J Orthopsychiatry, 17*:449-457, 1947.

Grossman, F.: *Brothers and Sisters of Retarded Children*. Syracuse, Syracuse U Pr, 1972.

Grunewald, K.: *The Guiding Environment: The Dynamics of Residential Living*. Washington, U.S. Department of Health, Education, and Welfare, Social and Rehabilitation Service, 1971, p. 4.

Guskin, S.: Research on labeling retarded persons. *Am J Ment Defic, 79*:262-264, 1974.

Guthrie, G., Butler, A., and Gorlow, L.: Patterns of self-attitudes between institutionalized and non-institutionalized retardates. *Am J Ment Defic, 67*:543-548, 1963.

Hebb, D.: The mammal and his environment. In Maccoby, E., Newcomb, T., and Hartley, E. (Eds.): *Readings in Social Psychology*. New York, Holt, Rinehart and Winston, 1958.

Heber, R.: Research on personality disorders and characteristics of the mentally retarded. *Ment Retard Abstr, 1*(3):304-325. 1964.

Heber, R., and Garber, H.: An experiment in prevention of cultural-familial retardation. In Primrose, D.: *Proceedings of the Second Congress of the International Association for the Scientific Study of Mental Deficiency*.

Warsaw, Polish Medical Publishers, 1972.

Henderson, N.: Brain weight increases resulting from environmental enrichment: A directional dominance in mice. *Science*, (169):776-778, 1970.

Hereford, S., Cleland, C., and Fellner, M.: Territoriality and scent-marking: A study of profoundly retarded enuretics and encopretics. *Am J Ment Defic*, 77:426-430, 1973.

Hobbs, M.: A comparison of institutionalized and non-institutionalized mentally retarded. *Am J Ment Defic*, 69(2):206-210, 1964.

Hobbs, N. (Ed.): *The Futures of Children*. San Francisco, Jossey-Bass, 1975a, pp. 3-4.

Hobbs, N. (Ed.): *Issues in the Classification of Children* (Two volumes). San Francisco, Jossey-Bass, 1975b.

Holowinsky, I.: IQ constancy in a group of institutionalized mental defectives over a period of three decades. *Training School Bull*, 59:15-17, 1962.

Irwin, O.: Effect of strong light on the body activity of newborns. *J Comp Psychol*, 32:233-236, 1941.

Jersild, A.: *Child Psychology*, Englewood Cliffs, P-H, 1968, pp. 201, 205.

Kay, C., and McKinney, J.: Friendship fluctuation in normal and retarded children. *J Genet Psychol*, 110:233-241, 1967.

Kershner, J.: Intellectual and social development in relation to family functioning: A longitudinal comparison of home vs. institutional effects. *Am J Ment Defic*, 75:276-284, 1970.

King, R., and Raynes, N.: Patterns of institutional care for the severely subnormal. *Am J Ment Defic*, 76:700-709, 1968.

Kirk, S.: *Early Education of the Mentally Retarded*. Urbana, U Ill Pr, 1958.

Klaber, M. (Ed.): *Conference on Residential Care*. West Hartford, U of Hartford, 1969.

Klebanoff, L.: Parental attitudes of mothers of schizophrenic, brain-injured and retarded, and normal children. *Am J Orthopsychiatry*, 29:445-454, 1959.

Kreger, K.: Compensatory environment programming for the severely retarded behaviorally disturbed. *Ment Retard*, 9(4):29-33, 1971.

Lambeth, H.: The self-concept of mentally retarded children in relation to educational placement and developmental variables. *Dissertation Abstracts*, 27:3726, 1967.

Lawrence, E., and Winschel, J.: Self-concept and the retarded: Research and issues. *Except Child*, 39:310-319, 1973.

Leiderman, P., Leifer, A., Seashore, M., Barnett, C., and Grobstein, R.: Mother-infant interaction: Effects of early deprivation, prior experience and sex of infant. In Nurnberger, J. (Ed.): *Biological and Environmental Determinants of Early Development*. Baltimore, Williams & Wilkins, 1973, pp. 154-171.

Lyle, J.: The effect of an institutional environment upon the verbal development of imbecile children. *J Ment Defic Res*, 3:122-128, 1959.

MacMillian, D., Jones, R., and Aloia, G.: The mentally retarded label: A theoretical analysis and review of research. *Am J Ment Defic, 79*:241-261, 1974.

McKenney, J., and Keele, T.: Effects of increasing mothering on the behavior of severely retarded boys. *Am J Ment Defic, 67*:361-365, 1963.

Miranda, S.: Response to novel visual stimuli by Down's Syndrome and normal infants. *Proceedings, 78th Annual Convention, American Psychological Association,* 1970, pp. 275-276.

Mitchell, A., and Smeriglio, V.: Growth in social competence in institutionalized mentally retarded children. *Am J Ment Defic, 74*:666-674, 1970.

Moss, S.: How children feel about being placed away from home. *Children, 13*:153-157, 1966.

Overbeck, D.: Attitude sampling of institutional charge attendant personnel: Cues for intervention. *Ment Retard, 9*(4):8-10, 1971.

Paluck, R., and Esser, A.: Controlled experimental modification of aggressive behavior in territories of severely retarded boys. *Am J Ment Defic, 76*:23-29, 1971a.

Paluck, R., and Esser, A.: Territorial behavior as an indicator of changes in clinical behavioral condition of severely retarded boys. *Am J Ment Defic, 76*:284-290, 1971b.

Peck, J., and Sexton, C.: Effects of various settings on trainable children's program. *Am J Ment Defic, 66*:62-68, 1961.

Perry, J., and Freedman, D.: Massive neonatal environmental deprivation: A clinical and neuroanatomical study. In Nurnberger, J. (Ed.): *Biological and Environmental Determinants of Early Development.* Baltimore, Williams & Wilkins, 1973, pp. 244-268.

President's Committee on Mental Retardation: *Residential Services for the Mentally Retarded: An Action Policy Proposal.* Washington, U.S. Government Printing Office, 1970, pp. 7-8.

Provence, S., and Lipton, R.: *Infants in Institutions.* New York, Intl Univs Pr, 1962, pp. 25-26, 131-134.

Provence, S., and Ritvo, S.: Effects of deprivation on institutionalized infants: Disturbances in development of relationship to inanimate objects. *The Psychoanalytic Study of the Child,* 1961, pp. 189-205.

Rheingold, H.: The modification of social responsiveness in institutional babies. *Monographs of the Society for Research in Child Development* (Serial No. 63), 1956.

Robertson, J.: *Young Children in Hospitals.* New York, Basic, 1958, p. 2.

Rosen, M., Diggory, J., Floor, L., and Nowakiwska, M.: Self-evaluation, expectancy and performance in the mental subnormality. *J Ment Defic Res, 15*:81-95, 1971.

Rosenzweig, M., Bennett, E., and Diamond, M.: Brain changes in response to experience. *Sci Am, 2*:22-29, 1972.

Rosenzweig, M., Krech, D., Bennett, E., and Diamond, M.: Modifying brain chemistry and anatomy by enrichment or impoverishment of experience.

In Newton, G., and Levine, S. (Ed.): *Early Experience and Behavior: The Psychobiology of Development*. Springfield, Thomas, 1968, pp. 258-298.

Rowitz, L.: Sociological perspective on labeling. *Am J Ment Defic, 79*:265-267, 1974.

Sayegh, Y., and Dennis, W.: The effect of supplementary experiences upon the behavioral development of infants in institutions. *Child Devel, 36*:81-90, 1965.

Schaffer, H., and Emerson, P.: The development of social attachments in infancy. *Monographs of the Society for Research in Child Development* (Serial No. 94), 1964.

Schlanger, B.: Speech examination of a group of institutionalized mentally handicapped children. *J Speech Hear Disorders, 18*:339-349, 1953.

Schlanger, B.: Environmental influences on verbal output of mentally retarded children. *J Speech Hear Disorders, 19*(3):339-343, 1954.

Sievers, D., and Essa, S.: Language development in institutionalized and community mentally retarded children. *Am J Ment Defic, 66*:413-420, 1961.

Smith, S.: Studies of small groups in confinement. In Zubek, J. (Ed.): *Sensory Deprivation: Fifteen Years of Research*. New York, Appleton, 1969, pp. 374-403.

Spradlin, J.: Language and Communication. In Ellis, N. (Ed.): *Handbook of Mental Deficiency*. New York, McGraw, 1963.

Stedman, D., and Eichorn, D.: A comparative study of growth and developmental trends of institutionalized and non-institutionalized mongoloid children. *Am J Ment Defic*, 69:391-401, 1964.

Sternlicht, M.: Dreaming in adolescent and adult institutionalized mental retardates. *Psychiatr Q Suppl, 40*(Part I):97-99, 1966.

Sternlicht, M., and Deutsch, M.: *Personality Development and Social Behavior in the Mentally Retarded*. Lexington, Lexington Books, 1972.

Sternlicht, M., and Siegel, L.: Institutional residence and intellectual functioning. *J Ment Defic Res, 12*:119-127, 1946.

Stimpson, C., Geake, R., and Weir, H.: Effects of early institutionalization on growth and development of young children with Down's Syndrome. *Mich Med, 67*:1212-1218, 1968.

Tizard, J.: The role of social institutions in the causation, prevention and alleviation of mental retardation. In Haywood, H. (Ed.): *Social-Cultural Aspects of Mental Retardation*. New York, Appleton, 1970, pp. 281-340.

Tizard, B., Cooperman, O., Joseph, A., and Tizard, J.: Environmental effects on language development. A study of young children in long-stay residential facilities. In Chess, S.: *Annual Progress in Child Psychiatry and Child Development, 1973*. New York, Brunner-Mazel, 1974, pp. 705-728.

Vogel, W., Kun, K., and Meshorer, E.: Effects of environmental enrichment and environmental deprivation on cognitive functioning in institutionalized retardates. *J Consult Psychol, 31*:570-576, 1967.

Warren, S., and Mondy, L.: To what behaviors do attending adults respond. *Am*

J Ment Defic, 75:449-455, 1971.

Yarrow, L.: *The Etiology of Mental Retardation: The Deprivation Model.* In Hellmuth, J. (Ed.): *Cognitive Studies 1.* New York, Brunner-Mazel, 1970, pp. 275-290.

Zigler, E.: Cognitive-developmental and personality factors in behavior. In Kauffman, J., and Payne, J. (Eds.): *Mental Retardation: Introduction and Personal Perspectives.* Columbus, Merrill, 1975, pp. 360-386.

Zigler, E.: Research on personality structure in the retardate. In Ellis, N. (Ed.): *International Review of Research in Mental Retardation.* New York, Acad Pr, 1966, pp. 77-108.

Zubek, R. (Ed.): *Sensory Deprivation: Fifteen Years of Research.* New York, Appleton, 1969.

Chapter 3

PRESENT STATUS OF
RESIDENTIAL SERVICES

PROGRAMMING for the mentally retarded and developmentally disabled, including residential services, is at the crossroads. If the present attitude of society that all persons have the right to live, learn and work in an open community is maintained and actively supported, then the present role of residential facilities can be considered as one in transition. If, however, society does not continue to perpetuate the present philosophy or provide adequate support and community services are not provided, residential facilities will revert to their more traditional role of serving a wide range of retarded persons with substantially varying needs and whose admissions may be based on reasons other than those directly related to their maximum well-being.

The discussion of the present status of residential services will take into consideration four aspects. These include (1) the generally recognized purpose of residential facilities, (2) historical precedents, (3) major influences on contemporary programming and administration, and (4) current status and trends based on a recent survey of public residential facilities.

PURPOSE OF RESIDENTIAL SERVICES

Today, most residential facilities subscribe to the statement of purpose offered by the President's Committee on Mental Retardation (1969),

> The prime purpose of residential services for the mentally retarded is to protect and nurture the mental, physical, emotional, and social development of each individual requiring full-time residential services. Inherent in this commitment is the responsibility to provide those experiences which will enable the individual (1) to develop his physical, intellectual, and social capabilities to the fullest extent possible; (2) to develop emo-

59

tional maturity commensurate with social and intellectual
growth; (3) whenever possible, to develop skills, habits, and
attitudes essential for return to contemporary society; and (4) to
live a personally satisfying life in the residential environment.

In addition to serving a resident population, most residential
facilities are also engaged in providing a variety of services to
retarded persons living in the community as well as to community agencies. The modern residential facility is no longer considered an isolated phenomenon but is viewed as one vital member in
a continuum of community services for the retarded. The nature
and extensiveness of community-oriented services will be viewed
in the section on current status and trends.

HISTORICAL PRECEDENTS

The present discussion will be limited to a few historical land-
marks primarily to illustrate several points — (1) the philosophy
of residential services has changed significantly over time; (2) no
philosophy, regardless of how humane or positive, is guaranteed
to persist; and (3) public residential facilities have always responded to society's image and expectations of the retarded. More
definitive surveys of historical trends are provided by Haskell
(1944), Sloan (1963), Kanner (1964) and Wolfensberger (1969).

The first acknowledged residential facility for the mentally
retarded was established by Johann Jacob Guggenbuhl in Abendberg, Switzerland, in 1839. His original intent was to provide a
"cure and prophylaxis" of cretinism. In order to accomplish his
goals he established a residential facility in the mountains for
cretin youngsters and adolescents. His basic program involved
pure mountain air; good diet; care of the body through baths,
massage and physical exercises; appropriate medication; and the
development of sensory perceptions. In the beginning, he and his
facility were hailed as a major reform and their fame spread
throughout western Europe. Regrettably, he was unable to cure
cretinism as promised, and owing to his frequent travels, he neg-
lected the administration of the facility. As a result, his efforts
with regard to both treatment and management were condemned.
Interestingly, while Abendberg was being closed, most other

countries in Europe as well as the United States were establishing residential facilities modeled after his ideas.

The first residential facility in the United States was developed by Samuel Gridley Howe in a wing of the Perkins Institute to serve ten "idiotic" children on October 1, 1848. Howe's initial effort led to the establishment of the Massachusetts School for Idiotic and Feeble-Minded Youth in 1855. Today, that facility is known as the Walter E. Fernald State School.

Howe's approach reflected a humane concern and positive intent to provide training for the retarded. His attitude was based on his own successful experiences in training three severely retarded blind children. He inferred that "if so much could be done for idiots who are blind, still more could be done for idiots who are not blind" (Kanner, 1964).

One of the earliest and most significant contributors to residential programming was Edouard Onesimus Seguin. Following considerable experience with the retarded at the Hospice des Incurables and at the Bicetre, France, Seguin came to the United States in 1848. He contributed not only to Howe's initial adventure but served as superintendent of the Pennsylvania Training School for Idiots and was instrumental in the creation of the American Association of Mental Deficiency in 1876. Many of the concepts and ideas advanced by Seguin in the 1840's and 1850's are identical to those presently being promulgated —

> Young children should be taught at home with the institution staff acting as advisors to the mothers.
>
> The institution's physical plant should be located where future inmates are born and raised.
>
> Living quarters should accommodate four to ten children with . . . numerous small dining rooms for family-modeled meals.
>
> The approximate size of an efficient institution should be 150-200 residents (Talbot, 1964).

In other words, Seguin believed that through education and training, retarded persons, though not cured, could function in an open society. Further, as indicated, the very positive attributes of contemporary philosophies concerning residential care were, in fact, described by Seguin as early as 1846.

It also should be noted that the early founders of residential care and training services were concerned with the more severely retarded, not the mildly retarded. For example, Seguin served the "idiot" who was defined as "an individual who knows nothing, thinks of nothing, wills nothing, and each idiot approaches more or less this summum of incapacity" (Talbot, 1964).

Unfortunately, residential care passed from the stage of making "deviant undeviant" to "removing the deviant from society" during the subsequent decades of 1870 to 1890 (White and Wolfensberger, 1969). It was at this time that residential facilities increased in size, were located in isolated rural areas, and established admission policies of accepting mildly retarded and normal epileptic persons.

This negative trend was further aggravated at the turn of the century by a subtle but significant revision in the concept underlying residential services. What had been considered *protecting the deviant from society* became *protecting society from the deviant*. These years saw laws forbidding marriage among retarded and epileptic persons, statutory sterilization requirements and the introduction of dehumanizing conditions which resulted in (1) overdependency, (2) lack of personal identity, (3) lack of privacy, (4) lack of meaningful relations and (5) lack of individual programs (National Association for Retarded Citizens, 1968).

This latter trend reflected society's basic image and fears of the retarded. The retarded were considered amoral and incorrigible. As summarized by Fernald in 1924,

> a composite portrait of a mythical person embodying all the bad qualities of many defectives appeared as the hero of what I like to call the *legend of the feeble-minded*. This legend conveyed the impression that the feeble-minded were almost all the highly hereditary class; they were almost invariably immoral; most of the women bore illegitimate children; nearly all were anti-social, vicious and criminal; they were all idle and shiftless and seldom supported themselves; they were highly dangerous people roaming up and down the earth seeking whom they might destroy (Sloan, 1963).

Though Fernald highlighted the fallacies of such concepts, especially those dealing with heredity and criminality, the attitudes and resultant patterns of programming had been set.

By World War I, residential facilities had developed throughout the United States consistent with the philosophy which encouraged large isolated facilities offering minimum programming, located primarily in rural areas. These practices were consistent with society's decision to remove the retarded and epileptic from within their midst; place them in a remote area beyond sight, thought and conscience; and treat them as indentured servants in order to reduce operational costs.

The period of 1918 to 1940 represented what Kanner (1964) termed "the great lull." Residential facilities were built around the country, serving primarily a mildly retarded and epileptic population with no significant changes in those philosophies advocated at the turn of the century.

It was not until World War II when the mildly retarded had an opportunity to demonstrate their effectiveness as citizens with regard to both military and industrial service that a major change in philosophy occurred. Following World War II, as a result of the demonstrated capabilities of the mildly retarded and an increased sensitivity to the dignity of all people, the mildly retarded began receiving vital services in the community including special education and appropriate vocational training and placement.

In 1952, the National Association for Retarded Children, now known as the National Association for Retarded Citizens (NARC), was established by parents. This organization played a tremendous role in promoting educational and vocational opportunities for the trainable or moderately retarded child. Subsequently, this subpopulation of the mentally retarded began to be served in the community, thereby reducing their need for extended residential placement. Today, the NARC is actively encouraging the development of similar opportunities for the severely and profoundly retarded as well as seeking improved residential services.

Another major impact upon residential programming involved the establishment of an advisory panel on mental retardation by President Kennedy in 1962 and his famous address to the Congress of the United States on February 5, 1963, which clearly outlined the challenge of our society in meeting the needs of both the mentally retarded and disabled,

> We as a Nation have long neglected the mentally ill and the mentally retarded. This neglect must end, if our Nation is to live up to its own standards of compassion and dignity and achieve the maximum use of its manpower.
>
> This tradition of neglect must be replaced by forceful and far-reaching programs carried out at all levels of government, by private individuals and by State and local agencies in every part of the Union.
>
> We must act —
>
> to bestow the full benefits of our society on those who suffer from mental disabilities;
>
> to prevent the occurrence of mental illness and mental retardation wherever and whenever possible;
>
> to provide for early diagnosis and continuous and comprehensive care, in the community, of those suffering from these disorders;
>
> to stimulate improvements in the level of care given the mentally disabled in our State and private institutions, and to reorient those programs to a community-centered approach;
>
> to reduce, over a number of years, and by hundreds of thousands, the persons confined to these institutions;
>
> to retain in and return to the community the mentally ill and mentally retarded, and there to restore and revitalize their lives through better health programs and strengthened educational and rehabilitation services; and
>
> to reinforce the will and capacity of our communities to meet these problems, in order that the communities, in turn, can reinforce the will and capacity of individuals and individual families.
>
> We must promote — to the best of our ability and by all possible and appropriate means — the mental and physical health of all our citizens. (Kennedy, 1963).

For the past twenty years, there has been a marked decrease in the proportion of mildly retarded and trainable persons served in residential facilities, and practically no one is being committed for reasons of epilepsy per se. Dehumanizing conditions, however, are still too prevalent.

MAJOR INFLUENCES AFFECTING
RESIDENTIAL PROGRAMMING

Contemporary residential programming and administration are being guided and, in some instances, directed by a number of forces. These include a growing recognition of the rights of the retarded, recent concepts of programming and standards. Let us consider each of these categories independently.

Generic Statements of the Rights of the Retarded

Perhaps the most significant trend in the field of mental retardation during the past ten years has involved the full recognition of the rights of retarded persons. This has taken two forms — (1) general statements of rights issued by various organizations and (2) specific litigation. The present discussion will be limited to several generic statements; specific court decisions will be reviewed in the next chapter.

A General Statement of the Rights of All Children

The mentally retarded are entitled to the same rights as all other citizens. For this reason, let us observe the general statement of rights for every child advanced by the Joint Commission on Mental Health of Children (1970),

All children have:
   The right to be wanted.
   The right to live in a healthy environment.
   The right to satisfaction of basic needs.
   The right to continuous loving care.
   The right to acquire the intellectual and emotional skills necessary to achieve individual aspirations and to cope effectively in our society.

With regard to exceptional children and youth, the Commission (1970) stated that they also have the "right to receive care and treatment through facilities which are appropriate to their needs and which keep them as closely as possible within their normal social setting."

Basic Rights of the Retarded According to the American Association on Mental Deficiency

The American Association on Mental Deficiency (AAMD) issued its basic rights statement in 1973. Accordingly,

specific rights of mentally retarded persons include, but are not limited to:

1. The right to freedom of choice within the individual's capacity to make decisions and within the limitations imposed on all persons.

2. The right to live in the least restrictive individually appropriate environment.

3. The right to gainful employment, and to a fair day's pay for a fair day's labor.

4. The right to be part of a family.

5. The right to marry and have a family of his or her own.

6. The right to freedom of movement, hence not to be interned without just cause and due process of law, including the right not to be permanently deprived of liberty by institutionalization in lieu of imprisonment.

7. The right to speak openly and fully without fear of undue punishment, to privacy, to the practice of a religion (or the practice of no religion), and to interact with peers (AAMD, 1973a).

The Association added specific extensions of the basic rights in view of the special needs of retarded persons. These included

1. The right to a publicly supported and administered comprehensive and integrated set of habilitative programs and services designed to minimize handicap or handicaps.

2. The right to a publicly supported and administered program of training and education including, but not restricted to, basic academic and interpersonal skills.

3. The right, beyond those implicit in the right to education described above, to a publicly administered and supported program of training toward the goal of maximum gainful employment insofar as the individual is capable.

4. The right to protection against exploitation, demeaning treatment or abuse.

5. The right, when participating in research, to be safeguarded

from violations of human dignity and to be protected from physical and psychological harm.

6. The right for retarded individuals who may not be able to act effectively in their own behalf to have a responsible impartial guardian or advocate appointed by the society to protect and effect the exercise and enjoyment of these foregoing rights insofar as this guardian, in accordance with responsible professional opinion, determines that the retarded citizen is able to enjoy and exercise these rights (AAMD, 1973a).

The "Declaration of General and Special Rights of the Mentally Retarded" of the United Nations

The most significant statement of rights which has appeared is the "Declaration of General and Special Rights of the Mentally Retarded." This statement, which was originally drafted by the International League of Societies for the Mentally Handicapped in 1968, was adopted by the United Nations General Assembly in 1971. The seven articles of the Declaration include

Article I

The mentally retarded person has the same basic rights as other citizens of the same country and same age.

Article II

The mentally retarded person has a right to proper medical care and physical restoration and to such education, training, habilitation and guidance as will enable him to develop his ability and potential to the fullest possible extent, no matter how severe his degree of disability. No mentally handicapped person should be deprived of such services by reason of the costs involved.

Article III

The mentally retarded person has a right to economic security and to a decent standard of living. He has a right to productive work or to other meaningful occupation.

Article IV

The mentally retarded person has a right to live with his own family or with foster parents, to participate in all aspects of community life, and to be provided with appropriate leisure time activities. If care in an institution becomes necessary, it should be in surroundings and other circumstances as close to normal living as possible.

Article V

The mentally retarded person has a right to a qualified guardian when this is required to protect his personal well-being and interest. No person rendering direct services to the mentally retarded should also serve as his guardian.

Article VI

The mentally retarded person has a right to protection from exploitation, abuse and degrading treatment. If accused, he has a right to a fair trial with full recognition being given to his degree of responsibility.

Article VII

Some mentally retarded persons may be unable, due to the severity of their handicap, to exercise for themselves all of their rights in a meaningful way. For others, modification of some or all of these rights is appropriate. The procedure used for modification or denial of rights must contain proper legal safeguards against every form of abuse, must be based on an evaluation of the social capability of the mentally retarded person by qualified experts, and must be subject to periodic reviews and to the right of appeal to higher authorities (Declaration . . . , 1969).

Supplement Statements

These initial statements concerning the rights of the retarded have been followed by a series of supplemental declarations, all of which are relevant to residential programming. In 1969, the International League reconvened in Germany to explore further basic principles for residential care. At that time the following conclusions were approved with the qualification that "they never be used as immutable principles or self-evident verities; they are hypotheses to be tested by time" (International League . . . , 1971):

All retarded children and adults are basically human beings, who must be treated with dignity and guaranteed fundamental human rights.

Efforts must be directed at eradicating "dehumanizing" conditions which still exist in some residential facilities. Conditions may be considered as dehumanizing to the degree to which they foster behavior which departs from the cultural norm.

Retarded individuals should be treated so as to promote emotional maturity. They should not be treated as children throughout their lifetime, lest childishness become fixed rather than replaced by adult patterns of behavior.

Most mental retardation programs have paid little attention to the goals of retarded persons themselves, and typically, few opportunities are provided for encouraging them to participate in decision making or goal setting.

Fostering happiness of retarded children and adults is a desirable goal, just as is fostering happiness of non-retarded individuals. Yet, as is true with the non-retarded, fostering happiness of the retarded should become secondary to the goal of developing their human qualities . . . Programs which are aimed simply at generating happiness in retarded individuals are failing to meet the more basic goal of maximizing their human qualities.

The Principle of Normalization is a sound basis for programming.

The most appropriate model for mental retardation programming is a developmental model . . .

The goal of programming for adjustment to community living is desirable and appropriate for most retarded individuals, yet it may be unrealistic and need to be modified for some seriously handicapped individuals, who may come closer to maximizing their human qualities by adapting to a specialized environment. Even profoundly retarded persons who may remain institutionalized should be stimulated to reach their optimal level of functioning.

Specific program goals must be tailored to meet the needs of each individual, and they will differ for different degrees of impairment. The most feasible and humane approach, in view of current limitations of knowledge, is to assume that all retarded persons have the potential for discharge from an institution until their response to programs clearly reveals the inappropriateness of this goal (International League . . . , 1971).

The American Association on Mental Deficiency has added two more significant rights to its basic list. These relate to the "right to life" and sterilization:

> The existence of mental retardation is no justification for the termination of the life of any human being or for permitting such a life to be terminated either directly or through the withholding of life sustaining procedures (AAMDb, 1973).

> Mentally retarded persons have the same basic rights as other citizens. Among these are the rights in conformance with state and local law, to marry, to engage in sexual activity, to have children and to control one's own fertility by any legal means available. Since sterilization is a method of contraception available to most North American adults, this option should be open to most retarded citizens as well. However, recent reports on cases involving the sterilization of mentally retarded individuals without even the most elementary legal and procedural safeguards raise serious questions concerning the adequacy of current efforts to protect the human and Constitutional rights of such citizens. Indications that retarded persons have been involuntarily rendered incapable of procreation because of presumed social irresponsibility, real or supposed genetic defects, or as a *quid pro quo* for release from an institution or receipt of financial assistance and social services are deeply disturbing . . . (AAMD, 1974).

Taken collectively, these principles simply reconfirm the fact that the mentally retarded and other developmentally disabled persons are first and foremost human beings with human needs which must be recognized and met in their entirety in as normal an environment as possible. Residential facilities should be used only when absolutely required for the shortest period of time necessary, regardless of the individual's degree of retardation or accompanying physical handicaps.

The need for these separate statements of rights in view of Constitutional guarantees for every citizen has been challenged. Fram (1974), for example, wrote, "The rights guaranteed by the

Constitution of the United States do not have exclusionary clauses. The legal profession, as a guardian of the Constitution, is obligated to enforce the legal mandates stipulated . . . When a separate Constitution for the retarded states in part, that the retarded shall have the 'same rights as other human beings,' this act recognizes the retarded as belonging to a separate class." Fram's observations are valid; there should be no need for a separate Bill of Rights for the retarded. On the other hand, the retarded have not always enjoyed the benefits of Constitutional protection; therefore, many believe that the rights of the retarded require greater visibility. It is assumed that when the rights of the retarded and other developmentally disabled persons are fully recognized by society as a whole, then such statements as have been reviewed can be retired to the ranks of historical documents.

Recent Concepts of Programming

Today there are two new, or to be more precise, two recently revitalized, concepts of programming for the retarded which are having a profound influence on residential programming. The first is the developmental model; the second is the Principle of Normalization.

The Developmental Model

The International League of Societies for the Mentally Handicapped was one of the first groups to proclaim that the most appropriate model for mental retardation programming was the developmental model "according to which retarded children and adults are considered capable of growth, learning, and development. Each individual has potential for some progress, no matter how severely impaired he might be. The basic goal of programming for retarded individuals consists of maximizing their human qualities." (International League . . . , 1971). The underlying concept of the developmental model requires that each retarded person be considered as a total human being capable of growth and development.

The developmental model has been accepted by nearly all organizations interested in and/or serving the mentally retarded and other developmentally disabled persons. For example, the National Association for Retarded Citizens has published several documents supporting the developmental model and its emphasis on facilitating each resident's degree of independence and control over his environment, e.g. 1972.

The developmental model is offered in contradiction to the medical model which some persons and groups contend has represented the major mode of residential treatment in the United States. Though there are numerous variations of the medical model, primary aspects which have been severely criticized by professionals, e.g. Roos, 1971; Wolfensberger, 1969, as well as the International League of Societies for the Mentally Handicapped (1971) and the President's Committee on Mental Retardation (1969) include

1. The overriding concept that mental retardation is an "illness" or "disease" with the subsequent tendency to treat the developmentally disabled as "sick" persons.
2. The emphasis on medical treatment to the neglect of the residents' total developmental needs.
3. The pronounced tendency to foster dependence among residents as a result of the "healer-patient" relationship plus an almost abnormal fear that a resident may hurt himself or come into contact with a communicable disease.
4. The frequent prognosis that the resident is so retarded that only custodial or skilled nursing care is required which readily becomes a self-fulfilling prophecy.
5. Administration, physical environment and programming (usually identified as "treatment") is developed along hospital lines rather than those of a home or total habilitation center.
6. The notion that all programming is to be delivered by medical personnel, e.g. physicians and nurses, with occasional consultation from a behaviorally-trained person.

Though the medical model has been in effect in some residential facilities and has probably affected programming for the severely and profoundly retarded in many facilities until recent years, the major tenets of the developmental model have been promoted by most superintendents and residential staff for many years. Unfortunately, most appeals for staff and environmental changes critical to meet the total developmental needs of the more seriously affected have fallen (and still fall) upon deaf ears.

Caution must be exercised when accepting any model of programming. While the developmental model places considerable emphasis on the psychosocial dimensions of behavior, at no time should the basic physical needs of the residents be sacrificed or the effectiveness of such services minimized. As witnessed earlier, many residents possess multiply handicapping conditions, and most of the more severely and profoundly retarded present major physical care problems. As stated by Scheerenberger (1975b), "The only model of significance involves the identification of a resident's total needs (mental, physical, emotional and social) and the delivery of appropriate programs and services which, of necessity, requires the integrated efforts of medical and nonmedical personnel."

The Normalization Principle

The Normalization Principle as defined by the International League of Societies for the Mentally Handicapped (1971)

> is a sound basis for programming which, by paralleling the normal patterns of the culture and drawing the retarded into the mainstream of society, aims at maximizing his human qualities, as defined by his particular culture. Retarded children and adults should, therefore, be helped to live as normal a life as possible. The structuring of routines, the form of life, and the nature of the physical environment should approximate the normal cultural pattern as much as possible."

Again, the Principle of Normalization has been generally accepted by most organizations serving the retarded and developmentally disabled. To illustrate, the Committee for the Handicapped Child of the American Academy of Pediatrics (1973) recently promulgated the following statement:

> All children, regardless of the *severity* and nature of their handicaps, have the *right* and should have the opportunity to receive services in educational, recreational, social, and medical settings equal to those available to their nonhandicapped peers. Such services should be in the same or specialized facilities as

their peers and manned by staff with special skills. To these ends the pediatrician should support the human management practice which enables a mentally or physically handicapped child to function in ways considered to be within acceptable norms for his society and advocate the mandating of resources which will provide families with the necessary support for the *maintaining of their children within the community.*

The Principle of Normalization, which was first developed in the Scandinavian countries, was imported to the United States and Canada primarily through the efforts of Nirje. In essence, this principle simply states that every effort should be made to enable the retarded to live a life as normal as possible. Specifically, Nirje (1969) defined normalization as "making available to the mentally retarded patterns and conditions of everyday life which are as close as possible to the norms and patterns of the mainstream of society." Further,

1. Normalization means a normal rhythm of the day for the retarded.
2. Normalization implies a normal routine of life, i.e. not always structured.
3. Normalization means to experience the normal rhythm of the year with holidays and family days of personal significance.
4. Normalization means an opportunity to undergo normal developmental experiences of the life cycle, i.e. experiences and opportunities should be consistent with the appropriate life cycle whenever possible; adjustments and special provisions should be made for the mentally retarded adult and elderly.
5. Normalization means that the choices, wishes and desires of the mentally retarded themselves have to be taken into consideration as frequently as possible and respected.
6. Normalization means living in a bisexual world.
7. Normalization means normal economic standards for the mentally retarded.
8. Normalization means that the standards of the physical facility should be the same as those regularly applied in society to the same kind of facilities for ordinary citizens (Nirje, 1969).

Taken in their totality, these concepts of normalization imply that each retarded person should live in the mainstream of society if at all possible, and that any environment in which the individual resides should provide as normal a way of life as the individual is capable of handling effectively. Also, every effort must be made to assist the resident, regardless of degree of retardation, to attain his maximum level of independence.

Reactions to the Principle of Normalization have varied among administrators of residential facilities. Warren and Jones (1973) conducted a survey among superintendents attending the 1973 annual convention of the American Association on Mental Deficiency. Thirty-nine administrators of public residential facilities and twenty-five administrators of private facilities responded. The results revealed that eighteen (46.2%) of the public administrators held a very positive attitude towards normalization. The remaining twenty-one superintendents (53.8%) were either neutral or negative in their attitude. Fifty-eight percent indicated that the normalization principle had a good chance of being realized in the near future. The results were similar among administrators of private residential facilities, i.e. 37.5 percent were very positive and 62.5 percent were neutral or negative. Sixty-two percent, however, indicated that they believed the goal of normalization could be attained in a reasonable period of time. The authors concluded that though the small sample precluded any firm conclusions, there was a lack of unanimity among administrators concerning their attitudes toward normalization, and "if pressure to pursue a normalization policy continues to grow, it would be advisable to explore in depth reasons for resistance among administrators and means of meeting the objections which they raise" (Warren and Jones, 1973).

Both the developmental model and normalization will be considered further when considering deinstitutionalization and institutional reform.

Standards

Each residential facility is guided (or directed) by several sets of standards: (1) self-determined, (2) state, (3) accreditation, and (4) federal. To some degree all four sets of standards are interwoven. The present discussion will be limited to a consideration of these standards associated with accreditation and with Title XIX of the

Social Security Act.

Accreditation Standards

Accreditation of residential facilities for the mentally retarded is a relatively recent innovation. According to the Accreditation Council for Facilities for the Menally Retarded of the Joint Commission on Accreditation of Hospitals (JCAH), the purpose of accreditation is to improve the "quality of services provided mentally retarded persons" (JCAH, 1971).

Standards used for accreditation purposes are based on the independent judgment of most knowledgeable persons in the respective field. This procedure has the advantage of being free from political sanction, fiscal considerations or the problem of accommodating existing facilities. Subsequently, accreditation standards frequently exceed those of state licensing regulations or codes.

In 1971, the Accreditation Council for Facilities for the Mentally Retarded (ACFMR) of the Joint Commission on Accreditation of Hospitals approved and distributed the standards. This represented the culmination of an effort started many years ago under the leadership of the American Association on Mental Deficiency.

The AAMD, which long has been concerned with quality of services rendered by a residential facility, appointed a committtee to study this entire area in the early 1950's. The committee filed its recommendations on standards for institutions in 1952. This report was followed by further study and refinement, and, in 1964, the AAMD published *Standards for State Residential Institutions for the Mentally Retarded*. These standards were used in evaluating residential facilities for several years.

In 1966, the National Planning Committee on Accreditation of Residential Centers for the Retarded was created and included representation from the AAMD and four other groups interested in the mentally retarded — American Psychiatric Association, Council for Exceptional Children, National Association for Retarded Children and the United Cerebral Palsy Association. Finally, the Joint Commission assumed responsibility for accrediting residential programs in 1969 with establishment of the ACFMR, which is composed of members from five professional organizations previously mentioned plus the American Medical Association.

The standards are divided into seven primary sections —

1. Administrative Policies and Practices
    Philosophy, Location and Organization
    General Policies and Practices
    Admission and Release
    Personnel Policies
2. Resident Living
    Staff-Resident Relationships and Activities
    Food Services
    Clothing
    Health, Hygiene and Grooming
    Grouping and Organization of Living Units
    Resident-Living Staff
    Design and Equipage of Living Units
3. Professional and Special Programs and Services
    Dental Services
    Educational Services
    Food and Nutrition Services
    Library Services
    Medical Services
    Nursing Services
    Pharmacy Services
    Physical and Occupational Therapy Services
    Psychological Services
    Recreation Services
    Religious Services
    Social Services
    Speech Pathology and Audiology Services
    Vocational Rehabilitation Services
    Volunteer Services
4. Records
5. Research
6. Safety and Sanitation
7. Administrative Support Services

The uniqueness of ACFMR's accreditation is not in its standards but rather in its procedures. One of the most frequent complaints about the typical licensing and accreditation process is that only written materials are surveyed, i.e. manuals and records. Rarely is there ever a check to see if the written documents actually reflect what is occurring nor is the quality of treatment assessed directly. In the case of ACFMR, however, accreditation is supposed to be based primarily on an evaluation of programs and services offered to a sample of residents individually studied.

The impact of the standards has taken several forms. First, most facilities are concerned with attaining accreditation. In many instances, this has or will require not only the introduction of new programs with additional staff, but lower rated bed capacities and extensive remodeling of the physical environment. Other agencies (state and local) as well as parents and parent groups are using the standards to assess the programmatic and administrative qualities of a residential facility.

Federal Standards

Since 1969, many states and their residential facilities for the mentally retarded have been participating in the Title XIX (Medicaid) program of the Social Security Act. Title XIX provides federal financial support for most mentally retarded persons in certified intermediate care and/or skilled nursing care facilities.

An intermediate care facility (ICF) for the mentally retarded is defined as an

> institution (or distinct part thereof) primarily for the diagnosis, treatment, or rehabilitation of the mentally retarded or persons with related conditions, which provides in a protected residential setting, individualized ongoing evaluation, planning, 24-hour supervision, coordination and integration of health or rehabilitative services to help each individual reach his maximum of functioning capacities (Intermediate care facilities, 1974).

Active treatment in an ICF for the mentally retarded includes

> (a) regular participation, in accordance with an individual plan of care in professionally developed and supervised activities,

experiences or therapies; and (b) an individual "plan of care" which is a written plan setting forth measurable goals or behaviorally stated objectives and prescribing an integrated program of individually designed activities, experiences or therapies necessary to achieve such goals or objectives. The overall objective of the plan is to attain or maintain the optimal physical, intellectual, social, or vocational functioning of which the individual is presently or potentially capable; and (c) an interdisciplinary professional evaluation consisting of complete medical, social and psychological diagnosis and evaluation, and an evaluation of the individual's need for institutional care, prior to, but not to exceed 3 months before admission to the institution or, in the case of individuals who make application while in such institution, before requesting payment under the plan; (d) re-evaluation medically, socially, and psychologically at least annually . . . including review of the individual's progress . . . , the appropriateness of the individual plan of care, assessment of continuing need for institutional care, and consideration or alternative methods of care; and (e) an individual postinstitutionalization plan (as part of the individual plan of care) developed prior to discharge by a Qualified Mental Retardation Professional and other appropriate professionals, including provision for appropriate services, protective supervision, and other follow-up services in the resident's new environment. (Intermediate care facilities, 1974).

Residential facilities participating in this program are affected in two major ways. First, an Independent Professional Review team (IPR) determines whether quality services are being rendered to each participating resident and if continued residential placement is required. This biannual evaluation by outside personnel is most critical. If in the judgment of the IPR team, for example, a resident does not require extended placement in a residential facility, it is incumbent upon the administration of that facility to seek an alternative, less restrictive placement.

Secondly, participating facilities must satisfy 563 standards which are collated under the following headings:

Administrative Policies and Practices
    General Policies and Practices
    Admission and Release

Personnel Policies
Resident Living
  Staff-Resident Relationships and Activities
  Clothing
  Health, Hygiene and Grooming
  Grouping and Organization of Living Units
  Resident-Living Staff
  Design and Equipage of Living Units
Professional and Special Programs and Services
  General Provisions
  Dental Services
  Training and Habilitation Services
  Food and Nutrition
  Medical Services
  Nursing Services
  Pharmacy Services
  Physical and Occupational Therapy
  Psychological Services
  Social Services
  Speech Pathology and Audiology
Records
  Maintenance of Resident Records
  Content of Records
  Confidentiality of Records
  Central Record Services
  Record Personnel
Research
Safety and Sanitation
  Safety
  Sanitation
Administrative Support Services
  Functions, Personnel and Facilities
  Communication
Engineering and Maintenance
  Laundry Services

It also is required that intermediate care facilities phase in higher standards. It is the intent of the federal government to incorporate all but perhaps a few of the JCAH accreditation standards into its regulations by 1977, and ICFs for the mentally retarded are expected to meet these standards as early as possible.

Title XIX rules and regulations were modified recently to include a statement enumerating the rights of retarded persons in ICF facilities. These rights include freedom from peonage, mental and physical abuse, and inappropriate utilization of chemical and mechanical restraints. Privacy, confidentiality of records and the right to communicate freely and participate in social, religious and community activities are to be guaranteed.

A "skilled nursing care facility" provides "24-hour service by licensed nurses, including the services of a registered nurse at least during the day tour of duty seven days a week . . . services are ordered by and under the direction of a physician, which as a practical matter can only be provided on an inpatient basis in a skilled nursing care facility . . . " (Skilled nursing care facility, 1974). In order to qualify for participation under Title XIX, a skilled nursing care facility must be duly licensed by the state. Some states have included specific reference to the mentally retarded in their nursing home regulations,

> Persons having a primary diagnosis of mental retardation or mental deficiency shall be admitted only on order of a physician and the recommendations of a qualified mental retardation professional, . . . The nursing home administrator shall provide a written program for those patients having a primary diagnosis of mental retardation or mental deficiency, and shall be reviewed by the department (i.e. State Department of Health and Social Services). This program shall be a statement of specific services and staff personnel assignments to accomplish and justify the goals to be attained by the nursing home. Services for patients and staff assignments shall be clearly expressed and justified in program terms. Such a program statement shall include at least the following:
>
> a. Specific admission policies for the mentally retarded and/or mentally deficient.
> b. Specific program goals for the mentally retarded and/or mentally deficient.
> c. A written description of program elements, by the administrator, including relationships, contracted services and arrangements with other health and social service agencies and

programs.
d. Statement of functions and staffing patterns as related to the program for the mentally retarded or mentally deficient.
e. Description of case evaluation procedures for the mentally retarded and/or mentally deficient.

. . . for mentally retarded patients placed in skilled or intermediate care homes and needing intermediate nursing care, there shall be 0.5 hours per patient per day, computed on a seven-day week, provided by physical therapists, occupational therapists, activity therapists, recreational therapists, social workers, vocational rehabilitation personnel, teachers or psychologists and their assistants. These requirements could be fulfilled by community activities approved by the department.

. . . for mentally retarded patients requiring personal care, there shall be one hour per patient per day, computed on a seven-day week, provided by activity therapists, social workers or vocational rehabilitation personnel and their assistants. These requirements could be fulfilled by community activities approved by the department (*Wisconsin Administrative Code*, 1974).

Most residential facilities as well as state governing bodies are basing their standards on those of Title XIX and JCAH. While such standards are effective and have been of considerable assistance in many areas, they are not without their problems —

1. While many of the standards can be readily met by new, relatively small residential facilities, they cannot be satisfied by some of the larger facilities constructed prior to 1965 without a significant financial outlay.

2. There is always the question whether one set of standards should apply equally to all residential facilities throughout the United States.

3. One frequently expressed concern is that federal regulations are too medically oriented.

4. Many of the surveyors are not professionally qualified in the field of mental retardation.

5. Some of the standards are vague and subject to individual interpretation.

6. Federal and JCAH standards are not always compatible.

7. Rigid fire and safety codes make it extremely difficult to create a normal physical environment.

Of particular concern is the fact that both federal and JCAH standards are based solely on professional judgment, and their validity in terms of actually increasing programmatic effectiveness and facilitating the return of mentally retarded persons to the community has not, in the opinion of many, been assessed adequately. As indicated, both reliability of ratings and qualifications of assessors also have been challenged,

> Any standards governing programs for the developmentally disabled person should be evaluated in a rigorous, scientifically acceptable manner. To date, the majority of standards reflect professional judgment. Their validity now needs to be established. Further, many questions have been raised about the reliability of assessment instruments and raters. Reliability studies are most essential to increasing acceptability of standards and related procedures established by many agencies (National Association of Superintendents of Public Residential Facilities for the Mentally Retarded, 1974).

The standards are both demanding and, in most instances, extremely expensive to implement. Each state is faced with the problem of meeting the standards either to qualify for federal funding and/or to be in compliance with the level of care deemed minimal by various federal court decisions. As indicated, the cost will be tremendous; hopefully, this fact will not result in the forced depopulation of residential facilities without adequate community programs.

CURRENT STATUS AND TRENDS

The information contained in this section is based on a survey of public residential facilities recently reported by Scheerenberger (1975a). The survey was conducted under the auspices of the National Association of Superintendents of Public Residential Facilities for the Mentally Retarded and was supported in part by a research grant from the President's Committee on Mental Retardation. It was intended to provide current information on the status and trends of public residential programs, which for purposes of the present discussion included basic demographic data, resident programs, services to nonresidents and parental participation.

Basic information was gathered through the use of a thirty-four item questionnaire which was forwarded to the superintendents of 250 public residential facilities (PRFs) listed in a continually updated directory maintained by the National Association of Superintendents. All data were collected in the fall of 1974.

Of the 250 public residential facilities, fifteen had not attained operational status at the time of the survey. Of the remaining 235 facilities, 192 (82%) responded; not all, however, completed each item. Forty-nine of the fifty states were represented, and the lowest return rate per state was 50 percent. Most of the states, including such larger ones as New York, California and Ohio, were represented by at least 80 percent of their facilities. Thus, the returns were substantial not only in terms of the number of responses, but also with regard to their distribution throughout the country.

Demographic Data

The results will be summarized briefly according to primary areas of inquiry.

Rated Bed Capacity

The total rated bed capacity of 191 PRFs (81% of the 235 operational facilities) providing data was 148,160 in the fall of 1974. The range was 10 to 3,178 with a median of 649. There was a significant difference between 106 PRFs established by 1964 and the eighty-five constructed since that date. The older PRFs ranged in bed capacity from 169 to 3,178 with a median of 1,014; the newer facilities ranged from ten to 1,508 with a median of 318. The total rated bed capacity for the 106 older facilities was reduced by 15 percent since 1964.

The total estimated bed capacity for the 235 operational facilities was 178,000.

While older facilities have reduced their capacities, these gains appear to be offset, at least partically, by the relatively large number of new, smaller facilities recently established. As stated, there were 135 operational facilities in 1964; in 1974, there were 235, a 74 percent increase.

Actual Resident Population

The actual resident population as reported by 191 PRFs (81%) in the fall of 1974 was 141,522. The range was ten to 3,094 with a median of 585. Again, there was a distinct difference between older and newer facilities. The range in actual number of residents in older PRFs was 150 to 3,094 with a median of 956; in newer facilities, the range was ten to 1,723 with a median of 198.

Analysis of the resident population for 176 PRFs from FY 1969-1970 through FY 1973-1974 revealed an overall decrease of 8.9 percent. The older PRFs reduced their populations by 15.9 percent since FY 1964-1965 (Scheerenberger, 1965).

Based on the information provided by this survey, it was estimated that the total number of residents in public residential facilities was approximately 176,000. The total rated bed capacity was estimated to be 178,000.

In 1964, the rated bed capacities for 135 PRFs was 180,133 with an actual population of 192,493 (Scheerenberger, 1965). In other words, the actual population exceeded the total rated bed capacity by approximately 7 percent. This pattern on a national scale is no longer evident, i.e. the number of residents is less than the rated bed capacity. This does not mean, however, that no PRFs were overcrowded. Twenty-seven (14%) of the reporting 191 facilities were overcrowded; sixteen of these were overcrowded by more than 10 percent. This small group of PRFs included both old and new facilities.

Sex Distribution

Of 138,183 residents, 72,907 (53%) were male and 65,276 (47%) were female.

Chronological Age and Level of Retardation

Approximately 42 percent of 130,973 residents reported by 178 PRFs were of school age, i.e. CA three to twenty-one; 53 percent were adults under age sixty-two; and less than 1 percent was under age three. Since 1964, there has been a definite increase in the number of residents over CA twenty-one and a significant decrease in the number of residents twenty-one years of age and younger.

Approximately 71 percent of the residents were profoundly and severely retarded; the remaining 29 percent were moderately or less retarded. There appeared to be a tendency toward lower levels of intellectual functioning among residents. The majority of residents were severely and profoundly retarded, three to twenty-one years of age.

Distribution of 91,436 residents of 141 PRFs (60%) by both chronological age and degree of retardation is presented in Table IV. Again, the majority of residents were severely and profoundly retarded, three to twenty-one years of age.

TABLE IV
DISTRIBUTION OF RESIDENTS OF 141 RESIDENTIAL
FACILITIES BY LEVEL OF RETARDATION
AND CHRONOLOGICAL AGE

Level of retardation	Chronological age:								Total	
	0-2		3-21		22-61		62+			
	n	%	n	%	n	%	n	%	n	%
Borderline+	4	.004	950	1.038	1247	1.363	215	.235	2416	2.64
Mild	9	.009	3096	3.385	3556	3.889	416	.454	7077	7.74
Moderate	21	.022	6054	6.621	8880	9.711	765	.836	15720	17.19
Severe	56	.061	11224	12.275	14067	15.384	1266	1.384	26613	29.10
Profound	218	.238	19065	20.850	19443	21.810	884	.966	39610	43.33
Total	308	.340	40389	44.170	47193	51.610	3546	3.880	91436	100.00

From: Scheerenberger (1975a)

Multiple Handicapping Conditions

As shown in Table V, approximately 50 percent of the resident population was multiply handicapped, and 34 percent of those affected had more than one handicapping condition. These data were based on reports by 126 PRFs (53%) with a total resident population of 105,442.

TABLE V
DISTRIBUTION OF MULTIPLY HANDICAPPED RESIDENTS
BY CONDITION AND CHRONOLOGICAL AGE

Handicapping condition	Chronological age:				Total
	0-2	3-21	22-61	62+	
Blind	27	2132	1561	105	3825
Deaf	10	1070	1053	93	2226
Deaf & blind	(13)	(492)	(156)	(10)	(671)
Emot. Dist.	3	3552	4225	240	8020
C. P. etc.	362	10426	7664	991	19443
Epilepsy	75	9245	9941	485	19746
Total	477	26425	24444	1914	53260
Total resident population	510	46394	53986	4552	105442
Percent multiply handicapped	94	57	45	42	50.51
More than one handicapping condition	149	9808	7766	572	18295
Percent	31	37	31	30	34

From: Scheerenberger (1975a)

Etiological Classification

One hundred sixteen PRFs (49%) recorded the associated etiological classification for 63,980 residents. Of the 116 PRFs, seventy-one used the new AAMD classification (1973); forty-five used the old (1959). Since the etiological categories of these systems are not entirely compatible, separate tables were prepared. Only the data recorded according to the new system will be reported. As will be observed from Table VI, sociopsychological causes of retarded functioning were most prevalent among the less severely affected. Also, in spite of recent advances in the medical sciences, the single largest etiological category for even the severely and profoundly retarded was *unknown prenatal influence*.

TABLE VI

DISTRIBUTION OF RESIDENTS BY MEDICAL (ETIOLOGICAL)
CLASSIFICATION ACCORDING TO NEW (1973) AAMD NOMENCLATURE

| Classification | Level of retardation: | | | | | | | | | | | |
| | PMR | | SMR | | Moderate | | Mild | | Borderline+ | | Total | |
	n	%	n	%	n	%	n	%	n	%	n	%
0. Infections & Intoxications	1880	16.25	1098	13.49	621	13.49	227	9.73	96	15.02	3922	14.38
1. Trauma or physical agent	1887	16.30	1231	15.41	673	14.62	334	14.32	100	15.65	4225	15.49
2. Metabolism or nutrition	395	3.42	216	2.65	108	2.35	37	1.59	8	1.26	764	2.80
3. Gross brain disease (postnatal)	483	4.17	328	4.04	200	4.35	90	3.86	39	6.10	1140	4.18
4. Unknown prenatal influence	3800	32.88	2560	31.46	1260	27.38	618	26.49	108	16.90	8346	30.60
5. Chromosomal abnormality	1495	12.93	899	11.05	317	6.89	38	1.62	2	.31	2751	10.08
6. Gestational disorders	768	6.64	396	4.87	223	4.85	117	5.01	46	7.19	1550	5.68
7. Following psychiatric disorder	107	.93	130	1.59	126	2.74	91	3.90	20	3.14	474	1.74
8. Environmental influences	751	6.48	1278	15.71	1074	23.33	781	33.48	220	34.43	4104	15.05
Total	11566	100.00	8136	100.00	4602	100.00	2333	100.00	639	100.00	27276	100.00

From: Scheerenberger (1975a)

Special Programs

One hundred forty-seven PRFs (58%) identified the number of persons engaged in five primary program areas — (1) formal education or training, (2) language and speech therapy, (3) occupational and/or physical therapy, (4) behavior management and (5) work activity/sheltered workshop. Distribution of these residents according to program category is presented in Table VII. A substantial number of residents eligible for formal training or education programs were receiving such services.

TABLE VII
NUMBER OF RESIDENTS ENROLLED IN SPECIAL
PROGRAMS AS REPORTED BY 147 RESIDENTIAL FACILITIES

Program	n	%
Formal education or training programs	37,809	84.9[1]
Language and speech therapy	14,606	32.8[1]
Occupational and/or physical therapy	17,902	18.0[2]
Behavior management	15,457	31.1[1]
Work activity, sheltered workshop	12,171	25.9[3]

[1] Of 44,527 residents of school age (i.e., CA 3-21)
[2] Of 99,409 residents CA 3-61
[3] Of 54,882 residents CA 21-61

From: Scheerenberger (1975a)

As shown in Table VIII, based on data reported by 133 PRFs (53%) with a total population of 83,484, considerable emphasis of these programs has been placed on providing for the severely and profoundly retarded. Not all residents, however, were receiving total programming. According to information provided by 124 PRFs (49%) with a total resident population of 81,009, approximately 34 percent of the residents still required some form of program which they were not receiving. The greatest need appeared to involve all forms of supplemental programming, e.g. occupational and physical therapy, for the severely and profoundly retarded.

TABLE VIII

NUMBER OF RESIDENTS ENROLLED IN SPECIAL PROGRAMS AS REPORTED
BY 133 RESIDENTIAL FACILITIES WITH A TOTAL POPULATION OF 83,484

Program	SMR/PMR		Moderate		Mild		Borderline		Total	
	n	%	n	%	n	%	n	%	n	%
Formal education or training programs	19621	60.8	7656	23.8	3444	10.6	1577	4.8	32298	100
Language and speech therapy	8062	64.5	2422	19.4	1862	14.9	158	1.2	12504	100
Occupational and/or physical therapy	8087	62.9	3644	28.4	886	6.9	233	1.8	12850	100
Behavior management	5167	60.5	1924	22.5	1081	12.7	368	4.3	8540	100
Work activity, sheltered workshop	4137	41.0	3664	36.3	1748	17.3	531	5.4	10080	100

From: Scheerenberger (1975a)

Services to Nonresidents

One item of the survey was concerned specifically with services offered to nonresidents from the community, and 152 (92%) of the 154 PRFs responded to this item. As shown in Table IX, only seventeen PRFs (11%) did not offer some form of service to nonresidents.

In addition to the categories specified in Table IX, a variety of additional services were offered by at least one residential facility. These included day care, audiology, job placement, education for the nonhandicapped, homemaking services, art and dance therapy, help for obtaining benefits, transportation, infant stimulation, sensory motor training, dental care, genetic counseling and preschool language programs.

TABLE IX
DIRECT SERVICES OFFERED TO NON-RESIDENTS
AS REPORTED BY 152 RESIDENTIAL FACILITIES

Service	n	%
Trainable or educable classes	41	27
Self-help or developmental classes	46	30
Counseling	65	43
Vocational training	44	29
Medical and/or nursing treatment	30	20
Diagnostic services	82	54
Physical therapy	31	20
Recreation	41	27
Sex education	10	7
Home visitation by staff	61	40
Respite care	117	77
None	17	11

From: Scheerenberger (1975a)

The results of the present survey were similar to those reported previously by Rosen and Bruno (1970) — trainable or educable classes, 34 percent; self-help or developmental classes, 32 percent; counseling, 59 percent; vocational training, 40 percent; medical and/or nursing treatment, 33 percent; diagnostic services, 70 percent; physical therapy, 23 percent; recreation, 32 percent; and home visitations by staff, 40 percent.

With regard to respite care, 117 (77%) of the 152 responding PRFs offered this service. There was, however, considerable variance in the number of residents served per year, i.e. the range was 0 to 256 with a median of 15.

Parental Participation in Residential Activities

Parents are becoming extremely active in many aspects of residential programming and services. For example, 94 percent of the

responding PRFs indicated that parents participated in selecting
a community placement facility for their son or daughter. Their
involvement with placement programs also included serving as a
member of the review team, outreach work and public education.

In addition, parents were actively engaged in many other programmatic areas. Table X presents the responses of 148 PRFs with
regard to the degree of parental participation in various activities.
Also included in this table are the data from Rosen and Bruno's
1970 study. In most instances, the fluctuation in percentages can
be attributed to variances in sampling with several exceptions.
First, it would appear that parents are much more active today in
such areas as treatment, training and sex education. Secondly,
there was no mention in the Rosen and Bruno (1970) report of
parents serving on committees. Parents now participate on advisory committees and are active in protecting the human and civil
rights of residents.

TABLE X
PARENT PARTICIPATION AS REPORTED
BY 148 RESIDENTIAL FACILITIES*

Activity	1970**		1974	
	n	% (of 108 PRFs)	n	% (of 148 PRFs)
Social	70	65	102	69
Treatment	24	22	63	43
Recreation	64	59	67	45
Training	22	20	59	40
Religion	35	32	53	36
Sex education	7	6	29	20
Public relations	62	57	90	61
Fund raising	56	52	87	59
Advisory committees:	--	--	94	64
Administrative	--	--	(61)	(41)
Program	--	--	(57)	(39)
Advocacy/Human & civil rights	--	--	(69)	(47)
None	10	9	11	7

* From: Scheerenberger (1975a)
**From: Rosen and Bruno (1970)

In spite of increased opportunities for greater participation in
the lives and affairs of their children, however, many residential
facilities reported little interaction between parents and resident.
As shown in Table XI, the percentages of visitations registered by
the responding facilities varied appreciably, i.e. 2 to 100 percent of

the residents enjoyed at least one parental visit per year. The median was 59.6 percent.

The data presented indicate many improvements in residential services. Residential facilities are serving an increasing number of severely and profoundly multiply handicapped residents. Though many facilities remain too large, there is a gradual trend toward reducing their size, and newer facilities are quite limited in terms of rated bed capacity. A variety of special programs are being offered to residents, regardless of degree of retardation; yet, significant gains in this area need to be made. Most residential facilities are extending their services to the community, and there are growing opportunities for parents to become involved in the broad aspects of residential programming.

TABLE XI
PARENTAL VISITS WITH RESIDENTS
AS REPORTED BY 143 RESIDENTIAL FACILITIES

Percent of residents visited at least once a year	n	%
90-100	22	15.4
80- 89	18	12.6
70- 79	21	14.7
60- 69	23	16.1
50- 59	24	16.8
40- 49	14	9.8
30- 39	7	4.9
20- 29	7	4.9
10- 19	5	3.5
0- 9	2	1.3
Total	143	100.0

From: Scheerenberger (1975a)

SUMMARY

Contemporary philosophies governing residental programming emphasize (1) meeting the total developmental needs of each resident including the severely and profoundly retarded; (2) providing a warm, normal physical environment; and (3) returning residents to their home communities as soon as possible. Philosophies of this nature have been reinforced by such concepts as the developmental model and the principle of normalization, a growing recognition of the rights of the retarded, standards for accreditation, and federal regulations.

Today, there are an estimated 176,000 retarded persons living in 235 operational public residential facilities with a total bed capacity of 178,000. Most of these facilities provide a comprehensive range of developmental activities and programs for all residents including the severely and profoundly mentally retarded. They also offer a variety of services to retarded persons from the community, e.g. diagnosis and evaluations, education and training, medical services and respite care. Though there is evidence to indicate that parents are becoming more active in residential programming and management, many need to be encouraged to resume a more active relationship with their son or daughter.

REFERENCES

American Association on Mental Deficiency: Rights of mentally retarded persons. *Ment Retard, 11*(5):56-58, 1973a.
American Association on Mental Deficiency: The right to life. *Ment Retard, 11*(6):66, 1973b.
American Association on Mental Deficiency: Sterilization of persons who are mentally retarded. *Ment Retard, 12*(2):59-61, 1974.
Committee for the Handicapped Child: *Normalization: A Guide to Services for Handicapped Children.* New York, American Academy of Pediatrics, 1973, p. 2.
Declaration of general and special rights of the mentally retarded. *Ment retard, 7*(4):2, 1969.
Fram, J.: The right to be retarded — normally. *Ment Retard, 12*(6):32, 1974.
Haskell, R.: Mental deficiency over a hundred years. *Am J Psychiatr, 100*:107-118, 1944.
Intermediate care facilities. *Fed Reg, 39*:2221, 1974.
International League of Societies for the Mentally Handicapped, Report of Frankfurt conference. *The Record,* June, 1971, p. 2.
Joint Commission on Accreditation of Hospitals: *Standards for Residential Facilities for the Mentally Retarded.* Chicago, Joint Commission on

Accreditation of Hospitals, 1971, p. vii.

Joint Commission on Mental Health of Children: *Crisis in Child Mental Health: Challenge for the 1970s.* New York, Har-Row, 1970, pp. 3-4.

Kanner, L.: *A History of the Care and Study of the Mentally Retarded.* Springfield, Thomas, 1964, p. 40.

Kennedy, J.: *Message from the President of the United States.* Washington, House of Representatives (88th Congress), Document Number 58, 1963, pp. 13-14.

National Association for Retarded Citizens: *Policy Statements on Residential Care.* New York, National Association for Retarded Citizens, 1968.

National Association for Retarded Citizens: *Residential Programming for Mentally Retarded Persons.* Arlington, National Association for Retarded Citizens, 1972.

National Association of Superintendents of Public Residential Facilities for the Mentally Retarded: *Contemporary Issues in Residential Programming.* Washington, President's Committee on Mental Retardation, 1974, pp. 7-8.

Nirje, B.: The Normalization Principle and its human management implications. In Kugel, R., and Wolfensberger, W. (Eds.): *Changing Patterns in Residential Services for the Mentally Retarded.* Washington, U.S. Government Printing Office, 1969, pp. 51-58.

President's Committee on Mental Retardation: *Residential Services for the Mentally Retarded: An Action Policy Proposal.* Washington, U.S. Government Printing Office, 1969, p. 1.

Roos, P.: Misinterpreting criticisms of the medical model. *Ment Retard, 9*(2):22-24, 1971.

Rosen, D., and Bruno, M.: *Trends: Residential Services for the Mentally Retarded.* Medical Lake, National Association of Superintendents of Public Residential Facilities for the Mentally Retarded, 1970, p. 22.

Scheerenberger, R.: A current census of state institutions for the mentally retarded. *Ment Retard, 3*(1):4-6, 1965.

Scheerenberger, R.: *Current Trends and Status of Public Residential Services for the Mentally Retarded: 1974.* Madison, National Association of Superintendents of Public Residential Facilities for the Mentally Retarded, 1975a, pp. 11, 12, 14, 34, 35, 39, 41, 42.

Scheerenberger, R.: *Managing Residential Facilities for the Developmentally Disabled.* Springfield, Thomas, 1975b, p. 13.

Skilled nursing care. *Fed Reg, 39*:35776, 1974.

Sloan, W.: Four score and seven. *Am J Ment Defic, 68*:6-14, 1963.

Talbot, M.: *Edouard Seguin.* New York, Columbia U Pr, 1964, pp. 72, 103, 104.

Warren, S., and Jones, S.: "Survey of Administrators of Residential Facilities for the Mentally Retarded." Unpublished paper. Boston University, 1973.

Wisconsin administrative code. *Nursing Home Rules.* Madison Department of

Health and Social Services. 1974.

White, W., and Wolfensberger, W.: The evaluation of dehumanization in our institutions. *Ment Retard,* 7(3):5-9, 1969.

Wolfensberger, W.: The origin and nature of our institutional models. In Kugel, R., and Wolfensberger, W. (Eds.): *Changing Patterns in Residential Services for the Mentally Retarded.* Washington, President's Committee on Mental Retardation, 1969.

Chapter 4

LITIGATION

IN the .preceding chapter several general statements concerning the rights of the retarded were reviewed. Let us now turn our attention to specific court decisions. Since 1971 the federal courts have had a tremendous impact on residential facilities, their policies, procedures and programming. Until that time admission criteria and practices as well as the quality of public residential services were determined primarily by individual states. While each state still retains both authority and accountability, various court decisions are setting the parameters within which the states must operate.

Judgments rendered by the federal courts always involve an interpretation of the Constitution and its provisions. Though several Constitutional amendments have been cited in decisions affecting the mentally retarded, none is more important than the Fourteenth Amendment (Section 1) —

> All persons born or naturalized in the United States and subject to the jurisdiction thereof, are citizens of the United States and of the State wherein they reside. No State shall make or enforce any law which shall abridge the privileges or immunities of citizens of the United States, nor shall any State deprive any person of life, liberty, or property without due process of law; nor deny to any person within its jurisdiction to equal protection of the laws.

Two clauses contained within the Fourteenth Amendment are of particular import — "due process" and "equal protection." According to Schwindler (1974), an authority on Constitutional law, the fundamental objective of the due process of law clause

> is to safeguard the individual and his well-being — i.e., his life, his independence of action, and his possessions. It is the basic standard of conduct in governments dealing with individuals, requiring that government abide by the required limits and procedures which the people have set up as guidelines to its

actions. In the twentieth century it has been distinguished both
as a procedural and a substantive right. . . .

The procedural dimension of the due process clause requires
that safeguards be established and followed to ensure each person
a fair and equitable hearing. This includes such aspects as prior
notice, adequate legal representation or counsel, and trial by jury.

The substantive right (or principles of liberty) associated with
the due process clause was well defined by Amos in 1938,

> . . . not only has the citizen the right to be free from the mere
> physical restraint of the person as by incarceration, but the term
> is deemed to embrace the right of the citizen to be free in the
> enjoyment of all his faculties; to be free to enjoy them in all
> lawful ways; to work and live where he will; to earn his liveli-
> hood by any lawful calling; to pursue any livelihood or avoca-
> tion; and for that purpose to enter into all contracts which may
> be proper, necessary and essential to his carrying out to a suc-
> cessful conclusion the purposes mentioned above (Boggs, 1966).

In other words, no individual can have any of his civil rights
denied without the full sanction of the courts and only when all
procedural safeguards have been assured. This clause also has
been interpreted to mean that any mentally retarded person involuntarily committed to a residential facility must receive a full
treatment program, not simply custodial care.

"Equal protection of the laws" refers to the fact that no group
of people, e.g. the mentally retarded or mentally ill, can be singled
out and treated as a group. Each person has the right to have his
particular case considered individually, irrespective of any com-
monalities he may share with other people.

Cases involving residential facilities in terms of both deinstitutionalization and institutional reform involve three broad categories — right to treatment, due process and involuntary servitude.
Let us examine each of these categories and several related cases.
No attempt will be made to review all court decisions and their
implications. Persons desiring a more extensive review of litigation are referred to a report prepared by the Mental Health Law
Project (1973), the proceedings of a conference on the rights of the
mentally retarded (1973), and the three-volume series edited by
Ennis and Friedman (1974). A general overview of the legal

aspects associated with mental retardation is provided by Woody (1974).

RIGHT TO TREATMENT

The celebrated landmark case relative to right to treatment was *Wyatt* v. *Stickney* (1972). This class action suit was brought against the Alabama Department of Mental Hygiene in 1970, alleging failure of the state to provide proper treatment for the mentally retarded in a public residential school. A *class action* suit is a case brought on behalf of both the plaintiffs, who are named, and all other persons in the same situation. In this instance, though the suit was filed in the name of Ricky Wyatt by his aunt who was also his legal guardian, the class action nature of the suit made the results applicable to all other residents, present and future, at Partlow State School.

In 1971, Judge Johnson of the District Court of the United States for the Middle District of Alabama, North Division, heard testimony from persons directly involved with the Partlow State School and from representatives of various professional organizations concerned with the mentally retarded. His final judgment was precedent setting not only because it declared the constitutional rights of the retarded were being violated, but the final document included a twenty-page appendix which defined minimum treatment standards for the state school to meet. An independent monitoring committee was created by the court to ensure the implementation of its judgment.

The standards, a copy of which has been placed in Appendix A, are specific and encompassing. They cover such areas as admission policies, resident rights to treatment and habilitation, staffing patterns, records and review, physical plant and environment, medication and resident labor.

The significance of this case is fourfold — (1) it held that the retarded have a constitutional right to appropriate habilitation and treatment; (2) it was the first such case to apply specifically to the mentally retarded; (3) it was the first case where the court set standards and established monitoring procedures; and (4) it was a class action suit.

In a subsequent class action suit, *Burnham* v. *Department of Public Health of the State of Georgia* (1972), an entirely different decision was reached. Though the allegations were very similar to those cited in *Wyatt* v. *Stickney*, Judge Smith of the United States District Court for the Northern District of Georgia granted the defendants' motion to dismiss the case. While he recognized that persons in mental institutions have a moral right to treatment, he disagreed that there existed a legal obligation to provide such treatment. Further, he found no legal precedent for assuming a federal constitutional right to treatment. It also was contended that a federal court could not require state expenditures in an area controlled by state law. Finally, Judge Smith did not hold that federal courts had the right to establish and police individualized treatment programs since such would be beyond the capabilities of the court and should be left to the discretion of professionals.

This resulted in a judicial situation where two courts faced with almost identical suits reached diametrically opposite conclusions. This conflict could be resolved only by appeal to a higher court.

In May, 1972, Governor Wallace of the State of Alabama filed an appeal to the United States Court of Appeals, Fifth Circuit. This case, known as *Wyatt* v. *Aderholt* (1974) consolidated the results of *Wyatt* v. *Stickney* and *Burnham* v. *Department of Public Health of the State of Georgia*. The Alabama appeal was based on the arguments put forth by Judge Smith.

A three-judge panel of the Fifth Circuit Court of Appeals reached their decision in November, 1974. In essence, the original judgment of the Alabama suit was upheld. The Court held that (1) the retarded have the constitutional right to treatment, (2) federal courts can enter into cases of this nature, and (3) the court can set standards and monitor their implementation.

The Fifth Circuit Court's decision paralleled their earlier judgment of *Donaldson* v. *O'Connor* (1974). Briefly, Donaldson was committed in 1957 by his father, following a hearing before a county judge, to the Florida State Hospital. Donaldson, who was released from the hospital in July, 1971, contended that the defendants confined him knowing that he was neither dangerous nor reckless and that they did not provide him with adequate treatment and therapy. For example, he stated that the defendants has unjustifiably withheld such forms of treatment as "grounds privileges," occupational therapy and psychiatric counseling. The jury returned a verdict in favor of the plaintiff. He was awarded 38,000 dollars in compensatory and punitive damages which were to be paid personally by the defendants — the superintendent and clinical director.

The Fifth Circuit Court upheld this decision on appeal, stating that the Fourteenth Amendment guarantees involuntary civilly committed mental patients a right to treatment. The court also found that the "attending physicians had acted in bad faith with respect to their treatment of the patient and were personally liable for injuries or deprivations of his constitutional rights." This is the first such court decision which held individual administrators and practitioners personally liable.

The *Donaldson* v. *O'Connor* case was appealed to the Supreme Court which reached its decision on June 26, 1975. Contrary to the expectations of many, the Court did not deal with the question of constitutional right to treatment; rather, it emphasized due process. Justice Burger, in his concurring opinion, made the following observations:

> As the Court points out . . . , the District Court instructed the jury in part that "a person who is involuntarily civilly committed to a mental hospital does have a *constitutional* right to receive such treatment as will give him a realistic opportunity to be cured," (emphasis added) and the Court of Appeals unequivocally approved this phrase, standing alone, as a correct statement of law. The Court's opinion plainly gives no approval to that holding and makes clear that it binds neither the parties to this case nor the courts of the Fifth Circuit . . . Moreover, in light of its importance for future litigation in this area, it should be emphasized that the Court of Appeals' analysis has no basis in the decisions of this Court (*O'Connor* v. *Donaldson*, 1975, Part II).

With regard to professional liability, the Supreme Court stated that "an official has, of course, no duty to anticipate unforseeable constitutional developments," and remanded that portion of the decision back to the Appeals Court. Subsequently, the question of personal liability remains unanswered at this time. The main force of the Supreme Court's decision will be discussed under the section concerned with due process.

It should be noted that the opinions of Judge Johnson and the Fifth Circuit Court of Appeals supported an earlier judgment by Judge Bazelon, one of the first leaders in the area of right to treatment. In 1966 Judge Bazelon, in an appeal decision in the case of *Rouse* v. *Cameron* (1966), included the following statement:

> The principle issues raised by this appeal are whether a person involuntarily committed to a mental hospital on being acquitted of an offense by reason of insanity has a right to treatment that is cognizable in habeas corpus and if so, how violation of this right may be established. The purpose of involuntary hospitalization is treatment, not punishment. The provision of commitment rests upon the supposed necessity for treatment of the mental condition which led to the acquittal by reason of insanity.

Later, Judge Bazelon (1969) wrote, "The most important fact of the right to treatment is not that the hospital does something for everyone, but that it does the right thing for the right patient. Because individual patients, particularly mental patients, vary so much in their needs, considerable attention must be paid to the patient as an individual."

DUE PROCESS

Though several of the court actions involving residential programs for the retarded referred to due process and equal protection under the law, none was more specific than the *Lessard* v. *Schmidt* decision of 1972 in which the United States District Court for the Eastern District of Wisconsin ruled that Wisconsin's civil commitment procedures were constitutionally defective. Since a copy of the Order of Judgment has been placed in Appendix B, the present discussion will be limited to a few key features. The existing procedures

1. Failed to require effective and timely notice of the *charges* under which a person is sought to be detained.

2. Failed to require adequate notice of all rights including the right to jury trial.

3. Permitted detention longer than forty-eight hours without a hearing on probable cause.

4. Permitted detention longer than two weeks without a full hearing on the necessity for commitment.

5. Permitted commitment based on a hearing in which the person charged with mental retardation was not represented by adversary counsel at which hearsay evidence was admitted and in which medical evidence was presented without the resident having been given the benefit of the privilege against self-incrimination.

6. Permitted commitment without proof beyond a reasonable doubt that the resident was both mentally retarded and dangerous.

7. Failed to require those seeking commitment to consider less restrictive alternatives to commitment.

The net effect of this decision was that all involuntarily committed residents eighteen years of age and older had to have their commitments reviewed in a formal court hearing, adhering to the principles and guarantees cited above. Not only did the courts take into consideration whether placement in a residential facility was appropriate, i.e. was the resident dangerous to himself or others, they also took into consideration whether less restrictive alternatives were available. Some residents were transferred to smaller residential facilities located in their home communities.

If a resident were found not to be dangerous to either himself or others, he could convert from an involuntary to a voluntary commitment. His rights, however, had to be explained in terms he could understand, and the applicant had to agree freely to remain in the residential facility. The decision had to represent a true voluntary application. In many instances this was not possible because the applicant could not comprehend the implications of the decision which included the right to leave at any time, nature of the treatment to be offered, and predicted outcomes of such treatment. When this situation did arise, the court usually ordered the residential facility to locate an alternative placement for the resident as soon as possible. Though the decision only affected residents eighteen years of age and older, greater attention is being paid to the "voluntariness" of all admissions.

On March 8, 1974, a three-judge Federal Court in Tennessee declared the admission procedures for mentally retarded in that state were unconstitutional (*Saville* v. *Treadway*, 1974). Briefly, a retarded person could be admitted on the following basis:

> Application to the superintendent by the parent or guardian or person having lawful custody of a mentally retarded minor or by the guardian of a mentally retarded adult or by a mentally retarded individual eighteen (18) years of age or over on his own behalf.

> Application to the superintendent by the spouse, adult or child or other close relative of the individual, or by any health or by any public welfare officer, or school official, with the consent of the individual or his parent, guardian or person having lawful custody of him, accompanied by a certificate of a licensed physician or licensed physician and a licensed psychologist that he has examined the individual within thirty (30) days of the date on which admission is sought and that he is of the opinion that the individual is mentally retarded and is in need of care and treatment in a hospital and school.

The court rejected this approach since it violated due process under the Fourteenth Amendment. In other words, the existing procedures for both minors and adults, *voluntary or involuntary,* did not provide adequate legal safeguards.

In view of the court order, admission procedures for the state were revised. Now when parents request admission of their child to a residential facility, the child first must receive a comprehensive diagnosis and evaluation by qualified mental retardation professionals. If, following the evaluation, it is recommended that the child be voluntarily admitted to a residential facility, then the case must be re-examined by an independent review board. This board is composed of three persons, one of whom must be a parent whose child is not in a residential facility and one a professional. None may be a state employee. If the review board concurs with the recommendation, the child may be admitted. If, however, the board rejects the recommendation, the child may be admitted only by court order. Following placement in a residential facility, a representative of the board must review the continued appropriateness of the residential placement at least annually (Tennessee Department of Mental Health, 1974).

The Tennessee procedure does provide that a retarded minor "may retain private counsel of his own choice or, absent such employment, said proposed resident shall be represented at the hearing by the Citizens Advocacy Council for the Developmentally Disabled, Inc., as advocate" (Tennessee Department of Mental Health, 1974). This approach establishes additional guarantees that the rights of due process are recognized for all retarded persons, regardless of chronological age. Historically, many minors have been admitted to residential facilities on a "voluntary" basis simply determined by parental desires. This practice has been severely criticized by legal authorities,

> In most states, parents may commit their children to mental institutions without a hearing or any other form of judicial scrutiny. If a parent wants a child committed, and a hospital will accept the child as a patient, no legal authority will hear the child's protest. Moreover, the child-patient has no standing to petition for release from the institution until he or she reaches the statutory age of majority. Until that time any request for discharge must be made by the parent. Thus the minor admitted to a mental hospital on application of a parent is denied access to virtually all procedural protections — notice, hearing, appellate review, and habeas corpus — rights afforded all other patients institutionalized against their will (Ellis, 1974).

These decisions by district-level federal courts would appear to have the full support of the Supreme Court based on its findings in *O'Connor* v. *Donaldson* (1975, Part I),

> A finding of "mental illness" alone cannot justify a State's locking a person up against his will and keeping him indefinitely in simple custodial confinement. Assuming that that term can be given a reasonably precise content and that the "mentally ill" can be identified with reasonable accuracy, there is still no constitutional basis for confining such persons involuntarily if they are dangerous to no one and can live safely in freedom!

> May the State confine the mentally ill merely to ensure them a living standard superior to that they enjoy in the private com-

munity? That the State has a proper interest in providing care and assistance to the unfortunate goes without saying. *But the mere presence of mental illness does not disqualify a person from preferring his home to the comforts of an institution!* Moreover, while the State may arguably confine a person to save him from harm, incarceration is rarely if ever a necessary condition for raising the living standards of those capable of surviving safely in freedom, on their own or with the help of family or friends . . .

May the State fence in the harmless mentally ill solely to save its citizens from exposure to those whose ways are different? One might as well ask if the State, to avoid public unease, could incarcerate all who are physically unattractive or socially eccentric. *Mere public intolerance or animosity cannot constitutionally justify the deprivation of a person's physical liberty!*

Involuntary Servitude

The question of involuntary servitude relates to the Thirteenth Amendment to the Constitution,

> Section 1. Neither slavery nor involuntary servitude, except as a punishment for crime whereof the party will be duly convicted, shall exist within the United States, or any place subject to their jurisdiction.
>
> Section 2. Congress shall have power to enforce this Article by appropriate legislation.

This amendment has been used as the basic appeal to end "involuntary servitude" or "peonage" in both mental hospitals and residential facilities for the retarded.

Historically, many residential facilities relied heavily upon resident labor to maintain their levels of operation. Older residents commonly worked in the laundry or in food service and frequently tended younger, less capable children. Many received little or no remuneration. This form of involuntary servitude was challenged.

A class action suit (*Townsend* v. *Treadway*, 1973) was filed with the United States District Court for the Middle District of Tennessee, Nashville Division, alleging that the "defendants subjected the plaintiffs during their residency at the defendant institution to peonage and involuntary servitude, failed to pay them the minimum wage required by the Federal Fair Labor Standards Act, and failed to provide them state retirement benefits as required by state law, and that these failures continue to the present time." In this particular case, the court denied injunctive relief on all issues. It was determined that residents were offered a range of job opportunities, could refuse all work, and that no one was ordered to work for "medical reasons." It was the opinion of the court that no proof of coercion or lack of choice was evident with regard to duties performed. Further, plaintiffs were not subject to state retirement or social security benefits since by state law they were not employees.

On March 13, 1973, a class action suit (*Souder* v. *Brennan*) was brought against the United States Department of Labor to compel the department to enforce provisions of the Fair Labor Standards Act of 1966 relative to resident workers in residential facilities for both the mentally ill and the mentally retarded. The American Association on Mental Deficiency, the National Association for Mental Health, and three individual plaintiffs filed the suit in the United States District Court in Washington, D.C. Named as defendants were the Secretary of Labor and four subordinate Labor Department head administrators. On December 4, 1973, a declaratory judgment and injunction order was issued stating, "The Secretary of Labor has a duty to implement reasonable enforcement efforts applying the minimum wage and overtime compensation provision of the Fair Labor Standards Act to patient-workers at non-Federal institutions for the residential care of the mentally ill and/or mentally retarded . . . " (*Souder* v. *Brennan*, 1973). In other words, the court held that the minimum wage, overtime and other provisions of the Fair Labor Standards Act applied to developmentally-disabled persons residing and working in a residential facility.

The preceding discussion has highlighted the major features of important litigation as it affects the mentally retarded in residential facilities. Let us review briefly their implications with regard to deinstitutionalization and institutional reform.

LITIGATION AND DEINSTITUTIONALIZATION

The court decisions, especially those related to right to treatment and due process, are playing a major role in deinstitutionalization. First, they have placed marked restrictions on who shall be considered for admission.

> No borderline or mildly retarded person shall be a resident of the institution (*Wyatt* v. *Stickney*, 1972).

> No person classified as borderline, mildly, or moderately retarded according to the standards of classification at Cambridge shall be admitted unless that person suffers from psychiatric or emotional disorders in addition to his retardation . . . (*Welsch* v. *Likens*, 1974).*

> No person shall be admitted unless he is 'dangerous to himself or others' (*Lessard* v. *Schmidt*, 1973).

Secondly, retarded persons, even those considered eligible under the court orders, shall not be admitted to a residential facility until all other community resources have been explored.

> No person shall be admitted to the institution unless a prior determination shall have been made that residence in the institution is the least restrictive habilitation setting (*Wyatt* v. *Stickney*, 1972).

> No mentally retarded person shall be admitted to Cambridge State Hospital on civil commitment if services and programs are available in the community (*Welsch* v. *Likens*, 1974).

Thirdly, no retarded person should remain in a residential facility longer than necessary,

> Residents shall have a right to the least restrictive conditions necessary to achieve the purposes of habilitation. To this end, the institution shall make every attempt to move residents from: (a) more to less structured living; (b) larger to smaller facilities; (c) larger to smaller living units; (d) group to individual residence; (e) segregated from the community to integrated living (*Wyatt* v. *Stickney*, 1972).

Welsch v. *Likens* (1974), which involved the Cambridge State Hospital in Minnesota, is the most recent right-to-treatment class actions suit to be decided. Judge Larson's decision was quite similar to that of Judge Johnson in *Wyatt* v. *Stickney*.

On the other hand, neither shall the retarded be returned to the community indiscriminately,

> No resident may be transferred to a community residential facility or foster home unless it has been duly licensed; and the defendants are to make a written determination of the eligibility of each resident at Cambridge for community placement and review such determination at least yearly. The defendants are to provide the court with a written plan to develop alternative residential care for all residents (*Welsch* v. *Likens*, 1974).

The intent of these decisions is clear. A residential facility shall be used only as a last resort and only if the retarded person's needs can be met.

LITIGATION AND INSTITUTIONAL REFORM

Institutional reform was one of the prime goals of the various court decisions as clearly indicated by the standards for Partlow State School (Appendix A). It should be realized that these standards were not developed by the judge himself. They were recommended by professionals knowledgeable about retardation. The judge accepted their recommendations and included them in his court order. Judge Larson, *Welsch* v. *Likens* (1974), required Cambridge State School to meet the federal standards associated with intermediate care facilities (ICF).

The court judgments and standards have emphasized five broad aspects of institutional reform. First, all retarded persons have basic rights which must be recognized. Secondly, as previously discussed, residential facilities should serve a very select population and prepare as many residents as possible for return to their home community. Thirdly, each resident is to have his/her total needs met on an individual basis,

> Resident shall have a right to habilitation, including medical treatment, education and care, suited to their needs, regardless of age, degree of retardation, or handicapping condition. Each resident has a right to a habilitation program which will maximize his human ability and enhance his ability to cope with his environment. The institution shall recognize that each resident,

regardless of ability or status, is entitled to develop and realize his fullest potential. The institution shall implement the principle of normalization so that each resident may live as normally as possible (*Wyatt* v. *Stickney*, 1972).

Each resident at Cambridge shall be provided with an individualized treatment program and these plans shall be periodically reviewed, evaluated, and altered to conform to the particular resident (*Welsch* v. *Likens*, 1974).

In this regard, Judge Larson prefaced his comments with the following positive observation: "Almost all of the residents, no matter the degree of severity of their retardation, are capable of some growth and development if given adequate care and suitable treatment" (*Welsch* v. *Likens*, 1974).

In order to realize these objectives, minimum staffing ratios were established by both Judge Johnson and Judge Larson.

Fourthly, restraints, certain aversive stimuli and other possible negative treatment procedures were restrictively circumscribed —

Resident shall have a right to be free from unnecessary or excessive medication. Medication shall not be used as punishment, for the convenience of staff, as a substitute for program, or in quantities that interfere with the resident's rehabilitation program (*Wyatt* v. *Stickney*, 1972).

Electric shock devices shall be considered a research technique for the purpose of these standards. Such devices shall only be used in extraordinary circumstances to prevent self-mutilation leading to repeated and possible permanent physical damage to the resident, and only after alternative techniques have failed. The use of such devices . . . shall be used only under the direct and specific order of the superintendent (*Wyatt* v. *Stickney*, 1972).

Finally, the residential facility must provide a humane physical and psychological environment. Standards under this category identified a broad array of resident rights such as the right to privacy and appropriate physical surroundings.

Some of the conditions found in residential facilities came close to being judged cruel and unusual punishment, which is specifically forbidden under the Eighth Amendment to the Constitution — "Excessive bail shall not be required, nor excessive fines imposed, nor cruel and unusual punishment inflicted." Such conditions included a lack of basic sanitation, overcrowding, absence of physical exercise, inadequate diet, unchecked violence of inmates against each other and of the employees against inmates, lack of adequate medical care and psychiatric care, abuse of solitary confinement and restraint. Restraints included both physical devices and medication.

Though the preceding comments were relatively few, the evidence would indicate that the federal courts are unequivocally committed to precluding the necessity of residential care whenever possible and are equally dedicated to the assurance that persons in residential facilities receive maximum services. Litigation, however, like most phenomena in life, has both its positive and negative aspects.

PROS AND CONS OF LITIGATION

The fact that the Constitution of the United States contains provisions which can be interpreted to protect the rights of all citizens reconfirms the integrity and creative intelligence of our forefathers. The fact that contemporary jurists are utilizing the Constitution to insure the rights of the retarded in residential facilities and to advance a new social policy are also of considerable merit. On the other hand, is it not regrettable that the courts had to be called upon to insure that the rights of the retarded and their needs for treatment were being honored?

The positive aspects of litigation are many. It is one of the few avenues available to many concerned residents, parents, guardians, professionals and interested citizens in general which can have a major impact on the legislature. When a class action suit results in a positive judgment, the legislature has to provide or improve services. Even the threat or potential threat of litigation has, in some states, produced significant changes in both residential and community programs.

Litigation also brings the plight of the mentally retarded in residential facilities to the public's attention. This, in turn, has had its effect.

Various federal regulations have been established or modified in response to court judgments. This is especially true with regard to admissions, length of stay and quality of services. Independent evaluations of residents and their programs are being required with increased frequency.

According to Turnbull (1975), an attorney, litigation has increased sensitivity to other rights of the retarded such as education, sterilization, sexual expression, guardianship, incompetency, commitment and voting. It also has aroused awareness of attorneys to the needs of retarded persons in residential facilities. For example, many attorneys are becoming involved with the development and implementation of advocacy programs.

This latter point is important. One of the conspicuous absences in the court decisions, especially since they dealt primarily with involuntary admissions, was any comment concerning the responsibility of attorneys and judges. No person has ever been involuntarily committed to a residential facility by a governor, a legislator, a director of a department of mental hygiene or a superintendent. They have been committed by judges. In the final analysis, much of the legal representation of the rights of the retarded has been forsaken by those who have a major responsibility in this area. Levy, for example, offered the following description of the guardian *ad litem:*

> The appointment of a guardian *ad litem* has been standard since the Minnesota Supreme Court recognized in the *Wretlind* case that the subject's interest and those of the petitioner (either his parents or the welfare department) may be adverse. In Hennepin County the guardian is appointed from a group of lawyers whose names are provided by the Bar Association. In Ramsey County, one attorney acts as guardian in all cases. The case workers are not sympathetic to the guardian's role and seem to believe that his presence deters parents' petitions. In fact, guardians have not often disturbed the placidity of commitment procedures. Many attorneys believe that the guardian serves no real function. In a recent session in Hennepin County, during which 13 persons were committed, the guardian asked only two questions. In one case, he asked the age of the petitioning father. In another . . . the guardian asked the parents whether they understood the petition and wanted state guardianship . . .

Only one of the Hennepin County guardians *ad litem,* of those interviewed, seemed to understand his role. He stated that he customarily opposed commitment unless the retardate needed treatment which could not be obtained without guardianship. But this attorney lacked basic information about the retardation program: He believed that case work services, foster care, and institutionalization could be obtained only after guardianship was established; and he had been informed that priority for institutional care was based solely on a "waiting list." In short, the guardian *ad litem* had not usually precluded necessary or improper commitments (Levy, 1965).

In essence, the legal profession needs to become more knowledgeable about and sensitive to the needs and rights of the retarded as well as alternatives to residential placement.

One final comment concerning the positive aspects of litigation — while many of the court decisions are or have the potentiality of being challenged at a higher court level, most of the states have responded positively by enacting legislation or creating policies to guarantee the rights of the developmentally disabled. For example, while the *Lessard* v. *Schmidt* decision is being contested, Wisconsin state law governing admissions has been modified to satisfy the intent and conditions of that decision. Many states are attempting to meet ICF standards or those of the Joint Commission on Accreditation of Hospitals. They are also attempting to comply with the Fair Labor Standards Act to insure that each resident receives a salary commensurate with his effort and productivity. At the same time, alternative community living systems are being developed.

There are several negative aspects associated with litigation. In some cases, it has been impossible to comply with the court's judgment within the time allotted. For example, Judge Johnson in his Interim Emergency Order dated March 2, 1972, required that

> within 15 days defendants shall completely eliminate all fire and safety hazards; that within 15 days they will engage a team of physicians to examine every resident . . . currently receiving anticonvulsants and/or behavior modifying drugs; within 10 days . . . defendants shall engage a team of physicians to conduct a program of appropriate immunization for all residents;

and within 30 days . . . defendants shall employ 300 additional resident care workers, including professionals of the various disciplines . . . .

Such requirements are difficult, if not impossible to meet. As observed by Turnbull (1975), a judgment of this nature is not only administratively difficult to comply with but may be expensive to satisfy and perhaps may not be productive, especially when it demands instant changes rather than the well-planned and systematic changes accomplished with reasonable speed.

There are other administrative difficulties. Most court cases require several years to resolve, and during this interval the residential facility is under constant scrutiny and reporting. Usually public statements such as newspaper articles concentrate solely on the negative aspects of the situation to the complete neglect of any positive features. This, in turn, has a marked demoralizing effect on staff. Further, because of the constant legal overtones to the investigation and proceedings, staff become hesitant to interact with residents or prescribe treatments in fear of being sued.*

Also, as aptly stated by Gettings (1973),

> There is a thin line between the proper exercise of judicial authority and the encroachment on the legitimate prerogatives of the administrator. The latter situation can stifle the proper exercise of administrative initiative by substituting judicial opinion for executive direction. In the final analysis, the success or failure of any public program is going to rest with the responsible governmental official. The courts can and should intervene to protect the individual's interests as a citizen; however, in doing so, they should not tie the hands of responsible administrative officials, since the ultimate and almost inevitable result will not be in the best interest of the patient.

Some of the standards, especially those concerning reimbursement for work, have presented problems. A few states apparently cannot afford to pay minimum wages to working residents. Subsequently, residents have been removed from any jobs which

---

*An extensive description of the adverse effects of litigation on staff and parents as reported by one superintendent will be found in *Labor, Litigation and Legal Rights of Residents* (1975).

would qualify under the Fair Labor Standards Act. This, in turn, has affected their sense of self-worth and respect.

Also, some of the standards set by the courts are inadequate to meet the basic charge of providing comprehensive, individualized programs. An overall ratio of one aide to two severely or profoundly retarded residents, for example, simply will not permit intensive programming. JCAH requires a staff/resident of 1:1, a 100 percent increase in direct care personnel. Standards set for one facility need not be appropriate for another. Yet, many state legislators and/or budget analysts look to Partlow standards when evaluating budget requests. This can result in significant cuts which may reduce the facility's effectiveness.

Also, rigid admission criteria may inadvertently prevent a retarded individual from getting services he desperately needs. The community simply may not have an alternative program. In order for court decisions to be fully realized many gains will have to be made in providing a broad spectrum of services at the community level.

Until recently, the only area of community programming considered by the courts involved educational opportunities. Several courts stipulated that at least education and training must be offered to retarded persons in the community. The two landmark cases involved Pennsylvania and Washington, D.C. In 1971 a three-judge federal district court panel upheld a consent agreement between the Pennsylvania Association for Retarded Children and the Commonwealth of Pennsylvania, guaranteeing every retarded child in the state the right to a free public education. This position was upheld and further expanded by *Mills* v. *The Board of Education* in 1972. The latter judgment contended that no child in Washington, D.C., could be denied a public education because of mental, behavioral, physical or emotional handicaps or deficiencies. Since the time of these decisions approximately 70 percent of states have passed appropriate special education legislation.

Historically, the federal courts have placed primary responsibility for deinstitutionalization on the residential facility and those responsible for its administration and financing. Little attention was devoted to where these youngsters were to go or how such programs were to be developed. In 1975, however, a consent agreement was reached between New York and the United States District Court, Eastern District of New York, which did address itself to the problem of alternative residential facilities. As stated in the consent agreement,

> Defendants shall take all steps necessary to develop and operate a broad range of non-institutional community facilities and programs to meet the needs of Willowbrook's residents and of the class. Within six years from the date of this judgment Willowbrook shall be reduced to an institution of 250 or fewer beds to serve the needs of residents who require institutional care and who come from the geographic area of Staton Island. A Review Panel shall annually evaluate progress toward this objective.

> To this end, the defendant shall each year for the next five years request the legislature to appropriate additional funds for the development and operation of community facilities and programs to serve the needs of the class to ensure that an increasing proportion, exclusive of increases in salaries, of the Department's budget, resources and expenditures relevant to the class, shall be devoted to the development and operation of such facilities and programs.

> Within twelve months of the date of this judgment, defendants shall develop and operate or cause to be developed and operated at least 200 new community placements to meet the needs of Willowbrooks residents and of the class. For purposes of this section, except for placement in hospitals currently under construction or development, which in no event shall exceed fifteen beds, a "community placement" shall mean a non-institutional resident in the community in a hospital, half-way house, group home, foster care home, or similar residential facility of fifteen or fewer beds for mildly retarded adults, and ten or fewer beds for all others, coupled with a program element adequate to meet the residents' individual needs. Promptly following the date of this judgment, defendants shall request an appropriation of not less than two-million dollars ($2,000,000.00) from sums already appropriated by the legislature for the 1975-1976 fiscal year (*New York State Association for Retarded Citizens et al. v. Carey et al.,* 1975).

One final observation concerning litigation and the mentally retarded. While federal and state agencies may revise their laws, rules and administrative practices, the ultimate realization of the rights of the retarded depends on the response of local communities and counties. For example, a state may pass appropriate legislation requiring special education for eligible retarded students, but only the local level can develop the needed programs. This requires staff, classrooms, equipment and instructional materials. Many local communities are confronted with innumerable fiscal problems which result in an inability to implement existing laws.

Counties are not only confronted with a similar fiscal problem, many seem to possess an inordinate inability to relate to each other effectively. A sizeable number of retarded persons remain in residential facilities because of county disagreements and disputes over authority and responsibility. One county may refuse to provide services for a retarded person if he was originally admitted from another county. The original county of origin, in turn, may refuse to reimburse the other county for services even though it is unable to provide the service itself.

It is interesting to observe that the above practice is almost identical to *warning out*, an early, deplored technique used by counties and local communities in the United States. In 1647, Rhode Island adopted as part of its legal code the responsibility to "provide for the poor and the impotent . . . and to appoint an overseer for that purpose" (Friedman, 1973). If a person were a resident of a county or town for three months, he then became the responsibility of that community. By 1671, Plymouth had revised the law to provide that a newcomer could be advised or *warned out* by a constable or other local official, that the community would not assume any responsibility for him. In that case, while the person could reside in that town or county, if he became a pauper or in any manner impotent, the burden of support would remain with his place of former residence. According to Friedman (1973), *warning out* represented a system that "discriminated against the deviant and the stranger." It would appear that while laws and policies may change, actual practices may not.

Finally, recent actions of the courts clearly identify another major trend — children have rights, and in some instances these rights supersede those of their parents. Let us examine this new area in more detail.

CHILDREN'S RIGHTS

Not only will the courts continue to play a prominent role in the affairs of residential facilities, they also will play an increasing role with regard to community services and to children's rights in general. Historically, the courts have devoted primary attention to adults rather than to children. Underlying this practice has been the general assumption that children are an integral part of a family constellation, receiving due attention and protection from their parents. Today, however, children are being viewed as possessing their own distinct rights, and there is growing concern over contemporary concepts of parental responsibility and childrearing practices.

Marker and Friedman (1973) succinctly summarized this changing attitude towards the legal rights of children,

> Eighty million Americans are under 21 years of age. Every day, a larger number of these youth are the recipients of state actions which have painful and even tragic consequences. The legal response to the rights of children, however, has been conspicuously weak. It was not until 1967, for example, that the United States Supreme Court considered its first case raising the constitutional rights of a child . . . Perhaps this disinterest in the legal rights of children has persisted so long because traditionally children have not been considered *persons* under the law. However, if the law is to become responsive to their special interest, it must recognize that children *are* persons. Moreover, it must recognize that they have points of view which may conflict with and should be considered separately from the views of parents and other adult authorities. The rights of children which are basic to human development include but are not limited to the right to be raised in a supportive and nurturing environment; the right to adequate medical care; the right to an appropriate education; the right to protection from severe physical and psychological abuse and neglect; and the right to have their own interest adequately represented in the making of decisions which affect their lives.

There appears to be growing evidence to indicate that children

are no longer as valued in our society as they have been in the past.
For example, in her address to the American Association for the
Advancement of Science, Boocock (1975), a sociologist with the
Russell Sage Foundation, enumerated a number of rather discon-
certing trends and characteristics of parental attitudes and be-
havior —

1. Some 60,000 cases of child abuse are reported annually in the
United States. This was considered to be a very conservative
estimate.

2. There have been significant increases in the number of di-
vorce cases in which *neither* parent wishes to assume custody of
the children.

3. A study by the Child Welfare League estimated that in 1965
almost 1,000,000 American children under fourteen years of age
were left on their own while their parents worked. Seven thousand of these were under age six. Another 1,000,000 were left in
the care of older brothers and sisters under sixteen or relatives
over sixty-five.

4. At recent federal and state hearings, working-class mothers
testified that they had left ill preschoolers unattended in locked
apartments because they feared losing their jobs if they stayed
home.

5. Children are spending most of their time alone or with other
children, mostly in relatively unorganized activities such as
watching television and eating snacks.

Based on these data and impressions, Boocock (1975) concluded
that "the status of children in our society is highly ambiguous
. . . It does seem that there is less wanting of children in America,
and in the developed nations generally, than in the past and that
people who do want children want fewer of them."

The concept of child abuse is also changing. No longer is it.
limited to gross physical harm or abandonment. As illustrated in
a recent definition proposed by the federal government, an attempt is being made to include the more subtle aspects of neglect,

> "Child abuse and neglect" means harm or threatened harm to a
> child's health or welfare by a person responsible for the child's
> health or welfare.

> "Harm or threatened harm to a child's health or welfare" can

occur through: non-accidental physical or mental injury; sexual abuse, as defined by State law; or negligent treatment or maltreatment, including the failure to provide adequate food, clothing, or shelter. *Provided,* however, that a parent or guardian legitimately practicing his religious beliefs who thereby does not provide specific medical treatment for a child, for that reason alone shall not be considered a negligent parent or guardian. However, such an exception shall not preclude a court from ordering that medical services be provided to the child, where his health requires it.

"Person responsible for a child's health or welfare" means a child's parent, guardian, or other person responsible for the child's health or welfare, whether in the same home as the child, a relative's home, a foster home, or a residential institution (*Federal Register,* 1975).

The courts are not going to abandon responsibility for protecting children, nor will they hesitate to intervene in cases where neglect is evident. Even today the courts no longer appear to be willing to assume automatically that each child is receiving proper nurturance and protection within the home. Nor is the court willing to accept the fact that parental protection is always a reasonable substitute for children's rights.

Parental decisions concerning residential placement of their child have been challenged by the court. In the case of *Horacek* v. *Exon* (1974), which involved the residents of the Beatrice State Home, the United States District Court for the District of Nebraska denied dismissal of a right-to-treatment suit on the basis that parents admitted their children voluntarily to the state residential facility. The judge stated, "Equating the plaintiffs with their parents will not do . . . I simply hold that parents cannot deprive their children of constitutional rights — rights of the children *vis-à-vis* the state."

In another instance a state superior court intervened directly to protect the life of a child. In *Maine Medical Center* v. *Houle* (1974) an apparently retarded child required intervenous feeding and surgery to sustain life. The father directed the physician not to offer the required treatment. The attending physician, after reviewing the case, concurred with the father. The court, however, stated, "At the moment of live birth there does exist a human being entitled to the fullest protection of the law. The most basic right enjoyed by every human being is the right to life itself." The court also indicated that while parents have a considerable degree of discretion when the condition of a child does not involve a serious risk of life and treatment does not involve this risk, they do not have the right to make the decision to terminate a child's life, nor is this within the realm of a doctor's expertise or opinion. Specifically, "The doctor's qualitative evaluation of the value of the life to be preserved is not legally within the scope of his expertise. The issue before the court is not the prospective quality of the life to be preserved, but the medical feasibility of the proposed treatment compared with the almost certain risk of death should treatment be withheld." The court, in essence, found that neither the parent nor the physician has the right to withhold treatment, and to do so would constitute neglect. The court ordered a guardian *ad litem* to consent to the surgical correction and to insure the provision of any other life supportive measures as might be required. The court also retained jurisdiction to determine the future custody of the child if such should become a question.

Another area in which the rights of both parents and states are being challenged involves sterilization. In *Relf* v. *Weinberger et al.* (1974) a federal court in viewing the guidelines promulgated by the United States Department of Health, Education, and Welfare declared that the guidelines were inadequate. Briefly, the regulations required that legally incompetent adults must give their "informed consent" to sterilization and legally competent persons under age eighteen must also give their informed consent. In the latter instance, a review committee of persons from the community was to evaluate the petition of the legally competent person under eighteen to determine if sterilization would be in his/her best interest. Parental consent was not required. The court determined that these regulations did not incorporate proper safeguards to insure that sterilization was "voluntary." The court concluded that no person who is mentally incompetent could meet the standard of "voluntary" consent nor could the consent of a representative, however sufficient under state law, impute voluntariness to a minor undergoing irreversible sterilization. This case is but one of many which has challenged the current practice concerning the sterilization of minors and/or mentally retarded persons.

The die has been cast; courts are and will continue to be highly concerned about the rights of all citizens, including the mentally retarded. It is important and encouraging to recognize that courts do not function in isolation. Their decisions usually reflect the prevailing attitudes and level of receptivity of the population in general. As stated by Friedman (1973), "as long as the country endures, so will its system of law, co-extensive with society, reflecting its wishes and needs . . . The law is a mirror held up against life." He also observed that the two most active legal interests of the twentieth century have been the idea of equality before the law and the demand for equality of opportunity which follows when formal equality fails in its purpose. Both trends clearly involve the mentally retarded and other developmentally disabled persons.

SUMMARY

Litigation has been used successfully in clarifying the rights of the retarded in three major areas — right to treatment, due process and involuntary servitude. In essence, court decisions have enunciated clearly the principle that no person, regardless of intellectual limitations, shall be denied the right to live in a free and open society without recourse to the full protection of the law and the assurance that appropriate care, treatment and training will be provided. Also, any work performed by a resident must be reimbursed in accordance with the Fair Labor Standards Act.

Residential facilities for the mentally retarded are no longer to be used as a substitute for inadequate or absent community services. While the initial impact of the court decisions has been on residential programming, its ultimate effect will be greater on the community, which now must provide more services for more retarded persons.

REFERENCES

Bazelon, D.: Implementing the right to treatment. *University of Chicago Law Review, 36*:742-754, 1969.

Boggs, E.: Legal aspects of mental retardation. In Phillips, I. (Ed.): *Prevention and Treatment of Mental Retardation.* New York, Basic, 1966, pp. 407-428.

Boocock, S.: Is U.S. becoming less child-oriented? *National Observer,* February 18, 1975.

Burnham v. *Georgia.* Civil Action No. 16385, U.S. District Court, Northern Division of Georgia, 1972.

Donaldson v. *O'Connor.* No. 73-1843, U.S. Court of Appeals, Fifth Circuit, 1974.

Ellis, J.: Volunteering children: Parental commitment of minors to mental institutions. *California Law Review, 62*: 840-916, 1974.

Ennis, B., and Friedman, P. (Ed.): *Legal Rights of the Mentally Handicapped* (Three volumes). New York, Practising Law Institute, 1974.

Friedman, L.: *A History of American Law.* New York, S & S, 1973, pp. 77, 595.

Gettings, R.: The implications of recent litigation involving the rights of the mentally retarded. In *The Rights of the Mentally Handicapped.* Washington, National Association of Coordinators of State Programs for the Mentally Retarded, 1973, p. 23.

Horacek v. *Exon.* Civil Action No. CV 72-L-299, U.S. District Court for the District of Nebraska, 1974.

Labor, Litigation, and Legal Rights of Residents. Madison, National Association of Superintendents of Public Residential Facilities for the Mentally Retarded, 1975.

Lessard v. *Schmidt.* Civil Action No. 71-C-602, U.S. District Court, Eastern District of Wisconsin, 1972.

Levy, R.: Protecting the mentally retarded: An empirical survey and evaluation of the state guardianship in Minnesota. *Minnesota Law Review, 5*:821-887, 1965.

Maine Medical Center v. *Houle.* Civil Action No. 74-145, Superior Court, Cumberland, Maine, 1974.

Marker, G., and Friedman, P.: Rethinking children's rights. *Children Today, 2*(6): 8-11, 1973.

Mental Health Law Project: *Basic Rights of the Mentally Handicapped.* Washington, Mental Health Law Project, 1973.

Mills v. *The Board of Education.* Civil Action No. 1939-71. U.S. District Court of the District of Columbia, 1972.

New York State Association for Retarded Citizens, et. al., v. *Carey, et. al.,* U.S. District Court, Eastern District of New York, 72 C., 356 and 357, 1975, p. 27.

O'Connor v. *Donaldson.* Supreme Court of the United States, No. 74-8, June 26, 1975, pp. 3, 11-12.

Provisions relating to child abuse and child neglect. *Federal Register, 40*(30): 6506, 1975.

Relf v. *Weinberger, et al.,* Civil Action No. 1557-73, U.S. District Court for the District of Columbia, 1974.

The Rights of the Mentally Handicapped: *Proceedings from a Bi-regional*

Conference. Washington, National Association of Coordinators of State Programs for the Mentally Retarded, 1973.

Rouse v. *Cameron.* 373 F. 2d 451, 1966.

Saville v. *Treadway.* Civil Action No. 6969. U.S. District Court, Northern District of Tennessee, 1974.

Schwindler, W.: *Court and Constitution in the 20th Century.* New York, Bobbs, 1974, p. 201.

Souder v. *Brennan.* Civil Action No. 482-73. U.S. District Court for the District of Columbia, 1973.

Tennessee Department of Mental Health. *Regulation on Voluntary Admission.* Nashville, Tennessee Department of Mental Health, 1974, p. 6.

Townsend v. *Treadway.* Civil Action No. 6500. U.S. District Court, Northern District of Tennessee, 1973.

Turnbull, H.: Effects of litigation on mental retardation centers. *Popular Government.* Winter: 44-52, 1975.

Welsch v. *Likens.* Civil Action No. 451. U.S. District Court, District of Minnesota, Fourth Division, 1974.

Woody, R.: *Legal Aspects of Mental Retardation.* Springfield, Thomas, 1974.

Wyatt v. *Aderholt.* No. 72-2634, U.S. Court of Appeals, Fifth Circuit, 1974.

Wyatt v. *Stickney.* Civil Action No. 3195-N. U.S. District Court, Middle District of Alabama, North Division, 1972.

Chapter 5

DEINSTITUTIONALIZATION

FROM the foregoing discussions we have seen that very few retarded persons require or have ever required residential care; residential services *may* repress intellectual, emotional and social functioning; recent philosophical programmatic trends as well as externally set standards are based on principles of total development and normalization, which, in turn, emphasize early discharge and community living; and courts at various levels of authority have stated repetitively that residential placements should not occur unless an individual is either dangerous to himself or others and only when a less restrictive alternative is not available. Taken collectively, these factors indicate that for many retarded persons in residential facilities, deinstitutionalization is not only desirable but critical.

The present discussion will concentrate on six aspects associated with deinstitutionalization — (1) deinstitutionalization as a concept, (2) community services, (3) integrants to successful deinstitutionalization, (4) public awareness and receptivity, (5) parental attitudes and problems and (6) the current status of deinstitutionalization.

DEINSTITUTIONALIZATION AS A CONCEPT

Deinstitutionalization involves an attitude, a principle and a complex process. Let us consider each of these aspects independently.

Deinstitutionalization as an Attitude

First and foremost, deinstitutionalization is an attitude which places great emphasis on freedom, independence, individuality, mobility, personalized life experiences and a high degree of interaction in a free society. In contrast, institutionalization *as an attitude* can be considered as one which emphasizes group living, regimentation and accommodation, limited choice, lack of privacy, and minimal independence and mobility in a restrictive society.

Deinstitutionalization as a Principle

The principle of deinstitutionalization pertains to the right of an individual to receive treatment and programming in the *least restrictive environment*. This concept, as we have seen, has served as the foundation for federal court decisions concerning right-to-treatment and is an integral part of due process, e.g. "No person shall be admitted to the institution unless prior determination shall have been made that residence in the institution is the least restrictive habilitation setting" (*Wyatt* v. *Stickney*, 1972). According to the Mental Health Law Project (1973) a least restrictive environment

> means a person should not be hospitalized, with drastic curtailment of liberty involved, if he can be treated in a community at outpatient clinics or community mental health centers.... The right to be treated in a setting less restrictive than an institution [is] required by the constitutional principle of the least drastic means. The Constitution required that whenever a government is going to restrict a person's liberty against his will in order to accomplish a legitimate governmental objective, it must impose the least drastic restriction necessary to accomplish the legitimate governmental objective.

Inasmuch as the concept of least restrictive environment is critical not only to deinstitutionalization but also to institutional reform, let us examine its implications in further detail. The key component is independence, i.e. the right to self-determination, the right to seek fulfillment or self-realization, the right to be an individual, and the right to move about at will. These involve several cardinal legal concepts —

> FREEDOM. The power of acting, in the character of a moral personality, according to the dictates of the will, without other check, hindrance, or prohibition and such as may be imposed by just and necessary laws and the duties of social life (Black, 1951).

LIBERTY. Exemption from extraneous control. Freedom from all restraint except such as are justly imposed by law (Black, 1951).

PERSONAL LIBERTY. The right or power of locomotion; of changing situation, or moving one's person to whatsoever place one's own inclination may direct, without imprisonment or restraint, unless by due course of law (Black, 1951).

As regards children and adolescents, the least restrictive environment implies a nurturing family setting, one which fosters independence, individuality and an ever-expanding world of contact and communication.

Independence for an adult implies the right to exercise one's full prerogative with regard to the conduct of his own affairs within the boundaries of legal sanction. This includes all rights which may be denied when an adult is judged legally incompetent, i.e. making a will; making a contract, deed, sale; being responsible for criminal acts; standing trial for a criminal charge; being punished for criminal acts; being married; being divorced; adopting a child; being a fit parent; suing and being sued; receiving property; holding property; being committed to a mental institution; being discharged from a mental institution; being fit for military service; operating a vehicle; giving a valid consent; giving a binding release or waiver; voting; being a witness; and receiving compensation for inability to work as a result of an injury (Metzer and Rheingold, 1962).

Independence is a critical component of normalization. Wolfensberger (1972a), for example, emphasizes independence when describing the physical and social integration of the retarded,

> For a (deviant) person, integration is achieved where he lives in a culturally normative community setting in ordinary community housing, can move and communicate in ways typical for his age, and is able to utilize, in typical ways, typical community resources: developmental, social, recreational, and religious facilities; hospitals and clinics; the post office; stores and restaurants; job placements; and so on.

> Ultimately, integration is only meaningful if it is social integration; i.e., if it involves social integration and acceptance, and not merely physical presence. However, social integration can

only be attained if certain pre-conditions exist, among these being physical integration, although physical integration by itself will not guarantee social integration.

Physical integration involves four factors — the home's location (in the community where the person is to be served), its physical context to other facilities and settings, its accessibility and its size (few residents). Again, however, even though foster homes and group homes, for example, may be located in the heart of the community in the midst of a nondeviant population, this alone will not guarantee social integration.

This brief discussion of independence, which is fundamental to both deinstitutionalization and normalization, clearly proposes that each retarded person live in the least restrictive environment possible and interact with the mainstream of society. This discussion also indicates what deinstitutionalization is not. It is not the simple transference of a retarded person from one restrictive residential setting to another.

Deinstitutionalization as a Complex Process

The National Association of Superintendents of Public Residential Facilities for the Mentally Retarded (1974) offered the following definition of deinstitutionalization:

> Deinstitutionalization encompassed three inter-related processes: (1) prevention of admission by finding and developing alternative community methods of care and training, (2) return to the community of all residents who have been prepared through programs of habilitation and training to function adequately in appropriate local settings, and (3) establishment and maintenance of a responsive residential environment which protects human and civil rights and which contributes to the expeditious return of the individual to normal community living whenever possible.

This tripartite definition identifies both the need to prevent admission as well as to return residents to their home communities adequately prepared to live in an appropriately programmed and protected (if necessary) setting. The third point, which reflects primarily on institutional reform, will be discussed in the next chapter.

Successful deinstitutionalization in terms of preventing residential placement facilitating early return of a resident to his home is largely dependent upon the community and its ability to provide a well-coordinated array of services. Though it is not the intent of this text to discuss the ramifications of such a statement in detail, it is imperative that community programming be considered at least briefly. Extensive deliberations concerning community services for the mentally retarded will be found in the annual reports of the President's Committee on Mental Retardation and in a number of basic books, including Gardner and Nisonger (1962), Meyen (1967), Gettings (1973), Dempsey (1975) and Cherington and Dybwad (1975).

COMMUNITY SERVICES

Prior to discussing community services, a concept of community should be posited. The term *community* can be considered from two points of view — (1) the sociopolitical community and (2) the individual's community. Sociopolitical definitions of a community usually refer to a group of persons with some common background residing within a relatively restricted geographical area —

> A community is "a social group of any size whose members reside in a specific locality, share government, and have a common cultural historical heritage" (Stein and Urdang, 1967).

> A community is "a general population having a common interest or interdependency in the delivery of services" (NARC Residential Services and Facilities Committee, 1973).

The individual's community is concerned with the experiences and mobility that he has within the sociopolitical community and his interactions with people, services and facilities contained within. Normally, the individual's community is smaller than the sociopolitical community as defined.

The residential facility's community also can be considered within the dual context of a sociopolitical area and its individual interactions. As shown in Figure 2, the residential facility exists within a sociopolitical community and may be part of the individual's community if he uses the services available. Although a residential facility may be located within or near a sociopolitical community, its services may extend to a number of such communities or, in some cases, throughout the state. Finally, communities also exist within the framework of a larger societal structure (county, state and nation), all of which may influence to some degree each community and its inhabitants.

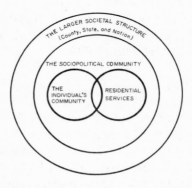

Figure 2: The Interrelationships of Communities. From: Scheerenberger (1974).

This concept of community is intended to illustrate three critical points —

1. An individual's community is not synonymous with the sociopolitical community. As indicated previously, simple placement into a community in no way assures that greater independence or normalization will be realized. It is the responsibility of all persons concerned with the retarded (parents, advocates or guardians, professionals and agencies) to assist each retarded individual in coping with as large and complex a sociopolitical community as possible.

2. The effectiveness of community placement depends upon the availability of local programs, support and guidance, which, in contemporary society are highly dependent upon the fiscal and regulatory policies of the larger societal structure.

3. By definition (and hopefully practice) a residential facility must be considered an integral part of any community. The

degree to which it is a successful member of that community depends upon the degree of its involvement and interaction. Regrettably, residential services, especially those of large state-sponsored facilities, are frequently considered distinct from local programming. Consequences of such polarization are most serious — (a) professionals do not work collaboratively to resolve problems which could benefit from the expertise of both community and residential personnel; (b) highly specialized services may not be extended by the residential facility to retarded persons in the community and vice versa; and (c) the community may assume that once a person has been placed in a residential facility, it no longer has any responsibility for his welfare. Effective programming and deinstitutionalization cannot be realized under such circumstances.

Most planners of community programs for the retarded emphasize three aspects — (1) required services, (2) the need for offering such services along a continuum of care, and (3) the utilization of both specialized and generic services. Let us examine each of these three areas.

Services Required by the Retarded

Though a number of models identifying required services have been developed over the past several years, none has been cited more frequently than that promulgated by the President's Panel on Mental Retardation in 1962. This model, which is shown in Table XII, displays the various services according to life stage and components of special need. In essence, an attempt was made to account for the total needs of retarded persons, including home and health care, education and training, vocational opportunities, leisure time activities, financial assistance and protection.

In order to assess the validity of this model, which was based primarily on professional judgment, let us review the relevant research. This falls into three categories — (1) reasons for seeking admission to a residential facility, (2) services required to retain a retarded person in the home, and (3) reasons for readmission.

Reasons for Seeking Admission to a Residential Facility

Many studies have investigated parental reasons for seeking

TABLE XII

ARRAY OF DIRECT SERVICES FOR THE RETARDED*

Life stage	Components of special need						
	Physical & mental health	Shelter nurture protection	Intellectual development	Social development	Recreation	Work	Economic security
Infant	Specialized medical follow-up; Special diets, drugs or surgery	Residential nursery	Sensory stimulation; Home training	Child welfare services			
Toddler	Home nursing; Correction of physical defects; Physical therapy	Foster care; Trained baby sitter	Nursery school; Environmental enrichment				
Child	Psychiatric care; Dental care; Day care	Homemaker service	Classes for slow learners; Special classes—educable; Special classes—trainable; Religious education	Scouting	Playground programs; Swimming		
Youth	Psychotherapy	Short stay home; Boarding school	Occupational training; Work-school programs; Speech training	Social clubs; Youth groups	Day camps; Residential camps		
Young adult		Halfway house; Facilities for retarded in conflict; Guardianship of person	Vocational counseling—Personal adjustment training	Marriage counseling		Selective job placement; Sheltered employment	Total disability assistance
Adult		Long-term residential care; Group homes	Evening school	Social supervision	Bowling; Evening recreation	Sheltered workshops	Guardianship of property; Life annuity or trust
Older adult	Medical attention to chronic conditions	Boarding homes					Old age assistance; OASI benefits; "Disabled child's" benefits; Health insurance

* Not included are diagnostic and evaluation services, or services to the family; the array is set forth in an irregular pattern in order to represent the overlapping of areas of need and the interdigitation of services. Duration of services along the life span has not been indicated here.

From: The President's Panel on Mental Retardation (1962).

residential placement. One consistent finding is that residential care is not sought solely for the reason of mental retardation. In some negative way, a retarded person presents problems beyond the coping ability of the family.

Tizard and Grad (1961) interviewed one hundred families with children or adults in residential facilities to determine why the moderately or severely retarded individuals were placed. The results, which were tabulated according to four major categories, were as follows:

1. Management, i.e. family no longer able to cope with a retarded person at home, 51 percent.
2. Family problems, i.e. death, illness, pregnancy, housing difficulties or adverse effect on other siblings, 26 percent.
3. Medical advice or social circumstances, i.e. inadequate home, 12 percent.
4. Mother's health, 11 percent.

Of the one hundred families, only 29 percent indicated that the availability of community services may have eliminated the requirement for residential placement. Services needed included nursery schools (14%), help with housing (14%) and medical treatment (1%). The remaining 71 percent of the families indicated that nothing would have prevented residential placement.

Downey (1965) was concerned specifically with parents' reasons for institutionalizing severely mentally retarded children. He also was interested in identifying those factors related to both early placement and low interest, and to late placement and high interest. A three-part theory of family crisis was advanced to explain differences in family response — (1) intrafamilial area, or interpersonal relations; (2) extrafamilial area, or family-community relations; and (3) retarded child area, or the family faced with a retarded child posing special problems of care, control or training. It was hypothesized "that parents placing younger children and demonstrating little interest offer reasons pertaining to the intrafamilial and extrafamilial social areas while those placing older children and demonstrating greater interest offer reasons pertaining to the retarded child area."

Trained staff interviewed sixty-nine families residing in the

Chicago area with the husband and wife being interviewed separately. The final sample consisted of fifty-eight fathers and sixty-three mothers. The results were collated according to major and minor reasons for placement. Major reasons, which had to be identified by two thirds of the subjects, included

1. Our doctor advised us to place him, 91 percent of both husbands and wives.
2. He needed more care than we could give him, 87.5 percent.
3. We had other children and could not give all of the children the care they needed, 83 percent.
4. He was too hard to handle, 82.5 percent.
5. There was too much strain in the home, 82.5 percent.
6. He was having harmful effects on his brothers and sisters, 69 percent.
7. He would have someone to watch over him when I am gone, 98.5 percent.

Downey's hypothesis was partially supported. Older parents cited reasons related to care, control and training. Younger parents gave primarily intrafamilial and extrafamilial reasons. Other findings included (1) both older and younger parents frequently indicated that child care needs were difficult to meet, (2) young fathers were most influenced by the advice of others, (3) both older and younger groups were concerned about the influence of the retarded child on other siblings, (4) a physician's recommendations were a major influence among all parents, and (5) parental education was a major factor, i.e. the more educated were concerned primarily with the child's effect on intrafamilial or intrapersonal relations.

With regard to sustained interest and age at placement, high interest parents tended to place their youngsters at an older age; however, many younger families did remain active in their children's lives. Education again was considered to be a major factor.

> By adding the fact that parents' education is related to both interest and age of placement, we may now summarize our findings in a predictive form. If the parents are well educated, if the wife feels she cannot provide care for all her children, if the husband's friends advise placement, then the child is likely to be

placed at an early age with subsequent low parental interest. If the parents are less educated, if the wife feels the child needs vocational training and fears neighborhood trouble, then it is likely the older child will be institutionalized and subsequent interest will be high (Downey, 1965).

A very significant series of studies concerning parental attitudes and problems associated with caring for retarded children at home as well as reasons for residential placement were conducted by Farber. His findings have been summarized in several publications, e.g. Farber and Ryckman (1965) and Farber (1968). In essence, a wide variety of factors were found to influence parental decisions concerning residential placement, including sex of child, sex of normal siblings, age of retarded child, family aspirations, period in family cycle, socioeconomic status (and its variable effect upon the willingness of fathers versus mothers with regard to placement), educational levels of parents, gratification of parents' needs as opposed to those of their children, and the personal impact of a retarded child on the parents.

Scheerenberger (1969) conducted a study of parents of retarded children on a waiting list for admission to one of a state's public residential facilities. Of the ninety-nine parents sampled, twenty had a mildly retarded child, thirty-nine had a moderately retarded child, and forty had either a severely or profoundly retarded child. Parents were from three sociogeographic areas — (1) middle-class, metropolitan Chicago (40 families); (2) poverty area, metropolitan Chicago (29 families); and (3) downstate communities (29 families). As will be observed from Table XIII, the primary reason for requesting residential placement, regardless of sociogeographic area, involved problems associated with care and management.

Based on a study of the social histories of a random sample of forty residents, Shellhaas and Nihira (1970) identified ten primary categories of reasons for admissions —

1. Arrest and court appearance
2. Cultural deprivation
3. Antisocial aggression
4. Incompatability with parents
5. School problems

TABLE XIII
PARENTAL REASONS FOR REQUESTING RESIDENTIAL PLACEMENT

Reason	Area I		Area II		Area III		Total	
	n	%	n	%	n	%	n	%
Care and management	21	51	16	55	18	62	55	56
Financial aid	11	26	3	10	4	14	18	18
"Insurance"	8	20	0	--	5	17	13	13
Training	1	3	6	1	2	7	9	9
Recommended by physician	0	--	3	10	0	--	3	3
Recommended by courts	0	--	1	4	0	--	1	1
Total	41	100	29	100	29	100	99	100

From: Scheerenberger (1969)

6. Sloppy individual, i.e. "slovenly manners and appearance and a history of illicit and promiscuous sexual relations"
7. Illegitimate child or broken home
8. School disruption
9. Generally good peer adjustment, but lied, ran away and/or wandered off
10. Vagrancy or disorderly conduct.

These results concerning reasons for admission support, directly or indirectly, the array of services specified by the President's Panel on Mental Retardation. Adequate counseling and support, home services and alternative home or residential settings were repetitively mentioned. Other major problems included the need for financial assistance and the assurance that adult retardates would be provided for properly in their advanced years. Indirectly, there was the strong identification of the need to develop adequate programs for adolescents and adults to avert such problems as vagrancy, slovenly appearance, wandering off and inappropriate sexual conduct.

The data also clearly demonstrate that parents of retarded children do not possess any common characteristics — some are poor, others are wealthy; some are well-educated, others are not; some are emotionally and personally secure, others are disturbed or ill;

some are young, others are older; some have strong family bonds, others do not. Each of these factors may influence the parents' decision to remove the child from the home. In brief, reasons for placing a retarded person outside of the home are highly individualized.

Of all the reasons presented by parents for seeking residential placement for their child, the most difficult to evaluate involves home care and management. In most studies this general category was not defined. It would be interesting to know the exact nature of the care and maintenance problems and how frequently such problems might evolve out of or reflect other family considerations. What may constitute a major problem in one family may be of little consequence to another. Thus, it is difficult to determine what services offered at which period in time may have resulted in a child remaining at home.

The study by Tizard and Grad would indicate that certain families simply are unable to cope with a retarded offspring regardless of what services may be available. The response of families who view mental retardation as jeopardizing either their careers or social life implies a need for attitude changes beyond those directly associated with any program or professional service. In other words, the stigma associated with retardation is the product of a real or perceived rejection of retardation by society in general. Also, such problems as adequate financial assistance and housing reflect broad social issues.

Services Required to Maintain Child at Home or in Community

Let us extend our consideration of parent-family difficulties by examining some of the services parents need to retain their retarded child at home. Fotheringham and Kershner (1970) studied parental responses to a personal interview intended to identify need similarities and differences between families of retarded persons admitted to a residential facility (n=116) and those remaining at home (n=38). Interestingly, the two parental groups were in agreement as to critically needed community services for the retarded — (1) education and training, (2) day care to give parents relief, (3) physical care and protection and (4) suitable recreation and companionship. They also shared common problems, e.g. the retarded person seriously interfered with family life; family problems unrelated to the retarded person interfered with their ability to care for him; the retarded person caused problems in the community.

In a study previously described, Scheerenberger (1969) requested parents with children on a waiting list for a state residential facility to identify needed community services. Only fourteen (14%) of the ninety-nine parents failed to indicate at least one service. As shown in Table XIV, the only consistent response across all three sociogeographic areas was the need to establish local residential facilities. This response by forty-three (43 percent)

TABLE XIV
NEEDED COMMUNITY PROGRAMS

Needed Services	Area I (n=41)		Area II (n=29)		Area III (n=29)		Total (n=99)	
	n	%	n	%	n	%	n	%
Local residential facilities	23	56	7	24	13	45	43	43
Expanded public school programs	9	22	4	14	3	10	16	16
Day centers	7	17	3	10	5	17	15	15
Increased financial aid	8	20	3	10	3	10	14	14
Central point of referral and information	7	17	2	7	3	10	12	12
Vocational training and sheltered workshops	4	10	0	--	5	17	9	9
More parent counseling and training	8	20	1	3	0	--	7	7
Home training programs	3	7	1	3	3	10	7	7
Home services	2	5	3	10	2	7	7	7
"Everything"	5	12	4	14	1	3	6	6
Better local diagnostic services	3	7	2	7	0	--	5	5
Better public information and support	1	2	2	7	2	7	5	5
Free transportation	3	7	2	7	0	--	5	5
Research (prevention)	2	5	0	--	0	--	5	5
Recreation	1	2	1	3	2	7	4	4
More qualified personnel	1	2	0	--	2	7	3	3
Better interagency cooperation	0	--	1	3	1	3	2	2
Speech therapy	0	--	1	3	0	--	1	1
Nothing	2	5	5	17	7	24	14	14

From: Scheerenberger (1969)

of the parents probably reflects the fact that residential placement had been sought for their retarded child. There were no statistically significant differences between the sociographic areas with regard to the need for additional community services.

Fanning (1973) forwarded a questionnaire concerning community services to various agencies and individuals, including parents with a child in a special education class, local pediatricians, social workers in public welfare and mental health clinics, county probation officers, the area association for retarded children, local vocational rehabilitation counselors, local psychologists and directors of special education of city and county school systems. The results, ranked according to priority were (1) child and adult training services, (2) group or residential homes, (3) guidance and counseling for families, (4) diagnostic and evaluation services, (5) consultation and education, (6) recreation and (7) temporary foster care. Group or residential homes were defined as a "live-in home without parents to supervise a structured program to help develop independence in the adult retardate while he is working or in a vocational setting." Thus, this study, which did not rely on parents who had requested residential placement, again gives high priority to the need for supplemental or alternative home settings.

Justice and associates (1971a) interviewed 156 families in Riverside, California, in an effort to identify problems in providing for a retarded sibling among Anglo-Americans, blacks and Mexican-American parents. Primary problems identified included learning, health, behavior, supervision and care and physical disabilities. Only 4.1 percent of the parents indicated that no difficulties were encountered. Responses among Anglo-Americans and Mexican-Americans were similar; black parents identified fewer problems.

In his study of twenty-four families of brain damaged children under ten years of age with IQ's less than fifty, Ehlers (1966) was concerned with services requested and received by parents. He found that most families with severely affected children seldom received services before two years of age. Services found to be particularly valuable were diagnosis and counseling, home training by a public health nurse, support from other members in the family, and parent associations. Additional services desired included expanded day school or nursery programs and speech or language therapy. Casework services were rated least valuable.

Thaman and Barclay (1967) found most of the parents sampled in their investigation rejected residential placement, but did believe it was necessary under certain circumstances, e.g. other siblings adversely affected, extreme aggressiveness, uncontrolled behavior and severe retardation with associated physical handicaps. Availability of community services, however, was considered critical to family decisions concerning possible placement, especially homemaking, day care, babysitting, temporary residential placement and recreation.

Foster families share problems in common with natural parents. Justice *et al.* (1971b) reported that forty-one (70%) of fifty-nine foster families studied encountered a number of problems in fulfilling their responsibilities. These included

1. Public misconceptions about mental retardation and lack of community acceptances, 34.1 percent.
2. School problems, i.e. programming inadequacies and personal conflicts, 26.8 percent.
3. Lack of other supportive programs, e.g. recreation, day care and workshops, 26.8 percent.
4. Behavior problems of residents, 21.9 percent.
5. Lack of medical and/or dental care in the community, 17.0 percent.
6. Problems with supervisory agencies, 17.0 percent.
7. Problems with natural parents, 17.0 percent.

Browder *et al.* (1974), in a study of twenty-two foster families for the retarded, indicated that some of the major obstacles to community training and management needs of foster retarded children included a lack of transportation, inability to afford services, care of other children in the home, distance to services and lack of parental time. Other problems encountered were indigenous to the foster home, e.g. foster mother's inability to see need for programs, elderly foster parents and child too difficult to manage.

In summary, services identified by the parents and foster parents lend further support to the model developed by the President's Panel on Mental Retardation as presented in Table XII.

Reasons for Readmission

Studies concerning reasons for readmission are scarcer than those concerning reasons for admission. Nevertheless, two studies were located which should prove informative.

Keys (1973) and her associates conducted a fourteen-month study of individuals placed in the community, number returned and reasons for return. All subjects were former residents of the Fairview State Hospital, California. During the fourteen-month period, the average number of former residents on leave was 1,270. Only 126 (9.9%) were readmitted, and only 1 percent of these were repeaters. Primary reasons for return included

1. Medical, 27.8 percent
2. Behavioral, 27.8 percent
3. Facility closed, 17.5 percent
4. Uncontrollable seizures, 6.3 percent
5. Caretaker could not cope with retarded person, 6.3 percent
6. Too old or too large, 4 percent
7. Psychotic episodes, 3.2 percent
8. Sexual behavior, 2.4 percent

As evidenced, the two major reasons for return involved medical and behavioral problems. Medical problems included "placements where medical needs could not be met in the community, acute medical episodes, and routine medical/dental needs." Behavioral reasons included "hostile, assaultive, aggressive, or unmanageable behavior, destruction of property, or noise, temper tantrums, smearing feces, or undressing inappropriately" (Keys, 1973).

In the study of national trends previously reported by Scheerenberger (1975), one of the questions dealt specifically with reasons for readmission. As shown in Table XV, primary reasons underlying unsuccessful placements as reported by 135 public residential facilities involved lack of community services (especially follow-along), community rejection of the retarded, the family and the retarded person himself.

TABLE XV
PRIMARY REASONS FOR READMISSIONS DURING FY 73-74
AS REPORTED BY 135 PUBLIC RESIDENTIAL FACILITIES

Reason	n	%
Community rejection	31	22
Lack of community services:	70	50
Activity centers & sheltered workshops	(12)	(9)
Advocacy services	(1)	(1)
Behavior management programs	(16)	(12)
Comprehensive services	(23)	(17)
Counselling	(5)	(4)
Day care	(11)	(8)
Education/Training	(13)	(9)
Employment	(9)	(6)
Family support	(2)	(1)
Follow-along services	(39)	(28)
Living accommodations	(27)	(19)
Medical services	(21)	(15)
Parent training	(4)	(3)
Failure to adjust	64	46
Family:	24	17
Could not adjust	(21)	(15)
Moved	(3)	(2)

From: Scheerenberger (1975)

The problem of inadequate supervision is of marked concern among superintendents. Several other studies have also indicated this problem.

McCarver and Craig (1974), in their extensive analysis of 175 published reports concerning postinstitutional adjustment of the mentally retarded, have noted a substantial decrease in successful placements in recent years. The mean success rate of community placements has dropped substantially from approximately 90 percent in 1954 to approximately 55 percent in 1970. Some of these failures undoubtedly could have been prevented if supportive follow-along services were available. McGarver and Craig (1974b), in a subsequent study, actually determined that only 29 percent of the thirty-four responding states described a follow-up program which seemed adequate.

Nihira and Nihira (1975) also found that community-placed retarded persons are potentially in danger. In this survey, intended to identify successful and unacceptable behavior among placed residents, 109 caretakers were interviewed. Of these, seventy-eight reported 203 incidents containing facts suggesting actual or potential jeopardy in one of three major categories — (1) jeopardy to health and/or safety, (2) jeopardy to general welfare where mental health or development were endangered, and/or (3) legal jeopardy. The investigators, taking into consideration the former resident's degree of retardation, concluded,

1. Moderately, severely and profoundly retarded clients in the community facilities are seemingly at greater risk in areas of health and safety than mildly retarded clients in need of appropriately closer supervision.

2. The general welfare of clients can be jeopardized with improper placement or retention in facilities that do not or cannot accommodate a variety of levels of functioning with individualized guidance to normalization. Individualization and groupings are important to the retarded person's social development.

3. Younger clients appear to be at risk when placed in the community. Like their nonretarded counterparts, child and adolescent clients are more prone to health and safety risks than the adult clients.

4. Borderline and mildly retarded clients are seemingly at greater risk of legal involvement than moderately, profoundly or severely retarded clients.

5. Heterosexual deviance can and does occur in the community-placed clients. This deviance can result in legal jeopardy.

Again, the need for follow-along services is implied. Taken collectively, the cited reasons for admissions, services required to maintain the child in his home and community as well as the readmission data all tend to validate the model proposed by the President's Committee on Mental Retardation. The research reviewed also indicated that parental assurances concerning the future of their retarded offspring, supplemental financial assistance for meeting special needs, and strong programs of postplacement supervision and support are essential.

Continuum of Care

As shown in the model, a variety of services are required by the retarded individual and/or his family at different stages in the life cycle. The effectiveness with which such services are easily secured refers directly to the concept of a "continuum of care." According to the President's Panel on Mental Retardation (1962), a continuum of care

> ... describes the selection, blending and use, in proper sequence and relationship, of the medical, educational, and social services required by a retarded person to minimize his disability at every point in his life span. Thus "care" is used in its broadest sense and the word "continuum" underscores the many transitions and liaisons within and among various services and professions, by which the community attempts to secure for the retarded the kind and variety of help and accommodation he requires. A "continuum of care" permits fluidity of movement of the individual from one type of service to another while maintaining a sharp focus on his unique requirements. The ongoing process of assuring that an individual receives the services he needs when he needs them and in the amount and variety he requires is the essence of planning and coordination.

One essential ingredient to a highly functional continuum of care is a central or fixed point of referral. Some very visible person or agency must be knowledgeable about all community services for the retarded and the criteria for their use. Without such a point of referral, programs may either not be used or not used in a timely manner.

Central points of referral may operate at three levels of sophistication. The first may be classified as a simple switchboard operation, i.e. one in which an agency is familiar with the various services and refers parent, a retarded person and/or professionals to those agencies which probably will be of assistance.

The second level involves a diagnostic program plus the services of an *expeditor* (or case manager) who deals specifically with mental retardation. The concept of an expeditor was adapted from industry for community health purposes by Reiff and Reissman (1965) and Hansell (1967). In essence, the expeditor serves as a link between parents (or retarded persons) and community resources. Working out of a professional agency, he

1. Provides continuous support and information to parents or the retarded person to assist in their decision making

2. Maintains a complete roster of service agencies and organizations within the community, including type of service rendered and rules and regulations

3. Establishes and maintains close liaison with all community agencies

4. Serves as an instrument through which interagency referrals are made and consummated

5. Exercises tracer and follow-through procedures to see that the client makes and keeps his appointment and continually checks to see that the client is receiving the maximum potential service of an agency with minimum delay

6. Receives complaints from parents about lack of or quality of service and investigates them in the client's interest

7. Consults with and provides other professional members serving the client with information about what resources are available which might meet the needs of the client as defined by other members of the professional team. He also takes responsibility for facilitating whatever disposition the team makes (Hansell *et al.*, 1968).

In brief, the expeditor or case manager is a competent, professional person, knowledgeable about mental retardation and community resources and who reaches out to the parents and/or the retarded client to assist them in whatever manner he can. He serves as a pivotal point or coordinator for meeting the needs of the retarded person and/or his parents.

The third level includes all components just described plus the recognition that retarded persons and their families frequently require many forms of assistance not directly related to retardation, e.g. family planning, parental job information, housing, legal counsel and financial aid. There is definite value in having a third-level community center(s) in a position to assist a family in meeting its broad human and social needs.

Generic as well as Special Services

Recent years have witnessed many advances in the development of local specialized services. Paralleling this development has been the growing realization that specialized programs should not constitute the sole approach to meeting the needs of the retarded. Total reliance on specialized services is neither desirable nor feasible. A successful community effort as well as deinstitutionalization will require the effective use of generic services.

A generic service is defined as any health, education, welfare, rehabilitation or employment agency in the community which serves a broad spectrum of persons (Jaslow, 1967). Excluded are those special programs intended only for the retarded.

From the standpoint of desirability and normalization, retarded persons should participate in the mainstream of society whenever possible, using all appropriate resources. The retarded need to participate in programs which permit interaction with other people, and they are entitled to receive services from a variety of agencies.

With regard to feasibility, the development of a local continuum of care based entirely on specialized services would prove impractical in terms of both human and financial resources. A blend of specialized and generic services is essential.

While generic services are of tremendous consequence, the little research data available would indicate that related agencies have yet to fulfill their anticipated role. The most comprehensive study located was conducted by Scheerenberger (1969, 1970). The purpose of this investigation was to determine the availability of generic services to the mentally retarded and their families in several Illinois communities. The sample included 504 representatives of medical, guidance and counseling, religious and socio-recreational agencies. As shown in Table XVI, most generic services were not serving the mentally retarded, nor were they particularly sensitive to their needs. This includes reference to both individual practitioners, e.g. physicians and community agencies. Problems identified included

1. There were too few generic agencies serving the retarded, especially in poverty areas.

2. Activities of generic agencies serving the mentally retarded were not coordinated with those of other generic agencies as well as specialized programs.

3. Services, especially among nonmedical agencies, had low visibility, and parents were unaware of their existence.

4. There was an absence of external support and guidance from persons professionally trained in programming for the retarded.

5. Financial considerations precluded the use of generic services by some parents.

6. There was an absence of specialized programs essential to complement generic services.

TABLE XVI

TOTAL RESPONSE DISTRIBUTED ACCORDING TO GENERIC SERVICE
CATEGORY AND NATURE OF RESPONSE

Category	n	Response		Serve the retarded		Do not serve the retarded		Don't know if served		Unable to participate for other reasons	
		n	%[a]	n	%[b]	n	%[b]	n	%[b]	n	%[b]
Medical services:											
Primary physician	110	108	98	22	20	67	62	8	7	11	11
Dentists	104	98	94	19	19	51	51	15	15	13	14
Community health agencies	25	25	100	3	12	22	88	0	--	0	--
Guidance and counseling	32	32	100	14	44	17	53	1	3	0	--
Religious programs (church)	130	123	95	47	38	58	47	7	6	11	9
Sociorecreational agencies	103	88	85	19	22	55	63	10	11	4	4
Parents	(232)	(143)	(61)	--	--	--	--	--	--	--	--
Generic agencies	504	474	94	124	26	270	57	41	9	39	8
Parents	232	143	61	--	--	--	--	--	--	--	--
TOTAL	736	617	84	--	--	--	--	--	--	--	--

[a]Percent of n, or total sample
[b]Percent of responses

From: Scheerenberger (1969)

One generic agency which frequently expresses high interest in and concern for the retarded is the mental health clinic. Yet, reports by Burton (1971) and Savino *et al.* (1973) challenge the depth of that interest and concern. Burton, for example, reported that during three fiscal years, 1963 to 1965, a total of 1,040 retarded persons had been seen by a clinic. Of these, 76 percent received no treatment, 10 percent received individual therapy, 8 percent received chemotherapy and 6 percent received some other form of therapy. In view of the relatively small number of retarded clients who actually received treatment, Burton concluded that those "who have criticized the strategy of assigning to mental health clinics the major responsibility for providing community programs are justified."

While caution must be exercised in generalizing the results of these studies reviewed, it is obvious that much remains to be accomplished. The four recommendations advanced by Jaslow in 1967 concerning generic service agencies still have merit — (1) open every generic community agency to the retarded insofar as the agency's competence and ability permits; (2) provide basic training and mental retardation for every health worker; (3) place a mental retardation specialist, either full-time or part-time, in every generic agency of any size or significance; and (4) establish a coordinating mechanism within each community to insure balanced services.

FIVE INTEGRANTS TO SUCCESSFUL DEINSTITUTIONALIZATION

The development of an adequate, well-coordinated system of community programs for the retarded, the return of many retarded persons to nonresidential settings, and the realization of appropriate roles and functions by both the community and residential facility require five integrants. These include local authority, independently determined standards, back-up services, an effective advocacy program and adequate financial support.

Local Authority

There must exist on a local or regional level a visible agency or body with *statutory* authority to plan, implement and coordinate programs for the retarded. These agencies must be *legally* accountable for services offered to the retarded in general and each individual in particular. Wisconsin recently passed legislation to create community boards on a county level with full authority, responsibility and accountability to provide the sixteen services associated with the Federal Developmental Disabilities Act (PL 91-517) — evaluation, diagnosis, treatment, day programs, training, education, sheltered employment, recreation, personal care, domiciliary care, special living arrangements, counseling, information and referral, follow up, protective and other sociolegal services and transportation. As of January 1, 1974, all state funds, excluding those for public schools and public residential facilities, were channeled through these boards and their professional staffs.

There is nothing new about the concept of local boards. Many states have tried similar arrangements, usually with minimal success. The difference is that in Wisconsin the boards have statutory sanction and control over funding. Whether or not this approach with its distinct advantages will prove more successful than preceding efforts remains to be fully demonstrated. Since the boards were established, however, there has been considerable local activity in providing a variety of services to the retarded and other developmentally disabled persons. Only two major problems have been encountered to date. First, some counties have refused to serve retarded persons from residential facilities if they were not placed from that county originally. This jeopardizes the rights of some residents. For example, a multiply handicapped youngster with serious orthopedic problems may not be able to have his needs met in his county of origin if that county happens to be in an isolated rural area. If another county with appropriate services denies placement of that resident in one of its communities, such action is incompatible with the stipulated rights of every retarded person as well as the intent of deinstitutionalization. Also, most boards have yet to receive from either the state or federal government adequate financial resources to provide the array of services required.

Standard Setting and Monitoring Agency

In addition to local boards, there must exist an independent standard setting and monitoring agency. This can be accomplished in several ways — by establishing within the state an independent standard setting group, by assigning such a task to a state agency, or by requiring accreditation through the Accreditation Council for Facilities for the Mentally Retarded (JCAH). Of these three alternatives, the least desirable is to have standard setting fall within the jurisdiction of a state agency. Regardless of the intentions and integrity of that state agency, the question of vested interest is never fully resolved.

The accreditation standards developed for community agencies by the Joint Commission on Accreditation of Hospitals (1973) follow the basic format and procedures as those described previously for residential facilities. The community standards are collated according to seven major sections —

1. Provision for an overall individual support program
2. Agency service components
3. Community organization
4. Program evaluation
5. Research and research utilization
6. Records
7. Administration

There is one drawback to the utilization of the standards of the Joint Commission. They do require that the entire community be taken into consideration. " ... an individual agency must be measured against the criteria of the total service delivery system's responsiveness to community need, and by its own ability to respond to the needs of individuals, whether voiced or silent" (JCAH, 1973).

For the agency which wishes to have its local services assessed, an alternative system is available — The Program Analysis of Service Systems (PASS). This approach, which is classified as a method for the quantitative evaluation of human services, was developed by Wolfensberger and Glenn for the Canadian National Institute on Mental Health in 1963. In essence, the PASS system for evaluating services is based on the rating of forty-one items collated under two generic categories — ideology and administration. Ideology includes such aspects as physical and social integration, age and culture-appropriate activities and structures, specialization, developmental orientation, the quality of the physical setting, utilization of generic services, consumer and public participation, ties to academia and innovativeness. Administration includes manpower considerations and operational effectiveness. A supplemental device entitled FUNDET also can be applied. FUNDET, an acronym for funding determination, is intended to assist the administrator and staff in setting fiscally related program priorities. Though developed in Canada, the system is available in the United States.

Regardless of the system used, however, the essential ingredient is that the setting of standards and their evaluation reflect only the needs of the retarded. Inadequate programs should be given a reasonable opportunity to improve; however, if the required improvements are not evidenced according to a set schedule, funding should be terminated. While local boards would neither set standards nor monitor them, they would retain responsibility and accountability to see that such standards were met.

Back-up Services

Local boards and agencies must have access to highly sophisticated back-up services, including technical consultancy. Many communities will, for a considerable period of time, require the expertise of persons who have had years of experience in dealing with the mentally retarded. This is especially true with regard to those retarded individuals making the transition from the residential environment to the community setting and the more severely and profoundly retarded, multiply handicapped child who rarely has been programmed in a nonresidential setting. In addition, many difficult-to-manage children, either for behavior or medical reasons, will require short-term treatment and/or training which can be best offered in a residential facility. Hopefully, residential staff, university personnel and representatives from established community agencies will pool their talents in a collaborative effort to provide the retarded with the finest programming possible.

Advocacy

In order to assure that the rights and needs of the retarded are recognized and met there must exist a tough-minded, strong-willed advocacy program. Commensurate with the growing recognition of rights of the retarded and developmentally disabled, as well as children in general, has been the concern for creating systems capable of protecting these rights.

Advocacy is an all inclusive term which, according to the

Random House Dictionary of the English Language (Stein and Urdang, 1967), means an "act of pleading for, supporting, or recommending active espousal." An advocate, in turn, is "one who pleads for or in behalf of another." Subsequently, advocacy assumes many forms, ranging from individual to class representation. There are many groups and national organizations as well as state and federal agencies which serve as advocates for the retarded as a *class*. For example, the President's Committee on Mental Retardation, the American Association on Mental Deficiency, the National Association of Superintendents of Public Residential Facilities for the Mentally Retarded, the Council for Exceptional Children, and the National Association for Retarded Citizens constantly advocate for the rights of the retarded, appropriate program standards and financial support at the federal level. Similarly, many groups and individuals advocate for the retarded at local and state levels. A number of professional groups have also adopted an advocacy role, e.g. educators (Hobbs, 1975), social workers (AD Hoc Committee on Advocacy, 1969) and physicians (Kenney and Clemmens, 1975).

While such advocacy endeavors are extremely important, the immediate concern is with individual advocacy. There must be some insurance that each retarded person in need of support or assistance during all or part of his life must find such help readily available. This is particularly critical in view of present deinstitutionalization trends where an increasing number of moderately, severely and even profoundly retarded persons are remaining in the community.

In view of the urgency associated with developing advocacy programs combined with the newness of this effort and limited resources, many different approaches are being tried. Nearly every state is attempting to establish some form of protective or advocacy program.

For purposes of the present discussion, the techniques being utilized can be classified into three broad categories — (1) state agency programs, (2) lay or citizen advocacy and (3) legal advocacy. Before considering each of these approaches briefly, let us examine three cardinal principles associated with any individualized advocacy or protective service.

1. No person, regardless of ability or limitations, shall be assigned an advocate with decision-making authority unless such action is absolutely warranted.

This principle highlights two essential facts. First, the mentally retarded as a class do not require an advocacy or protective service program. Only a few retarded persons need such assistance. As will be recalled from an earlier discussion, rights of the retarded include the right to take risks and to fail. Overprotection is as equally undesirable as no protection at all. Secondly, denial of one's personal decision making authority by another is most serious and must be approached circumspectively. Perhaps Professor Kindred of the Ohio State University College of Law expressed this caution best,

> Our basic task is to put ourselves in a position to critically evaluate [a protective services] bill, at first by asking this: If the bill did not say "for the mentally retarded," would we find it acceptable? If the bill allowed for the appointment of a protective service worker for any citizen, not just the sub-category of mentally retarded or developmentally disabled citizens, would we find the legislation acceptable? My answer to that is, "No way." Of course, some might say that they would not mind having a protector now and then, but it seems to me that a basic premise of our society is that we do not set up relationships in which someone is someone else's protector and controller. If that bill were to be applicable to all of us, we would either reject it or tighten it up considerably so that there were no safeguards, so that it was only used in the proper situations after adequate investigation. If we find it unacceptable when we are the targets, why do we find it acceptable when it is restricted to the developmentally disabled? (Kindred, 1974).

2. An advocate's authority must be limited to acting in behalf of a retarded person only in certain areas based on a comprehensive evaluation of the person's decision-making ability and interests.

One major problem which has plagued guardianship efforts in the past has been the statutory requirement that before a guardian could be appointed, the person must be declared legally incompetent which historically has denied that person most, if not all, of his civil rights. With the development of new concepts concerning advocacy and protective services, however, statutes are being revised to limit the authority of an advocate or guardian —

> Any finding of limited incompetency shall specifically state which legal rights the person is incompetent to exercise. Guardianship of the person shall be limited in accordance with the order of the court accompanying the finding of incompetence. No person determined to be incompetent in accordance with this subchapter shall be deprived of any legal rights, including the right to vote, to marry, to obtain a motor vehicle operator's license, to testify in any judicial or administrative proceedings, to make a will, to hold or convey property, and to contract except upon specific finding of the court. Such findings must be based on clear and convincing evidence of the need for such limitations *(Wisconsin State Statutes,* s 880.33, 1974).

3. No agency serving the retarded should be appointed advocate or guardian in order to avoid any possible conflict of interests.

Closely related to these three points is the role of an advocate. Regrettably, some individuals and groups view advocacy as involving a perpetual adversary relationship. While at times an adversarial situation will arise, this should not occur too frequently. Persons who approach advocacy from an adversarial point of view frequently overwhelm the retarded client with their activities (and hostility) and, in many instances, prove self-defeating. *The primary function of an advocate is to assist the retarded person to exercise his rights.* Fortunately, organizations interested in advocacy for the retarded have assumed a positive attitude, e.g. "Personal advocacy services are those that provide a competent individual to assist and befriend an impaired person in coping with problems, including the exercise of personal legal rights" (JCAH, 1973).

State Agency Programs

This approach vests broad protectorship in a state department or agency. Two well-recognized state programs are those of Ohio and New Jersey.

Ohio's protective service system, which became law in April, 1972, includes "those services undertaken by a legally authorized and accountable agency on behalf of a client who needs help in managing himself or his affairs. These services may be social or legal in nature and may involve counseling, monitoring, follow-along, program auditing, advocacy, legal intervention, trustee-ship, guardianship, and protectorship" (Helsel, 1974). Further,

1. The Director of the Division of Mental Retardation and Developmental Disabilities may accept public guardianship of the person.

2. Before entering the system, each client must have a comprehensive evaluation.

3. The protective service agency may provide protectorship, trusteeship and guardianship.

4. The state may provide protective services itself or may make contract for such services.

5. The Division must provide in writing, at least once a year, a review of the physical, mental and social condition of individuals for whom it is acting as a guardian, trustee or protector (Helsel, 1974).

Retarded persons may get into the protective system in a variety of ways, including voluntary admission on the part of the retarded person, parental request, by public agency referral, by voluntary agency referral, by protective service worker referral, and by court appointment.

Duties associated with the protective service system are quite comprehensive, including outreach, counseling, needs appraisal, referral for service and coordination with case managers and other agencies, follow-up and follow-along, monitoring, program auditing, advocacy for rights, legal intervention and guardianship. The protective services worker must be in a position to respond to a need on a twenty-four-hour basis.

New Jersey's program for retarded adults is of longer standing. In New Jersey the retarded population is defined according to mental retardation and mental deficiency in which mental deficiency is considered a special type of mental retardation defined as "The state of mental retardation in which the reduction of social competence is so marked that persistent social dependency requiring guardianship of the person shall have been demonstrated or anticipated" (White, 1966, p. 20).

Since 1965, the Division of Mental Retardation Services has had legal authorization to assume guardianship responsibilities,

> In the event that no guardian has been appointed when the minor has attained age 21, and if the commissioner has ascertained that such a person is mentally deficient as provided above, then the Division of Mental Retardation within the Department *shall perform such services for the mentally deficient adult as he may require, which otherwise would be rendered by guardian of his person* (White, 1966).

In brief, the adult retarded may receive guardianship services from the Division if he fulfills all of the following conditions:

1. He is over twenty-one years old.
2. He is receiving *functional services* from the Department, i.e. services rendered by the Division of Mental Retardation, such as care in a residential facility, family care, community supervision or day care in a state-operated facility.
3. He has been found by the Division of Mental Retardation to be "mentally deficient."
4. His parents (or guardian if one was appointed when he was a child) have not applied through the courts for determination of incompetence and appointment of themselves or someone else as a private guardian of the person (New Jersey Association of Retarded Citizens, 1966).

The Division of Mental Retardation Services has delegated the responsibility of guardianship to the Bureau of Field Services which operates independently from residential programs. Duties of the field services staff include guardianship of the person as well as determining if the present placement satisfies each client's health, safety, training and general welfare needs. Client programs are reviewed periodically and relevant adjustments are made. In contrast to the Ohio program, New Jersey is concerned with the adult and with providing services for retarded persons considered to be mentally deficient engaged in one of the Division's programs. Most states are modeling their protective services after the experiences in Ohio rather than New Jersey.

State agency programs are not without their criticisms. It is contended by many persons that state programs cannot avoid problems of vested interests — caseworkers or guardians, being state employees, may feel somewhat obligated to respond to the state's needs rather than those of their clients in conflict situations. Also, many retarded persons may be given protective services which are neither necessary nor desired. As observed by one critic,

> However well-intentioned, protective services (and particularly public guardianship laws and practices) have suffered from a number of major shortcomings. Among these are the unavailability or impracticality of many protective arrangements, the dull rigidity in which they are administered, the fact that conflicts of interest are built into the very structure and functioning of protective service agency personnel, the fact that agencies — again because of their very nature — can rarely provide the sustained individual relationships that many clients need, and the inability of protective services to match protected measures to protective needs. Characteristically, a person who needed protection received either too much or too little (Wolfensberger, 1972).

Lay or Citizen Advocacy

Citizen advocacy for the mentally retarded is a relatively recent innovation which is being received enthusiastically throughout the country. This concept, which was developed by Wolfensberger (1972b), has received support from various professional organizations. The National Association for Retarded Citizens (1974), for example, has issued an excellent set of guidelines for developing and implementing a citizen advocacy program.

Citizen advocacy has been defined "as a mature, competent citizen volunteer representing, as if they were his own, the interests of another citizen who is impaired in his instrumental competence, or who has major expressive needs which are unmet and which are likely to remain unmet without special intervention" (Wolfensberger and Zauha, 1973). The citizen advocacy program is not to be exercised by agencies or professionals acting in professional roles. It is truly a volunteer program, relying on both adults and youth.

Citizen advocacy can provide for both *formal roles,* i.e. adopted parenthood, guardianship and trusteeship for property, and *informal roles,* i.e. being a friend and guide. The latter concept is most commonly employed. Helsel (1974), for example, wrote that Ohio is initiating a citizen advocacy program modeled after the one successfully initiated in Nebraska. Accordingly, lay or citizen advocates would

1. Be a friend
2. Know the client's personal needs, interests and program
3. Know community resources
4. Raise questions and concerns about the adequacy of the client's program
5. Keep in contact with persons serving the client
6. Be familiar with the client's neighbors and neighborhoods
7. Keep promises to the client

Advantages of this system as described by its originators include its personalized nature, its avoidance of many problems associated with agencies and bureaucracies, and its economic feasibility. Special legislation is not required. Also, the voluntary aspect of this approach possesses the potential for eliciting the interest and enthusiasm of people not normally associated with mental retardation (Wolfensberger and Zauha, 1974).

Legal Advocacy

Simply stated, a system of legal advocacy emphasizes the rights of retarded persons and relies primarily on legally-trained advocates. This approach is predicated on the primary assumption that the retarded should share the same advantages and responsibilities as any other citizen in our society and that their rights as individuals and their rights to services must be recognized. Questions surrounding individual rights and rights to service frequently are a legal matter which best can be represented by professionals of that discipline. As stated by Gilhool (1973), "The language has changed. It is no longer the language of favor or benefit. It is no longer the fact that what comes to the retarded child and his family comes out of the good will and graciousness of others. It is now the language of rights. What comes, comes as a right. It is really not the language of love and kindness but of justice."

While legal advocacy possesses certain merits, especially with regard to its potential effectiveness, it also is not without its difficulties. First, there are very few highly interested attorneys and concerned judges. The cost of a relatively large-scale program probably would be prohibitive, and such a system would undoubtedly lack the personalized quality associated with citizen advocacy.

At this time, one cannot assess which of these three systems is most effective under what circumstances. No research data are available. It may well prove that when services are easily accessible for retarded persons and their rights are fully recognized by all, the citizen or lay approach may prove adequate. On the other hand, when appropriate programs do not exist or there is resistance to including the retarded, there is little question that legal representation is best. Both the citizen advocate and the state-employed protector are somewhat bound to approach an agency on a request basis. An attorney under such circumstances would be in a more advantageous position.

Before concluding this discussion of guardianship and advocacy, the role of the parent should be considered. Most states provide that parents are automatically guardians of retarded minors. This same privilege, however, normally terminates when a child reaches the age of majority unless specifically renewed through a proper court hearing. It is recommended that capable parents be encouraged to have themselves appointed guardians for their adult retarded if such supervision and support are required. As stated by Boggs (1966),

> It is true that many mentally deficient adults live for years as dependent or semi-dependent members of their families, without the formal protection of guardianship. Parents frequently assume the functions of guardian of the adult person without any judicial procedure. This omission produces an ambiguous situation and leaves the retarded vulnerable on two counts. In the first place, there is a hazard in encouraging the assumption by one adult of an attitude of control over another, except when the justification for this relationship has been impartially reviewed and sanctioned and when, in fact, the sanctioning

authority has considered not only the need for protection but the qualification of the protector. Secondly, by postponing the formal enunciation of the need for such protection, parents leave the retarded adult exposed at such time as the informal parental supervision is interrupted. By seeking judicial recognition of the retarded adult's incapacity and securing an appointment of himself or another suitable person as guardian of the person of the adult and establishing the relationship with a person or agency that can provide at least transitional continuity in an emergency, the parent can obviate these situations.

Not all parents, however, should be appointed guardians. Scheerenberger (1969) reported the experiences of a director of a sheltered workshop. The director indicated that several adult retarded persons had completed their training and were capable of assuming a job in the community. There was no question of competency. The parents, however, refused to let the respective retarded adults be placed in open employment for higher wages because it would affect their welfare allotments. This example illustrates the need for the adult retarded and professionals as well as parents to be better informed of laws regarding civil rights and guardianship. In this case the parents' ability to respond appropriately to the adult's needs might well be challenged. In general, however, many parents would make good guardians.

In summary, few retarded persons require any form of advocacy. If they do, however, such advocacy must be available, personalized, flexible and effective. Without such programs it is highly probable that some residents returned to the community may not be able to sustain themselves for more than a brief period of time. Perhaps the ultimate answer to the advocacy question is to create all three systems. This has happened in Ohio. In addition to the protective services system and citizen advocacy, it was announced in the summer of 1975 that a legal rights service for the retarded and their families was established within the Ohio Supreme Court by state law.

Adequate Financial Support

All community programs, including residential, must receive

substantial financial support. Neither the community nor its residential facilities can provide for the retarded unless it has access to an adequate resource of funding for programming, training and research. *Quality services are costly, regardless of where they are offered*!

PUBLIC AWARENESS

As we have seen, the courts have stated unequivocally that the retarded possess an inherent right to live in an open society and, in essence, that the realization of such a right is not subject to community approval. Yet, public awareness, knowledge and sensitivity remain critical aspects of deinstitutionalization. First, without community acceptance, the retarded will never attain a reasonable degree of social integration. Secondly, successful deinstitutionalization efforts as have been outlined will require considerable financial support which, in turn, is highly contingent upon public sentiment.

A review of the literature would indicate while there has been increased receptivity to the retarded in general, there still remains much misgiving and misunderstanding. The most recent study located was conducted by the Gallup Poll commissioned by the President's Committee on Mental Retardation (1975). The six questions posed by the Gallup Poll to 796 people as well as the answers are given in Table XVII.

The President's Committee was pleased with the results to the degree that most respondents would not object to the moderately or mildly retarded living in their block and that most believed the retarded should remain in the community. On the other hand, the relatively high percentage of respondents (49%) who indicated that most mentally retarded persons could not live independently or support themselves was somewhat disconcerting.

Several other studies which have been reported since 1970 would tend to support the ambivalence with which the retarded are viewed by society. Gottwald (1970) interviewed 1,515 people throughout the country to elicit or discern, in part, what attitudes the public had toward mental retardation. On the positive side, most respondents believed that the retarded could be tended at

162   *Deinstitutionalization and Institutional Reform*

TABLE XVII
ATTITUDES TOWARD THE MENTALLY RETARDED

Question	Response Category	Results (%)
1. Suppose mildly or moderately retarded persons have been educated to live in the general community. Would you object to six of them occupying a home on your block, or not?	Would object Would not Don't know	9 85 6 100
2. Would you object to having a trained worker who is mildly or moderately retarded employed where you work, or not?	Would object Would not Don't know	5 91 4 100
3. To the best of your knowledge, do all mentally retarded people, or only some, have to live in institutions?	All Only some Don't know	1 94 5 100
4. To the best of your knowledge, are all forms of mental retardation, or only some, inherited?	All Only some Don't know	3 76 21 100
5. Do you think there is reason to fear mentally retarded people?	Yes No Don't know	14 74 12 100
6. To the best of your knowledge, are most mentally retarded people able to support themselves and lead independent lives?	Yes No Don't know	33 49 18 100

From: President's Committee on Mental Retardation (1975a).

home (69.8%), only some of the retarded required residential placement (77.2%), only a few retarded persons could not learn to do anything for themselves (81.3%), the retarded have the right to a public education (81.1%), most would not object to their child attending a school with classes for the retarded (83.9%), and the retarded have the right to public residential facilities (71.3%). On the more negative side, 58.3 percent of the respondents contended that the retarded could not go downtown unattended; 83.8 percent believed the retarded should not consume alcoholic beverages; 77.5 percent felt that the retarded should not drive a vehicle; 49.0 percent would restrict voting privileges; and 53.9 percent would object to the retarded marrying and having families.

Latimer (1970) conducted an attitudinal survey sponsored by

the Tri-State Mental Retardation Project (Kentucky, Indiana and Ohio). A total of 1,113 subjects were interviewed personally, utilizing a household visit approach. Among the results were 80 percent of the respondents believed the retarded could be productive citizens; 75 percent believed the retarded had feelings; 91 percent contended that the retarded should remain in their own homes; 80 percent would not object to mixed social and educational activities. (Eighty percent, however, would object to the mixed dating between mentally retarded and nonmentally retarded persons). Unfamiliarity with retardation was revealed in the fact that most respondents were not acquainted with such basic services as clinic programs, residential facilities, sheltered workshops and parent associations. Also, 55 percent did not know that mental retardation could be prevented; 31 percent believed that mental retardation could be cured; and only 6 percent could distinguish between mental retardation and mental illness.

Lewis (1973) approached public sentiment from the standpoint of "social ambivalence." This study, which again involved household visits, included a sample of 2,641 citizens (one per household) in a southern California city with a population of 85,000. Nonambivalent attitudes were defined as (1) keep the retarded at home unconditionally or (2) institutionalize unconditionally. Ambivalence was measured by (1) keep the retarded at home conditionally and (2) institutionalize conditionally, i.e. depending upon the circumstances. The mildly and moderately retarded were separated from the severely and profoundly retarded. According to the responses, 23.1 percent advocated keeping the mildly and moderately retarded at home unconditionally, 36.4 percent would institutionalize this population unconditionally, and 40.5 percent were ambivalent. With regard to the severely and profoundly retarded, only 5.5 percent contended that they should remain at home unconditionally, 74.1 percent felt that they should be institutionalized unconditionally, and 20.4 percent were ambivalent. It was concluded,

> the community stance, although mixed, tends toward rejection — removal from the community setting — of both the educable-trainable and the severely-profoundly retarded child .... It [the results] would seem to indicate: (1) a disagreement in

principle with those in power who have worked out programs
for the educable-trainable, evidently without informing those
in the community to whom the retarded is unknown or relatively invisible; (2) a general lack of knowledge and confusion as to
the capabilities and potentialities of the less severely retarded
child; and (3) a continuing sense of fear and of threat by a substantial portion of the community.

These results would indicate that while there has been a growing awareness and sensitivity to the retarded, much remains to be
accomplished before the retarded will be fully accepted in contemporary society. It is interesting to note that American attitudes
are not as positive toward the mentally retarded as are those expressed in European countries. Lippman (1972), following his
visit to Europe, contended that Europeans view the mentally
retarded as human beings who should be treated with considerable dignity and that their potentiality should be realized with the
full cooperation and assistance of the state and society. While
Lippman did indicate that the United States was ahead in such
areas as research, professional training and voluntary citizen participation, fuller support by all of society for the retarded is
needed.

Another area of investigation which bears on the subject of
acceptance involves the integration or mainstreaming of the mentally retarded into regular as opposed to special classes. A classic
sociometric study in the field of mental retardation was conducted
by Johnson in 1950 with 659 normal and thirty-nine retarded
pupils in twenty-five regular public school classes serving as subjects. The retarded appeared to be markedly rejected; 69.23 percent
were isolated and 46.15 percent were rejected. Only 5.13 percent
were rated as "stars." Reasons for isolation and rejection were
attributed primarily to behavior rather than academic performance. For many years this study was used to support the notion
of special classes. Within recent years, however, sociopolitical as
well as educational reasons have once again encouraged the
mainstreaming of mentally retarded persons into regular classes.
One frequently-asked question involves the degree to which the
retarded are now being accepted in the regular class, "Are they
still isolated and rejected?" Several investigations have broached

this problem.

Goodman *et al.* (1972) conducted a study of normal boys and girls in each of the primary grades (1 through 6) using the *Peer Acceptance Scale* to determine the degree of acceptance of EMR children integrated into public classes. The results included (1) the EMR were accepted less and rejected more; (2) younger subjects were more accepting than older subjects; (3) girls were more accepting than boys; (4) integrated EMRs were more rejected than those in segregated classes, at least by male subjects. According to the author, the fact that normal children in the first three grades were more accepting than older students was similar to the results found among Norwegian children. Females at all ages were more "nurturing."

Lapp (1957) found that retarded persons integrated in the school on a part-time basis were neither rejected nor accepted. They simply were isolated and viewed neutrally.

Sheare (1974), in a study of ninth graders, found that the mentally retarded in ungraded schools were accepted. In other words, integration appeared to increase acceptance, with girls again being more accepting of mentally retarded persons than boys.

Gampel *et al.* (1974) studied the behavior of both integrated (n=12) and segregated (n=14) EMR students. After four months of integration, those students integrated revealed much less aggressive and hostile behavior. This was attributed to the fact that they no longer had to act "dumb," they were with new models for conduct, and they were afraid to misbehave in fear of either re-segregation or negative reaction by their new classmates. The actual degree of social acceptance, however, was not examined.

Bruininks *et al.* (1974) conducted a study to assess the social acceptance of retarded children enrolled in regular classrooms who were receiving supportive assistance in resource learning centers within either suburban or urban intercity schools. The prediction was that students in urban schools would be more accepting than those in suburban schools. The results did not support this hypothesis. The 1,234 elementary students tended to reject the sixty-five elementary-aged EMR's. One factor, which was mentioned in this study as well as others, involved busing. Apparently, the fact that many of the retarded youngsters did not live in the neighborhood but were bused may, in itself, have produced an isolating factor.

Similar to studies involving the general population, the school-related investigations concerning acceptance were equivocal. The single exception is that girls, at least at this time, appear more accepting of the retarded than normal male students.

Attitudinal problems associated with facilitating deinstitutionalization are by no means limited to the general public. There is considerable evidence that in many cases professional attitudes require modification. Most residential administrators and staff (and parents) have shared the experiences outlined by Rosen (1974) in his presidential address to the American Association on Mental Deficiency,

> Today, the institution is an easy and obvious symbol at which we may direct our outrage. The larger community, of which each of us is a part, on the other hand, is far less satisfying to attack. To sue the larger community for being arthritically slow in "readying" itself to accept the retarded entitled to leave the institution is something we have not learned to do. To direct our legal attention, in the place of helpless frustration, at our local societies, governmental and private agencies, and neighborhoods, which by their exclusions are violating the constitutional rights of the mentally retarded, is a formula we have not yet fully developed — but one that we will develop!
>
> Today many professionals in the community . . . are keeping a staunch vigil at the entrance to their domain. While there are many examples of good community programs, there are relatively few, if any, where the community is providing for all its own population of mentally retarded. More frequently, the lament that, "We need more *time* to develop appropriate resources," and "We need more time to get prepared" is heard. There is an irony to this lament in that the initial cries of outrage that institutions were being insensitive to the rights of retarded came from professionals in the larger community. Now, frequently, when this same citizenry is asked to take part in the revolution, they beg off because of a lack of preparation, funds, and so forth. Nobody can expect enough time or money, whether they be in an institution or community. It is not unusual to hear some professionals in the community ask instead that institutions modernize what they have and tell the adminis-

trators, "Not now — the time isn't quite right. We're getting ready."

The previous discussion concerning the unavailability of many generic services to the retarded also implies a need for attitudinal changes. In essence, while there is a growing acceptance of the retarded by both the general public and the professional community, much remains to be accomplished before the retarded individual will be viewed as just another person.

PARENTS

Parents today can be divided into two groups — (1) those whose retarded children have been born within recent years and who are receptive to the idea of maintaining their child in the local community and (2) those whose retarded children were born a number of years ago and are now confronted with the prospect of deinstitutionalization. Fortunately, though parents in the first group have suffered the traumatic experience of having a retarded child, they are finding a variety of services readily available to them in their local community. In most instances they need not suffer the second trauma associated with having to place their child in a residential facility for extended programming.

Fifteen years ago this was not the situation. Frequently, parents were confronted with one of two choices either (1) keep their child at home with little or no support or (2) place their child in a residential facility. As eloquently expressed by one parent, "An institution is only considered by desperate parents. Every parent I have known has moved heaven and earth to find another solution" (Jagar, 1974).

Other comments clearly illustrate the personal and emotional concerns of parents confronted with deinstitutionalization,

> As to deinstitutionalization plans, it seems to be of utmost importance that this should be done very slowly and with great care. The entire living conditions of a home must of necessity evolve around the retarded member. Parents have already gone through this "Garden of Gethsemane" by parting the first time with the child. Then if a child is returned home from an institution and the situation is again found an impossible one, to have to go through this traumatic experience a second time would

likely come very nearly to destroying mentally and physically the retarded child and the parents.

I realize that our institutions are presently overcrowded, and that this situation must be alleviated, but I do not agree with "deinstitutionalization" as it now stands. You can not deinstitutionalize the child without at the same time deinstitutionalizing his family. The child will not continue to develop educationally or emotionally unless the family finds it possible, perhaps with assistance in making the necessary adjustments.

As a parent, my great fears that many residents now in institutions will be returned home to unprepared and older parents and unprepared communities, and the gains over the years that have been made in institutions will be lost (Jagar, 1974).

These concerns cannot be ignored. No parent should be forced to have his retarded child or adult returned home if the situation is not appropriate. Though other community living alternatives are becoming available, parents are legitimately anxious about their quality. They are very sensitive to some of the unfortunate experiences associated with deinstitutionalization. Also, they are worried about the potential financial burden of deinstitutionalization. It is not uncommon for parents who are on Social Security or other limited income to express fear about the financial responsibility which they may have to assume. Others are concerned that their savings will be consumed or that they will be unable to leave anything to their children in the event of death.

While parental counseling during deinstitutionalization is of utmost importance (as is their involvement and participation with their child at all times), parents need a three-fold assurance — (1) their youngster will receive quality services with adequate supervision; (2) deinstitutionalization will not result in an undue personal financial burden; and (3) there will be appropriate back-up facilities other than the home in the event that community placement proves inadequate. Parental concerns and fears are genuine and should be so recognized.

CURRENT STATUS AND TRENDS

Deinstitutionalization today represents, at best, an ambiguous situation. On the one hand there is evidence to indicate that deinstitutionalization is effective to the extent of reducing residential populations in public residential facilities. On the other hand, there is evidence to suggest that what is being experienced in many cases is depopulation as opposed to deinstitutionalization as defined previously. Other data indicate that some components of deinstitutionalization are being implemented, some are not.

One can approach the subject of deinstitutionalization from two perspectives — (1) actual number of residents and (2) characteristics of the resident population. In both instances available data suggest that deinstitutionalization efforts are at least partially successful.

Number of Residents

As will be recalled from the previous discussion concerning the current status of residential facilities based on a recent survey of public residential facilities by Scheerenberger (1975), the overall reduction in total resident population during the period of FY 1969-1970 through FY 1973-1974 was 8.9 percent. This would indicate that deinstitutionalization, at least as it affects public residential facilities, is proving successful. The 8.9 percent reduction is of further significance when one considers the fact that the total population for the United States increased approximately 6 percent, from 202,599,000 in 1969 to 215,053,000 in 1974. It must be remembered, however, that the survey data were limited to public residential facilities. How many retarded persons were residing in private residential facilities, mental hospitals without identifiable units, and such other facilities as county homes was and is unknown.

Further, it was estimated that the total number of residents in public residential facilities was approximately 176,000. In 1960, there were 160,000 retarded persons in public residential facilities for the mentally retarded and 53,000 in private residential facilities and mental hospitals (President's Panel on Mental Retardation, 1962). By 1969, this number had increased to 190,000 retarded persons in public residential facilities and 65,000 in private facilities and mental hospitals (Office of Mental Retardation

Coordination, 1972). Thus, taking into consideration both the increase in total population and the estimated reduction of approximately 14,000 retarded persons in public residential facilities, it can be concluded that some programs of deinstitutionalization are successful.

Regrettably, while some data seem supportive of deinstitutionalization, others would indicate that many problems remain. For example, approximately 40 percent of retarded persons admitted during FY 1973-1974 were in the less seriously affected ranges. In fact, 25.6 percent of new admissions consisted of moderately, mildly and borderline retarded persons of school age (CA 3 to 21). Another major group (10.7%) was composed of the less seriously affected, ages twenty-two to sixty-one (Scheerenberger, 1975). These data not only suggest that community programs are not being developed as rapidly as desired, they also dispel the commonly-held belief that new admissions are limited to the very young and severely retarded.

Preadmission data followed a similar pattern. While the majority of readmissions were severely and profoundly retarded (56.5%), approximately 43.5 percent were moderately, mildly or borderline retarded (Scheerenberger, 1975). Such figures again suggest that a number of deficiencies exist in community programming.

A final consideration related to deinstitutionalization involves projected placements for FY 1974-1975. In the superintendents' judgment, 52 percent of the residents presently in a public residential facility could be placed in the community. Communities, however, are not prepared at the present to accept this many retarded persons. In contrast to 52 percent, the superintendents estimated that only 9.7 percent of the resident population would be placed during FY 1974-1975, a figure almost identical to reported placements during FY 1973-1974 (Scheerenberger, 1975).

Residents Characteristics

In addition to the fact that the total residential population in public residential facilities is decreasing, the changing characteristics of the residents also imply that deinstitutionalization is working. As shown in Table XVIII in FY 1922-1923, 40 percent of the first admissions were mildly retarded; in FY 1973-1974, only 17.6 were mildly retarded.

TABLE XVIII
FIRST ADMISSIONS
TO PUBLIC RESIDENTIAL FACILITIES

Year	Mild (+) %	Moderate %	Severe and Profound %
1922 - 23[a]	40.4	35.2	14.3
1931 - 35[a]	45.7	30.2	15.6
1941 - 45[a]	43.3	29.4	14.9
1951 - 55[a]	32.1	35.6	22.4
1963 - 64[b]	28.2	21.5	50.3
1973 - 74[c]	17.6	19.3	63.1

From: (a) Farber, 1968; (b) National Institute of Mental Health, 1966; (c) Scheerenberger, 1975.

As indicated previously, during FY 1973-1974, 71.2 percent of the resident population in PRF's was classified as severely or profoundly retarded. Only 17.9 percent were moderately retarded and 10.9 percent were mildly or borderline retarded. This latter pattern is similar to that reported by Scheerenberger in 1965. Thus, certain aspects of deinstitutionalization have been apparent for a number of years.

Community Placements

One major question that always exists with regard to any decrease in residential population involves the appropriateness of community placements. Table XIX shows the placement of 9,043 residents as reported by 115 PRFs. The total population for these PRFs dropped from 93,046 residents in FY 1972-1973 to 89,449 residents in FY 1973-1974, approximately a 4 percent decrease.

As shown, the results are relatively encouraging. Only 28.7 percent of the residents were transferred to other residential facilities. The remaining 71.3 percent was placed in smaller settings, ranging from total independence to group homes.

TABLE XIX
COMMUNITY PLACEMENTS AS REPORTED
BY 115 PUBLIC RESIDENTIAL FACILITIES

Placement	n	%
Independent living	137	1.5
Work placement	145	1.6
Parent's (or guardian's) home	2448	27.0
Other relative's home	261	2.9
Foster home	1182	13.1
Boarding home	51	.6
Group home	2227	24.6
ICF facility	501	5.5
Rest or convalescent home	248	2.7
Nursing home	1386	15.3
Intensive (nursing) care facility	457	5.2
Total	9043	100.0

From: Scheerenberger (1975)

The adequacy of these placements in terms of normalization and personal liberty are unknown. There is sufficient evidence, however, to indicate that all may not be right with community placements either in terms of alternative residential care or *less restrictive* settings.

Many of the reports available today would indicate that deinstitutionalization has *not* always been successful in terms of meeting the interests and needs of the retarded or mentally ill person. In some instances, community placements have proven extremely dehumanizing and degrading. *Time* magazine (Crackup . . . 1973) described deinstitutionalization experiences in California, " . . . chronically ill patients have been returned to communities poorly equipped to provide adequate treatment. With no one to care for them, former patients have ended up on welfare rolls, in boarding houses, cheap hotels, and even jail."

In New York, *Time* reported,

. . . since New York state started emptying its mental hospitals of thousands of inmates six years ago, many of them have been jammed into tiny rooms, basements, and garages and fed a semi-starvation diet of rice and chicken necks ... they are taken from the steps of mental institutions by operators who jam them into what can only be described as private jail and confiscate their monthly welfare checks.

Trotter and Kuttner (1974) summarized their study in the *Washington Post* with the following observations:

In larger cities, thousands of discharged mental patients have gravitated to the familiar skid rows, where instead of fending off the outraged middle-class, they must defend themselves against drug addicts, alcoholics, and prostitutes. The Uptown section of Chicago and the Times Square and Bowery Areas of Manhattan, which have recently experienced community protests over welfare hotels, now find the same hotels increasingly populated with former mental patients.

While it cannot be ascertained whether *Time* and the report by Trotter and Kuttner were referring to the mentally retarded as well as to the mentally ill, the circumstances associated with many placements of the retarded over the past several years have been quite similar.

Nor are foster and group homes immune from institutionalized attitudes. For example, Murphy, Rennee and Luchins (1972) studied foster home programs in Canada and concluded

1. There was very little interaction between residents and family. In fact, one of the authors observed that in most homes there was not "merely a lack of interaction, but a lack of *any* activities whatever."
2. Regimentation and uniformity were common, e.g. certain days were set aside for shaving and others for bathing.
3. In many cases, there was no interaction between resident and other persons or facilities within the community.

Luchins summarized his observations by stating, " ... it is my opinion that those who think foster home placement enables a patient to escape the disadvantages of an institutional life are mistaken. Foster homes can be as institutionalized as hospitals are while lacking the compensatory advantages that some hospitals might possess."

With specific regard to foster and group homes for the mentally retarded, little information is available. The newness of this program has precluded extensive research. The study by Tizard (1970), previously described, however, indicated that placement in group homes and hostels did not necessarily foster a high degree of independence.

A relatively recent study conducted by Browder *et al.* (1974) would indicate that foster homes are not proving as successful as desired. The authors' concluded their study of foster home placements of twenty-seven retarded children in twenty-two foster homes with the statement that "Over half of the placements assessed were in need of substantial improvement. Further reflections on the inadequacies observed included (a) a lack of realistic acceptance of the child's handicap, (b) failure in meeting in-home and out-of-home needs, (c) overloading of foster homes, (d) frequent changes in placement." Specifically, the investigators found that foster home children frequently lacked adequate transportation to services, lacked financial resources for such services, were far removed from community activities, and were in inadequate homes because of other children and minimal foster parent time. Other problems identified included the foster parent's inability to see the need for special programs, elderly foster mothers and the absence of sufficient training to manage the more difficult child.

According to Bjaanes and Butler (1974), there are four environmental components of any community facility — (1) physical, (2) supportive, (3) attitudinal and (4) behavioral. Their study was concerned with the behavioral aspects of two board-and-care facilities and two group homes for the mentally retarded. The two board-and-care facilities served thirty and fifty mildly retarded residents, respectively. The two group homes served four and six mildly retarded residents. The board-and-care facilities were located in an urban transitional area; the group homes were located in a suburban area, removed from parks, recreational facilities, transportation and businesses. Significant differences were found within as well as between board-and-care facilities and group homes. Though the amount of activity varied with each facility, six generalizations were proposed —

1. There were substantial differences in the behavioral component of the environment of community care facilities.

2. The board-and-care facilities examined were closer to the objective of normalization and developing social competence than were home care facilities.

3. Behavior was more independent in board-and-care facilities than in the group homes.

4. Exposure to the community was an important factor in normalization.

5. The development of independent functioning and social competence appeared to be related to the geographical location of the facility and the personal involvement of the caretaker.

6. Specific types of community involvement were associated with different outcomes.

O'Connor (1975) recently reported on a study of group homes for the mentally retarded conducted by the Rehabilitation Research and Training Center in Mental Retardation of the University of Washington. According to preliminary data, the three most serious problems in operating a group home were (1) inadequate funding, (2) finding qualified staff and (3) developing individualized client programs.

Of all facilities presently being used as an alternative to public residential programming for the mentally retarded, none is more questionable than the nursing home. This industry, which is under constant criticism and legal challenge in many parts of the country, has been and is being used indiscriminately for many placements. The author has visited a number of nursing homes in several states, and invariably the retarded were minimally programmed by understaffed, inadequately-trained personnel. The retarded frequently were viewed with little interest and low expectancy levels. Normalization, interaction, increased independence and application of the developmental approach were rarely found in a nursing home. The medical model, however, was prevalent.

On the other hand, there is a place for the nursing home in the continuum of care. Lyon and Bland (1969), for example, followed a sample of twenty-five nonpsychotic adults who had been placed in a nursing home from the state's psychiatric hospital. They found residents to be well attended and active. The residents interviewed were considered to be happy. O'Connor *et al.* (1970) reported that the quality of nursing home services for the disabled were improving and cited an example of a successful placement involving a sixty-nine-year-old, mildly retarded woman. While good nursing homes do exist, they still should be used judiciously and only for a limited subpopulation of the mentally retarded.

Two other major problems are associated with deinstitutionalization — isolation and lack of mobility. Many youngsters and adults, especially those from rural areas, are being returned to their home communities. In many instances, they are the only mentally retarded persons in that area. Subsequently, they frequently become isolated from the community in any genuine social sense. Greater consideration must be given to the placement of retarded persons in settings which will provide for peer interaction, especially among the more seriously affected.

Further, as indicated by a number of the studies cited, many retarded persons are being placed in facilities located in transitional neighborhoods. While such neighborhoods may be adequate for the time being, they have a tendency to deteriorate at a rapid rate. Unlike persons of normal or above intelligence, the moderately and severely retarded are not familiar with the community as a whole or the ramifications of making a move. Again, some of the retarded need strong support and advocacy to assure that they are living in an appropriate environmental setting, free from fear and harm.

This entire question of isolation and constraints placed upon a person living in a dangerous neighborhood gives rise to the question of how one wishes to interpret "normalization". In this context, Wolfensberger's (1972a) concept is of minimal assistance —

> From the proposed reformulation it is immediately apparent that the normalization principle is culture-specific, because cultures vary in their norms. For instance, normalization does not necessarily mean that human services should resemble Scandinavian services. It does mean that as much as possible, human management means should be typical of our own culture; and that a (potentially) deviant person should be able to emit behaviors and an appearance appropriate (normative) within that culture for persons of similar characteristics, such as

age and sex. The term "normative" is intended to have statistical rather than moral connotations, and could be equated with "typical" or "conventional." The phrase "as culturally normative as possible" implies ultimately an empirical process of determining what and how much is possible.

This definition appears to ignore the reality that the United States is a tremendously multicultural nation and that frequently any statistical data, such as an *average*, actually applies to no one. Nor should normalization or deinstitutionalization be considered independent of moral judgment. For example, no responsible administrator would place a basically defenseless retarded person in a high-risk neighborhood simply because he emanated from that environment and it is "normal" for some people in the United States to live in such areas.

Regrettably, there are a number of persons in the field who have placed the priority of their decision making on normalization and deinstitutionalization regardless of its potential impact upon the retarded person. In other words, some people, according to their own interpretations of normalization and deinstitutionalization, view these processes and concepts to be of greater consequence than taking into consideration the individual characteristics of the retarded. They have forgotten the most fundamental right of all — the right of a retarded person to be retarded. As expressed by Fram (1974),

> The right to belong as a retarded person always carries with it appropriate responsibilities for the retarded person as well as for the rest of society. In addition to the responsibility of giving equal protection to the retarded and normal, there is an obligation to insist that no one can declare the retarded extinct by proclamation. A retarded person should not be "hidden" nor should he be refused the right to be retarded.

Deinstitutionalization as a process is not a goal! Normalization per se is not a goal! *The genuine goal of both deinstitutionalization and normalization is the increased independence and quality of life for the mentally retarded.* The effectiveness of deinstitutionalization can be measured only in those terms.

The preceding negative comments and reservations about community programs were not presented for the purpose of condemning the idea of community placement for retarded persons. Nor were they intended in any way to justify inadequate practices or services in residential facilities. They do, however, clearly demonstrate that any program, regardless of the facility or location in which it is being implemented, must be assessed only in terms of individual needs. As stated by the National Association of Superintendents of Public Residential Facilities for the Mentally Retarded (1974),

> While the Association advocates without reservation the rights of the retarded to live in the least restrictive environment and to enjoy fully the benefits of a free and open society whenever possible, it does express concern over the manner in which this goal is being realized. First, the quality of community programs and services being offered to the mentally retarded and other developmentally disabled persons in many parts of the country is inadequate. All too often, "community back wards" and "closeting" are being substituted for institutional "warehousing." Neither community nor residential back wards or "closeting" are justified: the rights of the retarded must be respected wherever they reside. In essence, the Association calls attention to the need not only for continued upgrading of residential facilities ... but also for a greater interest in quality control for developing community programs.

It must be pointed out that there are many fine islands of excellence in community programming. Examples of innovative and promising services include

> Five counties in eastern Nebraska have implemented the EN-CORE system which provides for an integrated continuum of services and programs, including behavior shaping, specialized developmental units, adult training, and a series of graduated residential settings intended to facilitate maximum independence (Coleman, 1974, and Lensink, 1974).
> Specialized homes are being developed throughout the country. Variations, based on the needs of the specific clients served, include adoptive homes, foster care, five-day/weekend programs for the severely and profoundly retarded, special crisis intervention centers, group homes, adult residences, transitional homes or hostels, and special apartments (President's Committee on Mental Retardation, 1975b).

The California Instructional Television (ITV) Consortium at Cal State-Sonoma provides educational television for training parents and foster parents.

A special program was developed in Connecticut to stress family training. Five basic objectives were set — (1) to acquaint the parent-family with the child's handicap and current research relative to the handicapped, (2) to assist the parent-family in coordinating the program within the home, (3) to provide the parent-family with available assistance from an interpretation by the clinical team, (4) to promote a keener insight into the child's prognosis for future mental and physical growth and development, and (5) to provide the family with supportive assistance from parent groups.

Local church collaborates with the Winnebago-Boone Association for Retarded Children, Illinois, to establish a friendship coffee house.

Tennessee-Peabody establishes a hotline referral system so that parents of developmentally disabled children who don't know where to go for services can find a solution readily.

The Portland State University, Oregon, offers a summer vocational career program to trained students and persons with developmental disabilities to secure jobs.

In New Mexico, a special six and one-half mile marked nature trail for the mentally retarded and other disabled persons was developed.

The Austin Community College, Texas, offers special programming for the retarded in the evening.

The Spring Creek Early Childhood Center in New York State is a typical neighborhood day center which serves thirty-two clients, among whom are eight mentally retarded residents three to five years of age.

The mentally retarded themselves are beginning to organize. For example, mentally retarded adults in Oregon have established a group, People First, which was organized to establish their identity and to exhibit to their own communities not only their willingness but also their ability to contribute to society.

Most states and the federal government have initiated a number of programs intended to facilitate the retention of the retarded in the community. As indicated earlier, nearly all states have passed special education laws. Three states — Virginia, Tennessee and

West Virginia — have agreed to joint planning and programming to maximize services available to the retarded. The Georgia legislature recently adopted a special mentally retarded offender act to insure that offenders who are retarded receive appropriate training and programming. Commitment laws have been modified in many states, e.g. Wisconsin, West Virginia and Tennessee. The Florida legislature recently passed a "Bill of Rights" with very specific goals intended to improve services for the retarded — (1) upgrade the state's residential facilities by improving the quality of life and eliminating dehumanizing conditions, (2) provide individualized programming for all clients, and (3) strengthen regional services by offering necessary support programs to clients in the community and bring services to within an hour's travel time for most families.

The federal government, through various means and techniques, has been highly active in attempting to provide both legislative and financial support to assist the retarded person either remain or return to his home community. In 1974, there were twenty-six major pieces of legislation which offered benefits to the mentally retarded and other disabled persons (United States Department of Health, Education, and Welfare, 1975). Major legislation included extended programs of Social Security, rehabilitation, education and housing and community development. Other acts of significance involve such areas as maternal and child health, HEW — Labor appropriations, lead poisoning and transportation for the handicapped.

In essence, deinstitutionalization, like residential programming, is in transition. While many excellent programs have been implemented, many more need to be developed. Few areas have established a genuine continuum of care. Regrettably, a number of inhumane practices have been associated with deinstitutionalization, practices which cannot be tolerated by a responsible citizenry. The need for community standards is evident as it the need for effective support and advocacy programs for the retarded.

SUMMARY

Deinstitutionalization was defined as an attitude, a principle and a complex process. Of particular import is the realization that deinstitutionalization is an attitude which emphasizes freedom, independence, individuality, mobility, personalized life experiences and a high degree of interaction in a free society.

Deinstitutionalization, to a significant degree, depends upon each community being able to provide the array of services required by the retarded throughout their total life span. Such services should be offered along a continuum of care and place high priority on retaining as many retarded persons as possible in the community. Both generic and special services will be required.

Five integrants for successful deinstitutionalization were described — local authority, independently-determined standards, back-up services, effective advocacy programs and adequate financial support. Advocacy systems may involve state agency programs, citizen advocacy and/or legal representation. Public awareness of and sensitivity to the rights of the retarded are also essential.

Parents are confronted with many problems associated with deinstitutionalization. Among these are fears and legitimate concerns which require a three-fold assurance — (1) the retarded will receive quality community services with adequate supervision (2) deinstitutionalization will not result in undue personal financial burden, and (3) there will be adequate back-up facilities other than the home in the event that local placement proves inadequate.

There are a number of positive indices that deinstitutionalization is being implemented, including the reduction in the total number of residents being served in public residential facilities and the fact that most residents are severely and profoundly retarded. While a number of creative community programs have been implemented, inhumane treatment is also evident. In essence, while both the community and its residential facility are supportive of deinstitutionalization, much remains to be accomplished.

REFERENCES

Ad Hoc Committee on Advocacy: The social worker as advocate: Champion of social victims. *Social Work, 14*(2):16-22, 1969.

Bjaanes, A., and Butler, E.: Environmental variation in community care facilities for mentally retarded persons. *Am J Ment Defic, 78:*429-439, 1974.

Black, H.: *Black's Law Dictionary.* St. Paul, West Publishing Company, 1951, pp. 792, 1064, 1066.

Boggs, E.: Legal aspects of mental retardation. In Phillips, I. (Ed.): *Prevention and Treatment of Mental Retardation.* New York, Basic Books, 1966, 407-428.

Browder, J., Ellis, L., and Neal, J.: Foster homes: Alternatives to institutions? *Men Retard, 12:*33-36, 1974.

Bruininks, R., Rynders, J., and Gross, J.: Social acceptance of mildly retarded pupils in resource rooms and regular classes. *Am J Ment Defic, 78:*377-383, 1974.

Burton, T.: Mental health clinic services to the retarded. *Ment Retard, 9*(3):38-41, 1971.

Cherington, C., and Dybwad, G.: *New Neighbors: The Retarded Citizen in Quest of a Home.* Washington, U. S. Government Printing Office, 1974.

Coleman, R.: ENCOR: Some programs and their clients. In Menolascino, F., and Pearson, P. (Eds.): *Beyond the Limits.* Seattle, Special Child Publications, 1974, pp. 123-141.

Crackup in mental care. *Time,* December 17, 1973.

Dempsey, J. (Ed.): *Community Services for Retarded Children: The Consumer Provider Relationship.* Baltimore, Univ Park, 1975.

Downey, K.: Parent's reasons for institutionalizing severely mentally retarded children. *J Health Human Beh, 6*(3):147-155, 1965.

Ehlers, W.: *Mothers of Retarded Children.* Springfield, Thomas, 1966.

Fanning, F.: Coordinating community services. *Ment Retard, 11*(6):46-47, 1973.

Farber, B.: *Mental Retardation: Its Social Context and Social Consequences.* Boston, HM, 1968.

Farber, B., and Ryckman, D.: Effects of severely mentally retarded children on family relationships. *Ment Retard Abstracts, 2*(1):1-17, 1965.

Fotheringham, J., and Kershner, J.: Institution or family: A study. Ontario Assoc Ment Retard, 8(3):3-6, 1970.

Fram, J.: The right to be retarded — normally. *Ment Retard, 12*(6):32, 1974.

Gampel, D., Gottlieb, J., and Harrison, R.: Comparison of classroom behavior of special-class EMR, integrated EMR, low IQ, and nonretarded children. *Am J Ment Defic, 79:*16-21, 1974.

Gardner, W., and Nisonger, H.: *A Manual on Program Development in Mental Retardation.* Monograph Supplement to *Am J Ment Defic,* 1962.

Gettings, R. (Ed.): *Synergism for the Seventies: Conference Proceedings of the National Conference for State Planning and Advisory Councils on Services and Facilities for the Developmentally Disabled.* Reston, Virginia, Council for Exceptional Children, 1973.

Gilhool, T.: A commentary on the Pennsylvania Right to Education Suit. In *The Rights of the Mentally Handicapped*. Washington, National Coordinators of State Programs for the Mentally Retarded, 1973, p. 53.

Goodman, H., Gottlieb, J., and Harrison, R.: Social acceptance of EMRs integrated into a nongraded elementary school. *Am J Ment Defic, 76*:412-417, 1972.

Gottwald, H.: *Public Awareness about Mental Retardation*. Arlington, Virginia, Council for Exceptional Children, 1970.

Hansell, N.: Patient predicament and clinical service. *Arch Gen Psychiatry, 17*:204-210, 1967.

Hansell, N., Wodarczyk, M., and Visotsky, H.: The mental health expeditor. *Arch Gen Psychiatry, 18*:392-399, 1968.

Helsel, E.: Putting it together in Ohio. In Sigelman, C. (Ed.): *Protective Services and Citizen Advocacy*. Lubbock, Texas Tech Univ, 1974, pp. 23-36.

Hobbs, N.: *The Futures of Children*. San Francisco, Jossey-Bass, 1975.

Jager, E.: Institutional reform through the eyes of a parent. In *Region IV Staff Development Conference on Institutional Reform*. Columbia, South Carolina Department of Mental Retardation, 1974, pp. 82-84.

Jaslow, R.: *A Modern Plan for Modern Services to the Mentally Retarded*. Washington, U. S. Government Printing Office, 1967.

Johnson, G.: A study of the social position of mentally handicapped children in the regular grades. *Am Assoc Ment Defic, 55*:60-89, 1950.

Joint Commission on Accreditation of Hospitals: *Standards for Community Agencies*. Chicago, Joint Commission on Accreditation of Hospitals, 1973, pp. 2, 25.

Justice, R., O'Connor, G., and Warren, N.: Problems reported by parents of mentally retarded children — who helps ? *Am J Ment Defic, 75*:685-691, 1971a.

Justice, R., Bradley, J., and O'Connor, G.: Foster family care for the retarded: Management concerns of the caretaker. *Ment Retard, 9*(4):12-15, 1971b.

Kenney, T., and Clemmens, R.: *Behavioral Pediatrics and Child Development, A Clinical Handbook*. Baltimore, Williams & Wilkins, 1975.

Keys, V., Boroskin, A., and Ross, R.: The revolving door in a MR hospital: A study of returns from leave. *Ment Retard, 11*(1):55-56, 1973.

Kindred, M.: Protecting the civil and human rights of the developmentally disabled. In Sigelman, C. (Ed.): *Protective Services and Citizen Advocacy*. Lubbock, Texas Tech Univ, 1974, pp. 43-48.

Lapp, E.: A study of social adjustment of slow-learning children who were assigned part-time to regular class. *Am J Ment Defic, 62*:254-262, 1957.

Latimer, R.: Current attitudes toward mental retardation. *Ment Retard, 8*(5):30-36, 1970.

Lensink, B.: One service system at work. In Cherington, C., and Dybwad, G. (Eds.): *New Neighbors: The Retarded Citizen in Quest of a Home*. Washington, U. S. Government Printing Office, 1974, pp. 105-141.

Lewis, J.: The community and the retarded: A study in social ambivalence. In

Tarjan, G., Eyman, R., and Meyers, C. (Ed.): *Sociobehavioral Studies in Mental Retardation.* Washington, American Association on Mental Deficiency, 1973, pp. 164-183.

Lippman, L.: *Attitudes Toward the Handicapped.* Springfield, Thomas, 1972.

Lyon, R., and Bland, W.: The transfer of adult mental retardates from a state hospital to nursing homes. *Ment Retard, 7*(5):31-36, 1969.

McCarver, R., and Craig, E.: Placement of the retarded in the community: Prognosis and outcome. In Ellis, N. (Ed.): *International Review of Research in Mental Retardation.* New York, Acad Pr, 1974a.

McCarver, R., and Craig, E.: Current follow-up procedures of residential facilities for the MR. *Ment Retard, 12*(2):38, 1974b.

Mental Health Law Project: *Basic Rights of the Mentally Handicapped.* Washington, Mental Health Law Project, 1973, pp. 27-28.

Metzer, R., and Rheingold, H.: Mental capacity and incompetency: A psycholegal problem. *Am J Psychiatry, 18*:827-831, 1962.

Meyen, E. (Ed.): *Planning Community Services for the Mentally Retarded.* Scranton, International Textbook Company, 1967.

Murphy, H., Rennee, B., and Luchins, D.: *Foster Homes: The New Back Wards?* Monograph Supplement #71 to *Canada's Mental Health,* 1972, pp. 5, 14.

National Association for Retarded Citizens Residential Services and Facilities Committee: *The Right to Choose.* Arlington, National Association for Retarded Citizens, 1973, p. 72.

National Association for Retarded Citizens: *Avenues to Change.* Arlington, National Association for Retarded Citizens, 1974.

National Association of Superintendents of Public Residential Facilities: *Residential Programming.* Washington, President's Committee on Mental Retardation, 1974, pp. 2-5.

New Jersey Association for Retarded Children: *Guardianship of the Person for the Adult Mentally Retarded in New Jersey.* New Brunswick, New Jersey Association for Retarded Children, 1966.

Nihira, L., and Nihira, K.: Jeopardy in community placement. *Am J Ment Defic, 79*:538-544, 1975.

O'Connor, G., Justice, R., and Warren, N.: The aged mentally retarded: Institution or community care? *Am J Ment Defic, 75*:354-360, 1970.

O'Connor, G.: Trends in group homes examined. *New Direction, 3*(9):4, 1975.

Office of Mental Retardation Coordination: *Mental Retardation Source Book.* Washington, U. S. Government Printing Office, 1972.

President's Committee on Mental Retardation: Gallup poll shows attitudes on MR improving. *President's Committee on Mental Retardation Message,* April, 1975.

President's Committee on Mental Retardation: *People Live in Houses: Profiles of Community Residences for Retarded Children and Adults.* Washington, U. S. Government Printing Office, 1975b.

President's Panel on Mental Retardation: *A Proposed Program for National Action to Combat Mental Retardation.* Washington, U. S. Government

Printing Office, 1962, pp. 74, 76.

Reiff, R., and Riessman, F.: *The Indigenous Nonprofessional.* Monograph Supplement Number One to *Community Mental Health Journal,* 1965.

Rosen, D.: Observations of an era in transition. *Ment Retard, 12*(5):61-65, 1974.

Savino, M., Stearns, P., Merwin, E., and Kennedy, R.: The lack of services to the retarded through community mental health programs. *Comm Ment Health J, 9:*158-168, 1973.

Scheerenberger, R.: *A Study of Generic Services for the Mentally Retarded and their Families.* Springfield, Illinois, Department of Mental Health, 1969, pp. 56, 118, 120.

Scheerenberger, R.: Generic services for the mentally retarded and their families. *Ment Retard, 8*(6):10-16, 1970.

Scheerenberger, R.: *Current Trends and Status of Public Residential Services for the Mentally Retarded: 1974.* Madison, National Association of Superintendents of Public Residential Facilities, 1975, pp. 4, 22.

Sheare, J.: Social acceptance of EMR adolescents in integrated programs. *Am J Ment Defic, 78:*678-682, 1974.

Shellhaas, M., and Nihira, K.: Factor analysis of reasons retardates are referred to an institution. *Am J Ment Defic, 74:*171-179, 1970.

Stein, J., and Urdang, L. (Eds.): *Random House Dictionary of the English Language.* New York, Random, 1967, p. 298.

Thaman, A., and Barclay, A.: Parental attitudes toward institutionalization of mentally retarded children. *Child Welfare, 46*(3):156-159, 1967,

Tizard, J.: The role of social institutions in the causation, prevention and alleviation of mental retardation. In Haywood, H. (Ed.): *Social-Cultural Aspects of Mental Retardation.* New York, Appleton, 1970, pp. 281-340.

Tizard, J., and Grad, J.: *The Mentally Handicapped and their Families.* London, Oxford U Pr, 1961.

Trotter, S., and Kuttner, B.: The mentally ill: From back wards to back alleys. *Washington Post,* February 24, 1974.

U. S. Department of Health, Education, and Welfare. *A Summary of Selected Legislation Relating to the Handicapped: 1974.* Washington, U. S. Government Printing Office, 1975.

White, B.: Protective services for the mentally retarded in New Jersey. In Helsel, E., and Messner, S. (Eds.): *Conference on Protective Supervision and Services for the Handicapped.* New York, United Cerebral Palsy Association, 1966, pp. 20-24.

Wolfensberger, W.: *Normalization: The Principle of Normalization in Human Services.* Toronto, National Institute on Mental Retardation, 1972a, pp. 28, 48.

Wolfensberger, W.: *Citizen Advocacy for the Handicapped, Impaired, and Disadvantaged: An Overview.* Washington, President's Committee on Mental Retardation, 1972b.

Wolfensberger, W., and Glenn, L.: *PASS: Program Analysis of Service Systems.* Toronto, National Institute on Mental Retardation, 1973.

Wolfensberger, W., and Zauha, H.: *Citizen Advocacy.* Toronto, National Institute on Mental Retardation, 1973, p. 12.

Wyatt v. *Stickney.* Civil Action No. 3195-N. U. S. District Court, Middle District of Alabama, North Division, 1972, p. 3.

Chapter 6

INSTITUTIONAL
(RESIDENTIAL) REFORM

To many persons, residential reform simply implies compliance with federal regulations and/or the accreditation standards of residential facilities for the mentally retarded developed by JCAH. While the realization of such standards would greatly improve the existing situation, much of the existing situation itself requires change.

INSTITUTIONAL REFORM DEFINED

In the prior discussion of a definition of deinstitutionalization it was noted that one component of the tripartite concept offered by the National Association of Superintendents of Public Residential Facilities for the Mentally Retarded (1974) dealt primarily with institutional reform — "Establishment and maintenance of a responsive residential environment which protects human and civil rights and which contributes to the expeditious return of the individual to normal community living wherever possible." The inclusion of this statement in a definition of deinstitutionalization was most appropriate. Deinstitutionalization and residential reform are, to a large extent, inextricable. Residential reform in many instances will not be realized without a substantial decrease in existing residential populations while the return of many residents to their home communities will not be realized without significant reform.

The National Association of Superintendents of Public Residential Facilities for the Mentally Retarded did offer a specific definition of residential reform. Accordingly, reform "involves a modification or improvement in attitudes, philosophies, policies, effective utilization of all available resources, and increased financing to provide adequate programs to motivate and assist

187

individuals to reach their maximum level of functioning in the least restrictive environment possible" (National Association of Superintendents . . ., 1974).

Residential reform involves both preparing for the future and ameliorating present inadequacies or deficiencies. Let us initiate this discussion by looking ahead.

FUTURE ROLE OF RESIDENTIAL PROGRAMMING

There are basically four rather diverse viewpoints concerning the future of residential programming — (1) residential facilities should be "bigger and better;" (2) residential facilities should not exist at all; (3) residential facilities should offer only specialized services; and (4) residential facilities should offer comprehensive developmental services to special populations.

Of these four positions, only a few persons support the notion of "bigger and better" facilities. These same individuals usually oppose rather vigorously any significant efforts to deinstitutionalize.

A larger number of people believe that there will be no need for residential services in the future. This point of view was best advanced by Wolfensberger (1971), "I can see no reason why small, specialized living units (mostly hostels) can not accommodate all of the persons now in institutions." This observation was based on five noted trends —

1. The development of nonresidential services, e.g. day and public school programs.

2. New conceptualizations of and attitudes toward residential services, i.e. large, multipurpose residential facilities are undesirable and unnecessary.

3. Increased usage of individual rather than group residential placements, e.g. foster family care and five-day boarding homes.

4. Provision of small, specialized residential placements, e.g. hostels.

5. A decline in the prevalence of severely and profoundly retarded through continuing decline in birth rate among high risk groups, preventive health services for high risk groups,

increased legalization and practice of abortion, improvement of health and preventive services generally, environmental betterment and early childhood education.

According to Wolfensberger these trends will result in a natural phasing out of large-scale residential facilities. Though his desire for small, community-based facilities is well-supported, equally informed persons question the appropriateness of such facilities for the more multiply handicapped, severely and profoundly retarded; the degree to which conditions in point five will be realized; the ability of sparsely populated rural areas to provide adequate services; and the rate at which large facilities should be eliminated. Nevertheless, if all or even most of the conditions underlying Wolfensberger's predicted trends were satisfied, many of our existing residential facilities would no longer be required.

The third category, the specialized facility, was advocated by Dunn (1964). Types of specialized facilities recommended included medical special-purpose facilities for retarded persons requiring both generalized and specialized medical treatment (preferably in connection with a hospital), child developmental centers for severely retarded ambulatory persons, boarding schools for school-age eligible children, vocational centers and hostels. Dunn stipulated that responsibility for each facility should be assigned specifically to the discipline which provides the specialized treatment, e.g. physicians for medical-nursing programs, educators or psychologists for developmental centers. He contended that specialization of this nature would eliminate interdisciplinary struggles and bickering; emphasize intensive, specialized treatment programs; and reduce manpower needs.

The comment concerning disciplinary assignments for facilities reflects Dunn's apparent disappointment with the ability of representatives with various professional backgrounds to work together effectively. While problems occasionally are encountered as a result of professional "preciousness," most authorities still believe that an interdisciplinary approach is essential.

The fourth approach emphasizes total programming to select or limit groups of retarded persons, i.e. those who are severely and profoundly retarded with multiply handicapping conditions, including multisensory deficits, and those presenting severe behavior problems. In contrast to the specialized facility proposed by Dunn, each resident, regardless of the severity of his handicapping condition(s), would receive a comprehensive developmental program, planned, implemented and monitored by an interdisciplinary team. Children or adults requiring very specialized treatment on an outpatient basis also would be served.

The latter approach to meeting the needs of retarded individuals requiring extended residential services is believed to be most favored at this time. Extended programming, however, by no means exhausts the projected role of residential facilities. It is anticipated that residential facilities will also

1. Provide short-term programming for retarded persons with various needs to eliminate or reduce the need for extended services. At present, nearly all residential facilities offer comprehensive, diagnostic, evaluation and planning services for retarded infants, children and adults from the community. It is expected that these services will be extended to individuals with a variety of developmental disabilities. Further, a number of short-term, intensive treatment and training programs will be established with the intent of ameliorating specific problems and returning the child to his home community within several months. Such services may involve relatively minor behavior problems which cannot be resolved in the home environment (Kirkland, 1967 and Sternlicht and Deutsch, 1971). Another such program could involve physical restoration or habilitation for the child with a severe orthopedic handicap. Appropriate surgery, therapy and follow-up home services, including parental training and guidance would be offered. In a few instances, the very young multiply handicapped child or infant may be admitted for a brief period of time in order to develop a program which can be implemented by parents and/or representatives from a community agency. Genetic counseling and specialized dental services are other examples.

2. Collaborate more closely with community programs, including education and training, recreation, health services and vocational placements. Programming in the future will be a shared responsibility between the residential facility and community. Services of both shall be used simultaneously. For

example, while an individual may be receiving specialized medical treatment requiring short-term residential services, he also may be attending a local school.

3. Play a more significant role in assisting local communities develop, implement and evaluate appropriate programs for the retarded. Technical consultancy will become increasingly important as more community agencies (specialized and generic) become alert to and responsible for providing for the mentally retarded. Such programs frequently require the expertise of residential staff. Technical consultancy may relate to a variety of areas such as diagnosis and evaluation; education and training; language, speech and hearing therapy; activity therapy and recreation; nutrition; and domiciliary care. In essence, any aspect of residential services (administrative or clinical) may become involved in technical consultancy, depending upon evident needs. In some areas, technical consultancy services will be transitory, existing only until the community has an opportunity to develop its own cadre of well-experienced personnel and appropriate standards.

4. Expand training programs for persons from the community, including parents, aides and other personnel working in foster family, group or nursing homes. Parental training for home care of the developmentally-disabled child also will be offered. Many residential facilities will establish special training programs for adolescents to serve as babysitters for the multiply involved child. Special seminars and training sessions will be available to students and professionals in any health or behavior field concerned with the developmentally disabled.

5. Participate in community information programs in order to promote greater public understanding and acceptance of the mentally retarded as neighbors with special needs. Residential facilities may serve as central points of referral, conceivably at all levels of functioning previously described.

From this discussion, it can be seen that residential facilities will be providing a wide array of services to the community as well as establishing both short-term and long-term comprehensive treatment/training programs. One of the major tasks of residential facilities in the future will be to prevent the need for extended placement.

DIMENSIONS OF RESIDENTIAL REFORM

As evidenced by the preceding comments as well as earlier discussions pertaining to legal rights, potential adverse effects of residential experiences, and contemporary concepts of programming, reform may involve every aspect of residential living. Regrettably, the present discussion must be limited to highlighting a few of the more crucial dimensions of reform.

Philosophy

A key element of reform involves acceptance by all personnel of deinstitutionalization as an attitude and a principle. This, in turn, implies

1. Every effort must be made by both community and residential personnel to provide for the retarded person in the local setting if at all possible. A greater concentration of resources and energies should be devoted to maintaining the child in his natural or foster home. As succinctly expressed by Pursley (1973),

> Let's not waste our energies debating whether or not institutional care is better than community care — or whether or not a group is better than a foster home or nursing home.
> Let's stop talking about alternatives to institutionalization and speak instead of alternatives to home care. . . . Let's set about the task of providing the retarded with the service he needs at the time and place he needs it.
> There is one element of the care continuum that I feel we as professional planners may tend to overlook or at least fail to capitalize on. There is a great deal of strength within the bonds of the basic family unit. If we had emphasized and encouraged the maintenance of the family unit, I wonder if the overall development of programs for the retarded might not have been very different.

2. If a person cannot be served in the community, then his residential placement should be for as short a period of time as possible.

3. Presently misplaced retarded persons in residential facilities should be returned to the community.

4. Deinstitutionalization, which places great emphasis on individual freedom and growth, must be reflected in all aspects of residential programming as well as in the desirability for early community placement.

Though the validity of deinstitutionalization is being recognized throughout the country, its full acceptance within each residential facility will be contingent not only upon staff development and administrative support but also upon the judicious placement of residents. There must be the assurance that the quality of life for each resident returned to the community will be enriched. Unfortunately, early experiences with deinstitutionalization which did not reflect such an assurance have resulted in generating adverse reactions, e.g. "Health workers have had too many negative experiences with deinstitutionalization as a shell-game for budget cuts, layoffs, and profiteering not to be skeptical of the most impressive sounding plans" (Santiestevan, 1975).

Criteria for Admission

One of the prime reasons why residential facilities today accommodate an appreciable number of misplaced persons relates directly to the notion that residential programming is an "alternative." For example, residential facilities have served as an educational alternative to unresponsive school systems, as an orphanage for unwanted or abandoned children who happen to be retarded, and as a detention home for youngsters and adults whose minor infractions normally would not have resulted in extrusion from the community.

The net effect of this interpretation of residential programming as an "alternative" to any existing deficiencies within the community has resulted in many retarded persons being inappropriately admitted to residential facilities. This practice has not only denied the rights of such residents, it has also resulted in long waiting lists of youngsters in absolute need of residential services. In some cases, retarded persons were admitted regardless of overcrowded conditions. The latter experience was well described by Klebanoff (1964), "Officials who solemnly declare the financial inability to provide increased facilities will plead for admission of a worthy case. As the worthy cases spill over into the corridors, the already inadequate personnel-to-resident ratios become impossible and there is little the staff can do except to fold laundry and keep a fire watch."

While the described situation is improving, it still remains imperative that each residential facility clearly define its function and put forth unequivocal criteria for admission. In this way, residential facilities in the future will become one viable, but limited, service in the care continuum.

One residential facility, for example, has defined its role as offering extended care, treatment and training programs for severely and profoundly retarded, multiply handicapped children less than six years of age. Mentally retarded children considered for admission are those

1. Who require nasogastric or gastrotomy feedings due to difficulty in swallowing

2. With known history of respiratory or other infections requiring repeated local hospitalizations, or those with severe congenital cardiac disease requiring continuous medical supervision and treatment

3. With progressive hydrocephalus who have been denied shunting procedures for any reason in the community or continue to require skilled nursing care

4. With congenital or acquired neuromuscular disorders who are developing skeletal deformities due to the lack of appropriate medical, surgical or paramedical services in the community

5. With degenerative central nervous system diseases whose progressively deteriorating physical conditions require intensive medical and nursing care

6. With seizure disorders so poorly controlled that a protective environment is required to meet physical care and safety needs

7. With extensive cerebral damage due to congenital malformations, physical trauma, anoxia or infectious diseases who require intensive care and rehabilitative services

8. With limited life expectancy due to multiple congenital anomalies, including malformations of the brain and skull

9. With behavioral disorders so severe that management and training in a protective environment is required and no other community service is available

10. With severe sensory deficits that require rehabilitative services and no other community service is available

11. Who have utilized available community resources, but whose developmental disabilities are so severe as to require extended programming in a residential facility

These criteria reject the possibility of a moderately or mildly retarded infant or child being admitted for extensive residential services without major multiply handicapping conditions. This public residential facility has been quite successful in not only controlling the nature of the residential population to be served, but also in presenting a clear picture to the community as to its limited purposes.

Criteria for Placement

Ever since Fernald conducted the first recognized postplacement study of residents in 1919, a number of investigators have attempted to identify personal characteristics predictive of successful community adjustment. To date, none have produced any results of significance. In his extensive review of the literature, Windle (1962) found that many personal characteristics were not related to postplacement success, including sex, race, intelligence, physical handicaps and personality. Nor did psychiatric treatment, drug treatment, working ability, sterilization or original family interest appear to be of significance. One factor which did appear to be important involved the quality of the placement, "The more favorable the home to which the patient is released, the better the chances of success. However, this favorability applies to the emotional attitudes of the patients, guardians, not to material conditions in the home."

In a more recent review of the literature, McCarver and Craig (1974) concluded, "The literature concerning the postinstitutional adjustment of the mentally retarded is replete with inconclusive, discrepant, and contradictory findings. . . Perhaps the biggest reason that one cannot reliably predict who will or will not succeed on community placements is that most of the studies available are post hoc surveys rather than true experiments." Regardless of the reason, to date no significant predictors of community success have been isolated.

Let us examine several studies in order to gain a greater appreciation for the conclusions just cited. Tarjan *et al.* (1960) studied residents leaving a public residential facility between 1952 and 1956. Subjects who were followed for 700 days were of varying ages and intelligence and had been placed in several settings, including home placement and vocational leave. Sex, age, clinical diagnosis and IQ did not greatly affect success rate. Females, however, tended to remain out longer, indicating a greater community tolerance for retarded girls and women as compared to males.

Wolfson (1970) reviewed the socioeconomic adjustment of 163 male and female mildly retarded adults twenty years following discharge from a public residential facility in New York. Most of the residents had adjusted to community living. Fifty-seven percent of the males have been steadily employed for a number of years. Only seven (10%) were leading a "rather shiftless, vagabond existence"; ten (15%) developed psychosis; and one had returned to the residential facility. Fifty percent of the women were married and maintaining stable marital relationships; most had children. Fifteen (15%) of the women who were single, widowed or separated were working steadily and were self-supporting. Only nine (10%) of the women were making a poor adjustment; six developed psychosis and were in mental hospitals, and four had returned to the residential facility.

Albin (1973) compared the relationship of IQ to vocational success among thirty-five severely or moderately retarded individuals who had worked at least three months at the Southeast Nebraska Community Sheltered Workshop. The results indicated that IQ, even among the more seriously affected, is not a predictor of vocational adequacy.

Rosen *et al.* (1974) retested fifty previously institutionalized EMRs three years following discharge. The purpose of the study was to ascertain if community living resulted in either change in measured IQ or in academic achievement. The results indicated that no significant changes in either IQ or academically-oriented achievement occurred. Further, no relationship was found between the measured IQ or academic achievement level to overall community adjustment. The authors concluded that their study like so many others "failed to identify meaningful psychometric predictors of community adjustment for this population."

More recently, Fulton (1975) conducted a study of fifty-five adult retarded persons (IQ≤80) to determine which of a number of variables might be related to successful placement in competitive employment, e.g. IQ, academic achievement, previous work history, sex, whether client lived alone or with family, hourly pay rate and the presence of secondary emotional disability. The only variable to yield a statistically significant difference between successful and unsuccessful groups involved an emotional disability. While none of the successful clients had any emotional difficulties, approximately one-third of the unsuccessful participants revealed such problems.

In essence, these studies demonstrate that the future placement of residents, as in the past, will be based primarily on professional judgment. It is, therefore, very important to recognize that the research literature clearly indicates that given an appropriate setting and support, most retarded persons, even the more seriously involved, can adapt to community living. There also is evidence to indicate that foster parents and group home personnel are willing to work with the mentally retarded and are not expecting unrealistic levels of functioning. Desired attributes include the ability to care for self (or the potential for acquiring related skills), helping with chores around the house, and interacting with others in an acceptable manner (Wolfensberger, 1967; Eagle, 1968; Kraus, 1972; and Nihira and Nihira, 1975). Further, as demonstrated in the study by Nihira and Nihira, foster or group home parents take great satisfaction in witnessing even very minor changes in the retarded person's skill performance or attitude.

Historically, some residential personnel have been reluctant either to place a retarded person unless his behavior was near perfect, or to place the individual in a community which did not offer all services and programs available within the residential setting. As indicated, all but very few retarded persons can make a satisfactory community adjustment given the correct circumstances, and it is the task of residential and community personnel to locate an appropriate setting, train related personnel and provide the required supplemental services and support.

A decision always has to be made with regard to extensiveness of required programming. Occasionally one will encounter residential staff who believe firmly that a retarded person should not be returned to the community until all desired services are developed. Under such circumstances few retarded persons would ever leave the residential setting. In essence one has to weigh the advantages of increased opportunities for independence, freedom and privacy against those residential programmatic offerings which might be lost by an individual when placed in the community.

Having contended that all but a few mentally retarded persons should be served in the community, let us examine some of the reasons which may warrant extended programming. These include

1. Chronic or recurring medical or nursing care problems involving nutrition, respiration, circulation, elimination or temperature regulation which cannot be treated appropriately in a community facility

2. Progressively deteriorating general physical condition in which prolonged survival is doubtful

3. Progressive neuromuscular disorders which are likely to cause increasing discomfort and physical care difficulties unless constant active preventive measures are provided

4. Uncontrolled severe seizures

5. Uncontrolled aggressive or self-destructive behavior

6. Frequent acute intercurrent illnesses, particularly infections

7. Critical care, treatment, rehabilitative or training needs which cannot be met by the community at present

Resident Rights

A major portion of this text has been devoted to resident rights which require no further enumeration. The challenge is to provide a mechanism or system which will adequately insure that these rights are recognized and met within the residential facility. Ideally, each retarded person should have a guardian (or very active parent in the case of a minor) appointed prior to the time of admission to (1) assure that placement is the most appropriate course of action, (2) remain highly active in the child's programming during his stay at the residential facility, (3) encourage early release from the facility, and (4) assist in protecting the child's rights once he returns to the community. Unfortunately, a program of this nature is difficult to implement in view of the number of guardians that would be required as well as financial considerations. Therefore, other approaches are being tried.

Some states are establishing human rights committees with authority to examine the residential situation. Florida, for example, appointed several Human Rights Advocacy Committees to

> serve as a third-party mechanism for protecting the health, safety, welfare, civil and human rights of retarded individuals. Specifically, it shall discover, investigate, and determine the existence of abuse within any program or facility operated, funded, and/or regulated by the Division of Retardation, Department of Health and Rehabilitation Services. This abuse may consist of physical or mental punishment, unfair discrimination, withholding legal rights, the denial of social or community participation, the failure to recognize the retarded person as a human being, entitled to all rights of humans (*Human Rights Advocacy Committee*, 1973).

At least one residential facility is attempting to implement an advocacy program through the use of employees hired solely for that purpose. In other words, advocacy represents the staff member's sole responsibility. An alternative approach which is being tried by several residential facilities relies primarily on adult volunteers. As an advocate, either on a voluntary or employed basis, the person may

1. Serve as a friend and companion to the individual on a one-to-one basis
2. Monitor the individual's care, treatment and training programs —
   a. Participate actively in the individual's program and

attend staffings

b. Meet with all staff related to the individual's program regarding problems and progress and visit all appropriate living and activity areas

c. Raise questions with unit coordinator concerning signs of physical injury or bruises and any other form of abuse. If investigation is warranted, advocate shall be appraised fully of any results subject to the laws of confidentiality

d. Raise questions concerning any restraint measures for the individual, and attend any sessions of the resident human rights committee concerned with the utilization of restraint measures with the individual

3. Speak on behalf of the individual with regard to any requested participation in experimental research. He/she cannot, however, sanction or deny the individual's participation

a. Is totally familiar with the appropriate federal regulations and policies of the facility

b. Monitor the individual's progress and interests in the research project

4. Monitor the individual's rights as defined

5. Examine the individual's personal financial accounts and raise any questions which may be appropriate

6. Determine if the individual's wages (if any) are in compliance with the Fair Labor Standards Act

7. Continue to serve as a friend to the individual while on temporary discharge

8. Be invited to participate on various advisory committees serving the administrative and program delivery areas of the facility

In no instance may an advocate infringe upon the rights of a resident. Further, advocates do not possess the full authority of a guardian and may not engage in such activities as giving consent for medical treatment, authorizing participation in experimental research, signing official documents for the individual, or assuming control of the resident's property and financial resources.

As implied, implementing a strong advocacy program is difficult. Nevertheless, each residential facility must devise some means for guaranteeing the full expression of residents' rights.

Resident Programs

The main aspects of resident programming have already been cited, i.e. implementation of the developmental model, taking into consideration both normalization and the need for intensive interdisciplinary collaboration. Each child or adult, regardless of the degree or multiplicity of his handicapping conditions, must be viewed as a total person with individual needs. Each resident must also be trained to the highest degree of independence possible, and programming should emphasize community rather than residential living. As many experiences as possible should be offered each individual in the community setting.

A few residents, especially the more severely and profoundly retarded, may not be able to cope with the freedom associated with normalization. In all probability their environment and programming will require some modification to facilitate development and personal security.

Staffing

Programs require people, and nothing is of greater import than an adequate staff. Staffing ratios established by various regulations and standards for residential facilities for the mentally retarded, which, in many instances, exceed those presently available, will not be adequate to meet the needs of the very complicated population projected. Staffing requirements can be determined accurately only upon clearly delineated program goals for each resident, a task which can be accomplished only by residential personnel.

As demonstrated by several studies previously described, quantity per se offers no assurance that quality programs will be delivered. All persons responsible for residents will need not only to be sensitive to the implications of the developmental model and normalization, but should possess an insatiable curiosity and willingness to create and implement new programs. Quality in quantity must exist.

An ongoing program of staff development is essential. Historically, it has been difficult to acquire adequate financial support for such endeavors. Yet, at our stage of development, continuing education must be provided for all employees. This should involve university courses, professional meetings and other community-sponsored training as well as specialized programs offered by the residential facility. Without continuous training and the benefit of the many persons' expertise both within and without the residential facility, the generation of new ideas and programs will be seriously impeded.

New Programs and Research

With the change in priorities and approaches to funding human services as well as markedly elevated costs, monies to conduct research, either from the federal or state governments, are for all practical purposes no longer available. This is most regrettable since at no time in the history of residential services has the need for research been more evident. Very little actually is known about programming the more severely and profoundly multiply handicapped child or those with marked behavioral disorders. Though the use of psychopharmacology and various forms of behavior modification have proven somewhat successful, these techniques by no means provide the overall solution to many of the difficulties encountered. Nor, in the judgment of many, have these approaches always been applied judiciously or assessed adequately.

> Due in part to the previously stated emphasis on change in concepts, principles, practices, and strategies, valid concerns related to behavioral techniques have received relatively little attention.
>
> The general field of behavioral technology is advancing rapidly beyond our grasp of knowledge and control. Physical, pharmacological, and psychological behavioral techniques are in widespread use in residential and community programs (including the natural home and public school) for the mentally retarded. Properly prescribed, applied, and supervised, these techniques can be of valuable assistance to the mentally retarded person as well as to other members of our society. *Overused, ineptly prescribed, undersupervised,* a Pandora's box opens to

reveal a snake pit (Clements, 1975).

As indicated by Baumeister as early as 1969, while behavioral techniques have proven successful in many areas of skill acquisition, "the ultimate criterion hinges on far more complicated issues of cognition, socialization, and acculturation." Neither these areas nor other theories of learning as they relate to the more severely and profoundly multiply handicapped individual have been explored to any appreciable degree.

The need for research to generate new programs and techniques which will provide for the greater arousal and self-learning among the more seriously affected is critical. Complacent acceptance of our present level of knowledge is totally unwarranted.

Outreach Programs and Community Relations

As indicated previously, one of the contemporary concepts of future programming for residential facilities is to provide the community with a wide range of outreach and back-up services. While this general philosophy has been accepted by most persons, attitudinal problems are still encountered — "In many parts of the country today, a dichotomy exists between 'community' and 'residential' programming. This polarization of persons with a common dedication to meeting the needs of the mentally retarded is unwarranted and should be resolved as rapidly as possible to insure maximum services for the retarded, both within the community and within a residential environment" (National Association of Superintendents..., 1974).

Effecting highly integrated community-residential services is contingent upon the mutual respect and appreciation of the talents and integrity of all persons. Community representatives must acknowledge the residential facility as one active member in the care continuum, and, at the same time, residential personnel need to gain a greater knowledge of and appreciation for community programming.

The Physical Environment

One of the most significant changes which must occur in all

but the most recently designed and constructed residential facilities involves a rather substantial alteration of the physical environment. Fortunately, the warehousing phenomena which has inflicted the residential scene for many years is gradually disappearing. As indicated previously, the physical environment is tremendously important not only in terms of recognizing each individual's dignity and right to private possessions and privacy, but also in terms of facilitating his total development and fostering familiarity with normal living.

A number of guidelines or statements of principle have been developed to assist both programmers and designers provide an appropriate physical setting,

> An important part of the normalization principle implies that the standards of the physical facilities . . . should be the same as those regularly applied in society to the same kind of facilities for ordinary citizens (Nirje, 1969).

> Retarded children need opportunity to explore, to experiment, and to create . . . the retarded child responds well to a lively, colorful stimulating environment . . . retarded children need an atmosphere of structured informality in which they are offered intensive adult support, the opportunity for social involvement and withdrawal, for physical movement, for intellectual and esthetic stimulus. Like mankind in general the retarded child is happy when he is creating, when he is modifying the world in which he lives (Norris, 1969).

Elliot and Bayes (1973) were more elaborate,

> Whatever the pattern of care, whatever the degree of handicap, whether the site be in or out of the hospital, the residential facility is a substitute family home and the overriding principle of homeliness must apply so it should:

> Be known by its own individual name or street number.

> Create a family atmosphere, where individuals can develop within a small group and with their own interests and possessions.

> Encourage residents to do the sort of household jobs people normally do in their own homes as far as their handicaps permit.

> Separate children from adults.

Not usually separate the sexes.

Have single rooms for most adults and no rooms with more than four beds.

Have plenty of space for recreation, indoors and out of doors.

Enable its residents to use local parks, sportsgrounds and shops.

Be small, for a maximum of twenty-five adults or twenty children.

Most of the recently-constructed facilities as well as current remodelling efforts have attempted to realize these principles. Regrettably, however, the more subtle aspects of design and decoration in terms of influencing human behavior are not understood. What physical dimensions, for example, should be modified in order to provide the most desirable environment for the deaf-blind severely and profoundly retarded? What colors, textures and layouts are most effective in arousing and/or stimulating curiosity and play activity among seriously affected' infants? As stated by Elliot and Bayes (1972), "Not enough is yet known about the potential of those handicapped people with antisocial habits or whose behavior is severely disordered; we need to explore and learn more about how they will respond to extensive training in a more normal environment. Staff with much practical experience should combine with researchers to undertake further studies, or, better still, practical experiments . . . ."

The appropriate size of a residential facility, i.e. number of residents, is also an unresolved problem which has been of long-standing interest. Over one hundred years ago, Sequin, for example, proposed that no facility should exceed 150 to 200 residents so that the chief administrator could know each individual personally (Talbot, 1964). Other estimates have ranged from 500 beds for new facilities to 1,000 beds for older ones (President's Panel on Mental Retardation, 1962). Cleland (1965) reviewed the question of size from various viewpoints and concluded, "It may be possible that at some future date it will be proved as it is now assumed that the big institution is a bad institution, but it has not been proven yet!" The studies by Tizard and his associates previously reviewed suggested that size per se did not influence the actual quality of service.

Size, however, is important not only in terms of single living units but also in terms of the total residential population. Large dwelling units simply do not provide the homey, normalized atmosphere desired. As regards total size, the large facility poses many problems. First, as indicated previously, residents should interact with the community as much as possible, including attending public school classes. A relatively small community simply cannot absorb 500 or 600 residents into its educational system. Secondly, as most administrators will concede, once a facility expands beyond 350 to 400 persons (residents *and* staff), there is a tendency for interrelations to become less personal, the organizational structure and procedures become increasingly bureaucratic, and many services become centralized for reasons of economy. Thirdly, any physical modifications in a large facility tend to be very costly, thus reducing the probability of garnering adequate funds. Fourthly, buildings within a large complex which are no longer programmatically adequate or physically appropriate cannot be used by other agencies. Finally, the large institution undoubtedly presents a different aura to the community than does a smaller, home-like facility.

The question of size, however, may, in fact, be simply academic when one considers site selection and the actual retarded population which needs to live in a residential setting offering comprehensive services. One contemporary principle of programming is that all services should be offered within or at least near the community from which the clients emanate. Accordingly, the practice of locating large residential facilities for the retarded in isolated rural areas is no longer acceptable.

According to the superintendents surveyed by Scheerenberger in 1975, at least 50 percent of the existing residential population could be served in the community (Table XX). In other words, of the total estimated residential population of 176,000, only 88,000 may actually require the extended programming associated with a public residential facility.

Taking into consideration the need for home-like living units, the broad aspects of normalization, the principle of site selection,

TABLE XX

ESTIMATES BY 130 SUPERINTENDENTS AS TO THE
PERCENTAGE OF RESIDENTS WHO COULD LIVE IN
THE COMMUNITY

Level of retardation	Percent that could live in community (median)
Borderline	98
Mild	96
Moderate	81
Severe	53
Profound	33

From: Scheerenberger (1975)

and the few retarded persons who actually require extended residential services, it is not difficult for one to conclude that future residential facilities should be substantially different than most of those which presently exist. Tomorrow's facility should consist of six to eight homes, each accommodating eight to twelve persons. At least one unit should be set aside for specialized short-term programming and respite care. Large communities may have several such facilities located in different areas.

Parents

Parents as well as children suffer from separation. As described by Mandelbaum (1962),

Many parents consider residential treatment as meaning that they have no value to their child whatsoever. The good things they have done for him, the warm, tender moments are swept

away by the totality of their bitter thoughts. They no longer
have a useful function; the parental rights are entirely severed.
They feel that the treatment center will now do all the work and
this confirms their helplessness, their inadequacy, and their
feelings of being unwanted . . . And because some parents tend
to undervaluate themselves, they depreciate the child and his
potential strengths.

A study by Thaman and Barclay (1966) concerning parental
attitudes toward placing a retarded child in a residential facility
supports Mandelbaum's observation. Of the eighty-five families
completing the fifteen-item questionnaire, 71 percent agreed with
the statement, "Parents who have retarded children removed from
their care experience feelings of guilt and self-recrimination."

The implications of such statements in terms of reform are
obvious. Parental support and counseling must be continued
following admission of the child or adult. As one parent implied
rather bitterly, "Once the child had been admitted, she and other
members of the family were simply forgotten" (Scheerenberger,
1969).

Closely allied to continued support and counseling is the corol-
lary need to keep parents involved with their retarded resident.
Scheerenberger (1975) reported that at least 40 percent of retarded
persons in public residential facilities did not receive even one
visit from their parents or family during the year. Hammond *et al.*
(1969), in a study involving parents of 5,395 residents at Willow-
brook State School found a shocking lack of parental interest.
Only 1.5 percent of the respondents indicated any interest or desire to have their offspring return home. This was true regardless
of the age, sex or intellectual functioning of the retarded person.

At least some of the abandonment and lack of interest demonstrated by parents may be a function of expectancy. In many
instances, parents either assume or are assured by the residential
facility that it will take care of their child for the rest of his life.
The administration of each facility should make it unequivocally
clear that parental involvement is critical to the child's well-being
and development. At the same time, all but very few admissions
should be viewed as possessing some potential for return to the
community, and parents should be aware of this attitude at the

time of admission.

In terms of residential reform, parents must be encouraged and given every opportunity to participate in nearly all aspects of residential life, ranging from active involvement with their child's program and progress to policy formation. Visitation hours should be completely open, and parents should be given all desired information concerning their child, the residential facility and the total state program. Parents also should be approached as partners in working with the child and in facilitating early community placement.

INTEGRANTS TO RESIDENTIAL REFORM

In the discussion concerning successful deinstitutionalization programs, five integrants were identified — local boards, independently determined standards, back-up services, an effective advocacy system and adequate financial support. As shown in Figure 3, these same five features apply to residential reform. If residential facilities are to become an integral phase of total community programming, they must relate closely with local authorities, sharing professional services and expertise. Two independent standard setting and monitoring agencies are involved with residential services — the federal government (Title XIX) and the Joint Commission on Accreditation of Hospitals. As discussed previously, advocacy is vitally important, and the most desirable approach is for community persons to serve as guardians or advocates. Considerable financial support will be required to realize adequate staffing patterns and to develop appropriate physical environments.

CURRENT STATUS AND TRENDS

Residential reform, as community programming and deinstitutionalization, has been evolutionary in nature. Many if not all of the items recorded under future trends are being implemented by at least some of our residential facilities.

Several indicators of residential reform have been cited previously —

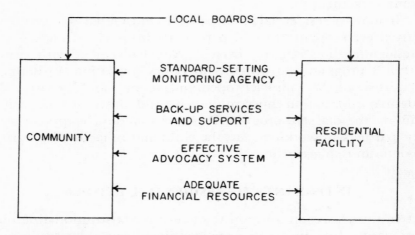

Figure 3: Integrants to Effective Programming.
From: Scheerenberger (1974).

1. Older residential facilities have reduced their size, i.e. the median number of actual residents dropped from 1146 to 956 during the period of FY 1969-1970 through FY 1973-1974.
2. Newer residential facilities are relatively small in size, providing for a median population of 198 residents (FY 1973-1974).
3. Most residential facilities are providing a variety of services to the community.
4. The majority of residents are severely and profoundly retarded, and many have multiply handicapping conditions.
5. An increasing number of programs are being developed and implemented for the severely and profoundly retarded.
6. Parents are becoming more involved with all aspects of residential programming.

Specific examples of reform programs include

The Utah Training School is implementing a special multidisciplinary unit for youngsters with orthopedic handicaps. The program provides occupational, developmental and physical therapy; academics; sensory and perceptual motor development; and allied recreational therapy skills.

The Western Carolina Center, North Carolina, has created a

special advocacy program for residents.

Special deaf/blind retarded units are being established in many residential facilities, e.g. Hissom Memorial Center, Oklahoma; Dixon State School, Illinois; Central Wisconsin Colony: Pinecrest State School, Louisiana; and the Costal Center, South Carolina.

Training for families in areas of behavior modification, physical and occupational therapy, and certain kinds of transportation related to programming is offered to parents with retarded children at home through an in-house trainer made available through the Macomb-Oakland Regional Center, Michigan.

Special short-term training programs to assist the youngsters adjust to the community and, at the same time, minimize their need for extended residential programming are provided by the Walter Fernald State School, Massachusetts (Fingado *et al.*, 1970), The Cloverbottom Developmental Center, Tennessee, (Ray, 1974), and the Muskegon Developmental Center, Michigan (Harvey and Christensen, 1975).

Retarded adults without occupational opportunities enroll in a productive workshop offered by the Conway Center, South Carolina.

Massachusetts has established statewide educational support services for parents and teachers of the developmentally disabled. The instructional materials workshop is located at the Walter Fernald State School, Massachusetts.

Four severely and profoundly retarded residents of the Elisabeth Ludeman Center, Illinois, are enrolled in the public school training program, while four public school students attend Ludeman for half days for training in self-care skills and speech (Gold Award . . . , 1975).

Central Wisconsin Colony and Training School offers training for babysitters of severely and profoundly retarded children.

The Allis Training Center, an outreach program of the Corpus Christi State School, Texas, is providing training experiences for younger residents in the community. Classroom curriculum evolves around improvement of self-help skills along with activities to increase physical competency, language, intellectual development and social and emotional growth.

Austin State School, Texas, provides outreach services to two rural areas to stimulate the development of local programs (Talkington, 1971).

The Mental Retardation Center of the New York Medical College extends many services to Harlem, partly in an effort to motivate the development of community programming (Goodman and Chernesky, 1971).

A special speech and hearing services mobile clinic provides services to communities in rural areas through the Anna State Hospital Unit for the Mentally Retarded, Illinois.

Fernald State School, Massachusetts, and Leslie College combine to prepare teachers to meet the new challenge of the state's educational law for all children between three and twenty-one years of age.

TABLE XXI
COMPARISON OF STAFFING RATIOS[*]

Professional category	FY 64-65[**] Staff:Resident (135 PRFs)	FY 73-74 Staff:Resident (140 PRFs)
Medical (including physicians, dentists, and RNs)	1:50	1:28
Resident care workers (including aides and LPNs)	1:4.4	1:1.8
Educators	1:84	1:20
Therapists (including recreational, occupational, and physical therapists)	1:193	1:19
Social workers	1:314	1:84
Psychologists	1:501	1:161

From: [*] Scheerenberger (1975)
        [**] Scheerenberger (1965)

While these examples highlight positive current trends, most residential facilities are still plagued with inadequate staffing and inappropriate physical facilities. Though, as shown in Table XXI, staffing ratios have improved within recent years, most facilities cannot satisfy related accreditation standards.

Another major concern involves the extent to which residents actually participate in community programs. As reported by Scheerenberger (1975), 86 percent of the 154 responding superintendents indicated that some of their residents participated in off-campus programs sponsored by community agencies. Twenty-one (14%) of the PRFs neither identified the population served nor the program involved. Of the remaining 112 PRFs, seventy-one (63%) indicated that some residents were enrolled in recreational programs; forty-four (39%) in social activities; seventy-seven (69%) in educational activities; sixty-seven (60%) in occupational programs; and sixty-eight (61%) in outside religious activities. Distribution of the resident population in terms of the various community programs is presented in Table XXII. Though the results are highly significant to the extent that a large number of severely and profoundly retarded persons as well as the less seriously affected are participating in community programs, the relative percentages of *participating residents* were less than

TABLE XXII
NUMBER OF RESIDENTS PARTICIPATING IN OFF-CAMPUS
PROGRAMS SPONSORED BY COMMUNITY AGENCIES AS REPORTED
BY 112 PUBLIC RESIDENTIAL FACILITIES WITH A TOTAL
POPULATION OF 68, 983 RESIDENTS

Program	SMR/ PMR	Moderate	Mild	Border- line+	Total	%
Recreational	5701	4306	1476	435	11918	17
Social	2943	2173	948	241	6305	9
Educational	462	519	1259	105	2345	3
Occupational	284	1001	1290	121	2696	4
Religious	1494	2546	1373	168	5581	8

From: Scheerenberger (1975)

reported previously by Rosen and Callan (1972), i.e. recreation, 34 percent; social activities, 30 percent; educational activities, 10 percent; occupational programs, 7 percent; and religious programs, 11 percent.

Also, only 5 percent of capable residents of school age were receiving their education in the community. Even in those states in which all educational programs were under the direct auspices of the public schools, only 23 percent of the residents were receiving their education in a public school. Whether this practice reflects an attitude or lack of facilities or lack of staff, many communities are not offering experiences vital to both deinstitutionalization and residential reform.

Every effort must be made by the residential facility to promote a greater utilization of community resources for residents capable of participation. Regrettably, in many areas of the country, a reverse trend seems to be evident, i.e. retarded persons from the community are being programmed in a residential facility. This practice appears inconsistent with the principle of normalization.

In essence, there are numerous positive indicators of residential reform; many of these, however, simply represent islands of excellence. While the principles of residential reform are widely accepted, the realization of such principles is only at the beginning stage. Much again remains to be accomplished.

This entire text can be concluded with the observation that deinstitutionalization is both desirable and feasible. A successful program of deinstitutionalization will require not only residential reform, but community reform, juridical reform and legislative reform. Each residential facility must assess its philosophy and services to insure that every resident is receiving a total developmental program, individually designed, intended to facilitate community return. Further, residential services, including technical consultancy, must be extended to the community at large to assist in developing local programs and averting the need for extended residential placement whenever possible. The community, in turn, must express a greater willingness to include the retarded in the mainstream of everyday life and make a concerted effort to provide adequate services. The juridical system must recognize and protect the rights of the retarded and respond to existing inequities with alacrity. Legislators at both state and national levels also must recognize and protect the rights of the retarded and provide those laws and resources necessary to enable them to live as full and rich a life as possible within our total society.

SUMMARY

Residential reform presents multifarious problems in terms of both planning for the future as well as ameliorating present deficiencies. Extended residential programming in the future will emphasize services for multiply handicapped, severely and profoundly retarded individuals and those with severe behavioral disorders. In addition to extended services, residential facilities will provide intensive short-term programs; collaborate closely with the community, assisting in the development of services for all levels of retarded persons; offer a variety of training to parents and representatives from local agencies; and participate in public informational programs. A primary task of residential facilities will be to prevent the need for extended placement whenever possible.

Dimensions of residential reform include acceptance by all personnel of deinstitutionalization as an attitude and as a principle. Criteria for admission should be restrictive while criteria for community placement should be broad. If a resident has any chance of succeeding in an appropriate community setting with adequate support, he should be released regardless of intelligence, age, sex or other such considerations.

Resident rights should not only be recognized by all residential personnel but should be protected by an effective advocacy system.

Resident programs should emphasize total development and the principle of normalization to the fullest degree possible. The need for adequate staff to provide such services is well recognized as is the need for continuing education. Many new programs have to be created for the multiply handicapped individual, and this, in turn, will require research funds not presently available.

The physical environment of most residential facilities requires substantial modification. It is anticipated that future residential facilities will accommodate a maximum of fifty to one hundred residents in home-like, single dwelling units.

Not only should parents receive continuous counseling and support following admission of their retarded child, they also should be encouraged to take an active role in their child's life during his residency and participate in nearly all aspects of residential living.

The current status of residential reform, as deinstitutionalization and programming, is in its inchoate stage. There are numerous islands of excellence, and many new programs are being implemented for the more severely and profoundly retarded and to facilitate community placement. Nevertheless, much remains to be accomplished before residential reform in all of its ramifications will be achieved.

Both deinstitutionalization and residential reform are worthy goals. These goals, however, will be realized only through the concerted effort of local, county, state and national representatives who place a high priority on meeting the needs and recognizing the rights of developmentally disabled citizens.

REFERENCES

Albin, T.: Relationships of IQ and previous work experiences. *Ment Retard, 11*(3):26, 1973.
Baumeister, A.: More ado about operant conditioning — or nothing? *Ment Retard, 7*(5):49-51, 1969.
Cleland, C.: Evidence on the relationship between size and institutional effectiveness. A review and analysis. *Am J Ment Defic, 70*:423-431, 1965.
Clements, J.: President's message. *Ment Retard, 13*(2):52, 1975.
Dunn, L.: Small special purpose residential facilities for the retarded. In Kugel, R., and Wolfensberger, W. (Ed.): *Changing Patterns in Residential Services for the Mentally Retarded.* Washington, President's Committee on Mental Retardation, 1969, pp. 211-226.
Eagle, E.: Prognosis and outcome of community placement of institutionalized retardates. *Am J Ment Defic, 72*:232-243, 1968.
Elliot, J., and Bayes, K.: *Room for Improvement: A Better Environment for the Mentally Handicapped.* London, King Edward's Hospital Fund for

London, 1972, pp. 6, 12.

Fernald, W. E.: After-care study of the patients discharged from Waverly for a period of twenty-five years. *Ungraded, 5*:25-31, 1919.

Fingado, M., Kini, J., Stewart, K., and Redd, W.: A thirty-day residential training program for retarded children. *Ment Retard, 8*(6):42-45, 1970.

Fulton, R.: Job retention of the MR. *Ment Retard, 13*(2):26-27, 1975.

Gold award: A community-oriented center for severely and profoundly retarded children. *Hosp Comm Psychiatry, 26*:667-670, 1975.

Goodman, L., and Chernesky, R.: Community intervention in planning for the mentally retarded in the inner city. *Ment Retard, 1*(9):3-6, 1971.

Hammond, J., Sternlicht, M., and Deutsch, M.: Parental interest in institutionalized children: A survey. *Hosp Comm Psychiatry, 20*:338-339, 1969.

Harvey, E., and Christensen, D.: Programs for retarded children combine behavior modification, training for parents, teachers. *Hosp Comm Psychiatry, 26*:421-422, 1975.

Human Rights Advocacy Committees. Tallahassee, Department of Health and Rehabilitative Services, 1973, p. 1.

Kirkland, M.: Institutions for the retarded: Their place in the continuum of services. *Ment Retard, 5*(2):5-8, 1967.

Kraus, J.: Supervised living in the community and residential and employment of retarded male juveniles. *Am J Ment Defic, 77*:283-290, 1972.

Klebanoff, L.: Out of mind — out of sight: Some dilemmas of institutional care. *J Educ, 147*:82-86, 1964.

Mandelbaum, A.: Parent-child separation: Its significance to parents. *Social Work, 7*:26-34, 1962.

McCarver, R., and Craig, E.: Placement of the retarded in the community: Prognosis and outcome. In Ellis, N. (Ed.): *International Review of Research in Mental Retardation,* New York, Acad Pr, 1974, p. 194.

National Association of Superintendents of Public Residential Facilities: *Residential Programming.* Washington, President's Committee on Mental Retardation, 1974, pp. 3-4.

Nihira, L., and Nihira, K.: Normalized behavior in community placement. *Ment Retard, 13*(2):9-13, 1975.

Nirje, B.: The normalization principles and its human management implications. In Kugel, R., and Wolfensberger, W.: *Changing Patterns in Residential Services for the Mentally Retarded.* Washington, President's Committee on Mental Retardation, 1969, 179-195.

Norris, D.: Architecture and mental subnormality: The environmental needs of the severely retarded: *J Ment Subnormality, 15*:45-50, 1969.

President's Panel on Mental Retardation: *A Proposed Program for National Action to Combat Mental Retardation.* Washington, U.S. Government Printing Office, 1962.

Pursley, N.: Institutional reform from the superintendent's view. In *Region IV Staff Development Conference on Institutional Reform.* Columbia,

South Carolina Department of Mental Retardation, 1973, pp. 77-80.

Ray, J.: The family training center: An experiment in normalization. *Ment Retard, 12*(1):12-13, 1974.

Rosen, D., and Callan, L.: *Trends, Residential Services for the Mentally Retarded: Focus — Community Facility Interaction.* Macomb, National Association of Superintendents of Public Residential Facilities for the Mentally Retarded, 1972.

Rosen, M., Floor, L., and Baxter, D.: IQ, academic achievement of the discharge from the institution. *Ment Retard, 12*(2):51-53, 1974.

Santiestevan, H.: *Out of their Beds and into the Streets.* Washington, American Federation of State, County and Municipal Employees, 1975, p. 34.

Scheerenberger, R.: A current census of state institutions for the mentally retarded. *Ment Retard, 3*(1):4-6, 1965.

Scheerenberger, R.: *A Study of Generic Services for the Mentally Retarded and their Families.* Springfield, Department of Mental Health, 1969.

Scheerenberger, R.: *Current Trends and Status of Public Residential Services for the Mentally Retarded: 1974,* Madison, National Association of Superintendents of Public Residential Facilities for the Mentally Retarded, 1975, pp. 23, 38, 45.

Sternlicht, M., and Deutsch, M.: The value of temporary institutionalization in habilitating the mentally retarded. *Ment Retard, 9*(3):37-38, 1971.

Talbot, M.: *Edouard Sequin.* New York, Columbia U Pr, 1964.

Talkington, L.: Outreach: Delivery of services to rural communities. *Ment Retard, 9*(5):27-29, 1971.

Tarjan, G., Dingman, H., Eyman, R., and Brown, S.: Effectiveness of hospital release programs. *Am J Ment Defic, 64*:609-617, 1960.

Thaman, A., and Barclay, A.: Parental attitudes toward institutionalization of mentally retarded children. *Child Welfare, 64*(3):156-159, 1967.

Windle, C.: *Prognosis of Mental Subnormals: A Critical Review of Research.* Monograph Supplement to the *Am J Ment Defic,* 1962, p. 136.

Wolfensberger, W.: Vocational preparation and occupation: In Baumeister, A. (Ed.): *Mental Retardation.* Chicago, Aldine, 1967, 232-273.

Wolfensberger, W.: Will there always be an institution? I. The impact of epidemiological trends. *Ment Retard, 9*(5):14-20, 1971.

Wolfson, I.: Adjustment of institutionalized mildly retarded patients twenty years after return to the community. *Ment Retard, 8*(4):20-23, 1970.

District Court of the United States for the Middle District of Alabama, Northern Division

COURT STANDARDS FOR PARTLOW STATE SCHOOL

I. *Definitions*

The terms used herein below are defined as follows:
   a. *Institution* — Partlow State School and Hospital
   b. *Residents* — All persons who are now confined and all persons who may in the future be confined at Partlow State School and Hospital.
   c. *Qualified Mental Retardation Professional* —
   1. A psychologist with a doctoral or master's degree from an accredited program with specialized training or one year's experience in treating the mentally retarded.
   2. A physician licensed to practice in the state of Alabama, with specialized training or one year's experience in treating the mentally retarded;
   3. An educator with a master's degree in special education from an accredited program;
   4. A social worker with a master's degree from an accredited program with specialized training or one year's experience in working with the mentally retarded;
   5. A physical, vocational or occupational therapist licensed to practice in the State of Alabama, and a graduate of an accredited program in physical, vocational or occupational therapy, with specialized training or one year's experience in treating the mentally retarded;
   6. A registered nurse, with specialized training or one year of experience treating the mentally retarded under

219

the supervision of a Qualified Mental Retardation Professional.

d.   *Resident Care Worker* — an employee of the institution, other than a Qualified Mental Retardation Professional, whose duties require regular contact with or supervision of residents.

e.   *Habilitation* — the process by which the staff of the institution assists the resident to acquire and maintain those life skills which enable him to cope more effectively with the demands of his own person and of his environment, and to raise the level of his physical, mental and social efficiency. Habilitation includes but is not limited to programs of formal, structured education and treatment.

f.   *Education* — the process of formal training and instruction to facilitate the intellectual and emotional development of residents.

g.   *Treatment* — the prevention, amelioration, and/or cure of a resident's physical disabilities or illnesses.

h.   *Guardian* — a general guardian of a resident, or if the general guardian is missing, indifferent to the welfare of the resident, a guardian appointed by an appropriate court on the motion of the superintendent, such guardian not to be in the control or the employ of the Alabama Board of Mental Health.

i.   *Express and Informed Consent* — the uncoerced decision of a resident who has comprehension and can signify assent or dissent.

II.   *Adequate Habilitation of Residents*

1.   Residents shall have a right to habilitation, including medical treatment, education and care, suited to their needs, regardless of age, degree of retardation, or handicapping condition.

2.   Each resident has a right to a habilitation program which will maximize his human abilities and enhance his ability to cope with his environment. The institution shall recognize that each resident, regardless of ability or

status, is entitled to develop and realize his fullest potential. The institution shall implement the principle of normalization so that each resident may live as normally as possible.

3. a. No person shall be admitted to the institution unless a prior determination shall have been made that residence in the institution is the least restrictive habilitation setting.

b. No mentally retarded person shall be admitted to the institution if services and programs in the community can afford adequate habilitation to such person.

c. Residents shall have a right to the least restrictive conditions necessary to achieve the purposes of habilitation. To this end, the institution shall make every attempt to move residents from (a) more to less structured living; (b) larger to smaller facilities; (c) larger to smaller living units; (d) group to individual residence; (e) segregated from the community to integrated living in the community; (f) dependent to independent living.

4. No borderline or mildly mentally retarded person shall be a resident of the institution. For purposes of this standard, borderline retarded person is defined as an individual who is functioning between 1 and 2 standard deviations below the mean on a standardized intelligence test such as the Stanford Binet Scale and on measures of adaptive behavior, such as the American Association on Mental Deficiency Adaptive Behavior Scale. A mildly retarded person is defined as an individual who is functioning between 2 and 3 standard deviations below the mean on a standardized intelligence test, such as the Stanford Binet Scale and on a measure of adaptive behavior, such as the American Association on Mental Deficiency Adaptive Behavior Scale.

5. Residents shall have a right to receive suitable educational services, regardless of chronological age, degree of retardation, or accompanying disabilities or handicaps.

a. The institution shall formulate a written statement

of educational objectives that is consistent with the institution's mission as set forth in Standard 2, *supra,* and the other standards proposed herein.

b. School-age residents shall be provided a full and suitable educational program. Such educational programs shall meet the following minimum standards:

	Mild	Moderate	Severe/Profound
(1) Class size	12	9	6
(2) Length of school year (in months)	9-10	9-10	11-12
(3) Minimum length of school day (in hours)	6	6	6

6. Residents shall have a right to receive prompt and adequate medical treatment for any physical ailments and for the prevention of any illness or disability. Such medical treatment shall meet standards of medical practice in the community.

III. *Individualized Habilitation Plans*

7. Each resident shall have a comprehensive social, psychological, educational, and medical diagnosis and evaluation by appropriate specialists prior to his admission to the institution to determine if admission is appropriate.

   a. Unless such preadmission evaluation has been conducted within three months prior to the admission, each resident shall have a new evaluation at the institution to determine if admission is appropriate.

   b. When undertaken at the institution, preadmission diagnosis and evaluation shall be completed within five days.

8. Upon admission, all residents shall have an evaluation by appropriate specialists for programming purposes within 14 days of admission to the institution.

9. Each resident shall have an individualized habilitation plan formulated by the institution. This plan shall be developed by appropriate Qualified Mental Retardation Professionals, and implemented as soon as possible, but

no later than 14 days after the resident's admission to the institution. An interim program of habilitation, based on the preadmission evaluation conducted pursuant to Standard 7, *supra,* shall commence promptly upon the resident's admission. Each individualized habilitation plan shall contain:

a. a statement of the nature of the specific limitations and specific needs of the resident;

b. a description of intermediate and long-range habilitation goals, with a projected timetable for their attainment;

c. a statement of and reasons for the plan of habilitation for achieving these intermediate and long-range goals;

d. a statement of the least restrictive setting for habilitation necessary to achieve the habilitation goals of the resident;

e. a specification of professional and staff responsibility for the resident in order to attain these habilitation goals;

f. criteria for release to less restrictive settings for habilitation including criteria for discharge and a projected date for discharge.

10. As part of his habilitation plan, each resident shall have an individualized post-institutionalization plan. This plan shall be developed by a Qualified Mental Retardation Professional who shall begin preparation of such plan prior to the resident's admission to the institution, and shall complete such plan, as soon as practicable. The guardian or next of kin of the resident and the resident, if able to give informed consent, shall be consulted in the development of such plan and shall be informed of the content of such plan.

11. In the interests of continuity of care, one Qualified Mental Retardation Professional shall be responsible for supervising the implementation of the habilitation plan, integrating the various aspects of the habilitation program, and recording the resident's progress as measured

by objective indicators. This Qualified Mental Retardation Professional shall also be responsible for ensuring that the resident is released when appropriate to a less restrictive habilitation setting.

12. The habilitation plan shall be continuously reviewed by the Qualified Mental Retardation Professional responsible for supervising the implementation of the plan and shall be modified if necessary. In addition, six months after admission and at least annually thereafter, each resident shall receive a comprehensive psychological, social, education and medical diagnosis and evaluation and his habilitation plan shall be reviewed by an interdisciplinary team of no less than two Qualified Mental Retardation Professionals and such resident care workers as are directly involved in his habilitation and care.

13. Complete resident records shall be maintained and shall be readily available to Qualified Mental Retardation Professionals and the resident care workers who are directly involved with the resident. All information contained in a resident's records shall be considered privileged and confidential. The guardian, next of kin, and any person properly authorized in writing by the resident, if such resident is capable of giving informed consent, or by his guardian or next of kin shall be permitted access to the resident's records. These records shall include:

    a. Identification data, including the resident's legal status;

    b. The resident's history, including but not limited to:
        (1) family data, educational background, and employment record;
        (2) prior medical history, both physical and mental, including prior institutionalization;

    c. The resident's grievances if any;

    d. An inventory of the resident's life skills;

    e. A record of each physical examination which describes the results of the examination;

    f. A copy of the individual habilitation plan and any

modifications thereto, and an appropriate summary which will guide and assist the resident care workers in implementing the resident's program;

g. The findings made in periodic reviews of the habilitation plan (see Standard 12, *supra*) which analyze the successes and failures of the habilitation program and direct whatever modifications are necessary;

h. A copy of the post-institutionalization plan and any modifications thereto, and a summary of the steps that have been taken to implement that plan;

i. A medication history and status, pursuant to Standard 21, *infra;*

j. A summary of each significant contact by a Qualified Mental Retardation Professional with the resident;

k. A summary, recorded at least monthly, by a Qualified Mental Retardation Professional involved in the resident's habilitation of the resident's response to his program. Such response, wherever possible, shall be scientifically documented;

l. A monthly summary of the extent and nature of the resident's work activities described in the Standard 32(b), *infra* and the effect of such activity upon the resident's progress along the habilitation plan;

m. A signed order by a Qualified Mental Retardation Professional for any physical restraints, as provided in Standard 25(a), *infra;*

n. A description of any extraordinary incident or accident in the institution involving the resident, to be entered by a staff member noting personal knowledge of the incident or accident or other source of information, including any reports of investigations of mistreatment, as required by Standard 27, *infra;*

o. A summary of family visits and contacts;

p. A summary of attendance and leaves from the institution;

q. A record of any seizures, illness, and treatment thereof, and immunizations.

IV. *Humane Physical and Psychological Environment*

14. Residents shall have a right to dignity, privacy and humane care.
15. Residents shall have all rights enjoyed by citizens of Alabama and of the United States, except as expressly determined by an appropriate court.
16. No person shall be presumed mentally incompetent solely by reason of his admission or commitment to the institution.
17. The right to religious worship shall be accorded to each resident who desires such opportunities. Provisions for such worship shall be made available to all residents on a non-discriminatory basis. No individual shall be coerced into engaging in any religious activities.
18. Residents shall have the same rights to telephone communication as patients at Alabama public hospitals, except to the extent that a Qualified Mental Retardation Professional responsible for formulation of a particular resident's habilitation plan (see Standard 9, *supra*) writes an order imposing special restrictions and explains the reasons for any such restrictions. The written order must be renewed semi-annually if any restrictions are to be continued. Residents shall have an unrestricted right to visitation.
19. Residents shall be entitled to send and receive sealed mail. Moreover, it shall be the duty of the institution to facilitate the exercise of this right by furnishing the necessary materials and assistance.
20. The institution shall provide suitable opportunities for the resident's interaction with members of the opposite sex.
21. *Medication:*
    a. No medication shall be administered unless at the written order of a physician.
    b. Notation of each individual's medication shall be kept in his medical records (Standard 13(i) *supra*). At least weekly the attending physician shall review the drug regimen of each resident under his care. All prescriptions shall be written with a termination

date, which shall not exceed 30 days.

c. Residents shall have a right to be free from unnecessary or excessive medication. The resident's records shall state the effects of psychoactive medication on the resident. When dosages of such are changed or other psychoactive medications are prescribed, a notation shall be made in the resident's record concerning the effect of the new medication or new dosages and the behavior changes, if any, which occur.

d. Medication shall not be used as punishment, for the convenience of staff, as a substitute for program, or in quantities that interfere with the resident's habilitation program.

22. (Omitted)

23. Behavior modification programs involving the use of noxious or aversive stimuli shall be reviewed and approved by the institution's Human Rights Committee and shall be conducted only with the express and informed consent of the affected resident, if the resident is able to give such consent, and of his guardian or next of kin, after opportunities for consultation with independent specialists and with legal counsel. Such behavior modification programs shall be conducted only under the supervision of and in the presence of a Qualified Mental Retardation Professional who has had proper training in such techniques.

24. Electric shock devices shall be considered a research technique for the purpose of these standards. Such devices shall only be used in extraordinary circumstances to prevent self-mutilation leading to repeated and possibly permanent physical damage to the resident, and only after alternative techniques have failed. The use of such devices shall be subject to the conditions prescribed in Standard 23, *supra,* and Standard 29, *infra,* shall be used only under the direct and specific order of the superintendent.

25. Physical restraint shall be employed only when absolutely necessary to protect the resident from injury to himself

or to prevent injury to others. Restraint shall not be employed as punishment, for the convenience of staff, or as a substitute for program. Such restraints shall be applied only if alternative techniques have failed and only if such restraint imposes the least possible restriction consistent with its purpose.

a. Only Qualified Mental Retardation Professionals may authorize the use of restraints. Such restraints shall be applied only if alternative techniques have failed and only if such restraint imposes the least possible restriction consistent with its purpose.

   (1) Orders for restraints by the Qualified Mental Retardation Professionals shall be in writing, and shall not be in force for longer than 12 hours.

   (2) A resident placed in restraint shall be checked at least every thirty minutes by staff trained in the use of restraints, and a record of such checks shall be kept.

   (3) Mechanical restraints shall be designed and used so as not to cause physical injury to the resident, and so as to cause the least possible discomfort.

   (4) Opportunity for motion and exercise shall be provided for a period of not less than ten minutes during each two hours in which restraint is employed.

   (5) Daily reports shall be made to the superintendent by those Qualified Mental Retardation Professionals ordering the use of restraints summarizing all such uses of restraint, the types used, the duration, and the reasons therefor.

b. The institution shall cause a written statement of this policy to be posted in each living unit and circulated to all staff members.

29. Residents shall have a right not to be subjected to experimental research without the express and informed consent of the resident, if the resident is able to give such consent, and of his guardian or next of kin, after opportunities for consultation with independent specialists

and with legal counsel. Such proposed research shall first have been reviewed and approved by the institution's Human Rights Committee before such consent shall be sought. Prior to such approval the Committee shall determine that such research complies with the principles of the Statement on the Use of Human Subjects for Research of the American Association on Mental Deficiency and with the principles for research involving human subjects required by the U.S. Department of Health, Education and Welfare for projects supported by that agency.

30. Residents shall have a right not to be subjected to any unusual or hazardous treatment procedures without the express and informed consent of the resident, if the resident is able to give such consent, and of his guardian or next of kin, after opportunities for consultation with independent specialists and legal counsel. Such proposed procedures shall first have been reviewed and approved by the institution's Human Rights Committee, before such consent shall be sought.

31. Residents shall have a right to regular physical exercise several times a week. It shall be the duty of the institution to provide facilities and equipment for such exercise.

32. Residents shall have a right to be outdoors daily in the absence of contrary medical considerations.

33. The following rules shall govern resident labor:

   a. *Institution Maintenance*

      (1) No resident shall be required to perform labor which involves the operation and maintenance of the institution or for which the institution is under contract with an outside organization. Privileges or release from the institution shall not be conditioned upon the performance of labor covered by this provision. Residents may voluntarily engage in such labor if the labor is compensated in accordance with the minimum wage laws of the Fair Labor Standards Act, 29 U.S.C. Sec. 206, as amended, 1966.

      (2) No resident shall be involved in the care (feeding,

clothing, bathing), training, or supervision of other residents unless he:

(a) has volunteered;

(b) has been specifically trained in the necessary skills;

(c) has the humane judgment required for such activities;

(d) is adequately supervised; and

(e) is reimbursed in accordance with the minimum wage laws of the Fair Labor Standards Act, 29 U.S.C. sec. 206, as amended, 1966.

b. *Training Tasks and Labor*

(1) Residents may be required to perform vocational training tasks which do not involve the operation and maintenance of the institution, subject to a presumption that an assignment of longer than three months to any task is not a training task, provided the specific task and any change in task assignment is:

(a) An integrated part of the resident's habilitation plan and approved as a habilitation activity by a Qualified Mental Retardation Professional responsible for supervising the resident's habilitation;

(b) Supervised by a staff member to oversee the habilitation aspects of the activity.

(2) Residents may voluntarily engage in habilitative labor at non-program hours for which the institution would otherwise have to pay an employee, provided the specific labor and any change in labor is:

(a) An integrated part of the resident's habilitation plan and approved as a habilitation activity by a Qualified Mental Retardation Professional responsible for supervising the resident's habilitation;

(b) Supervised by a staff member to oversee the habilitation aspects of the activity; and

      (c) Compensated in accordance with the minimum wage laws of the Fair Labor Standards Act, 29 U.S.C. Sec. 206, as amended, 1966.

c. *Personal Housekeeping.* Residents may be required to perform tasks of a personal housekeeping nature such as the making of one's own bed.

d. Payment of residents pursuant to this paragraph shall not be applied to the costs of institutionalization.

e. Staffing shall be sufficient so that the institution is not dependent upon the use of residents or volunteers for the care, maintenance or habilitation of other residents or for income-producing services. The institution shall formulate a written policy to protect the residents from exploitation when they are engaged in productive work.

34. A nourishing, well-balanced diet shall be provided each resident.

a. The diet for residents shall provide at a minimum and Recommended Daily Dietary Allowance as developed by the National Academy of Sciences. Menus shall be satisfying and shall provide the Recommended Daily Dietary Allowances. In developing such menus, the institution shall utilize the Moderate Cost Food Plan of the U.S. Department of Agriculture. The institution shall not spend less per patient for raw food, including the value of donated food, than the most recent per person costs of the Moderate Cost Food Plan for the Southern Region of the United States, as compiled by the U.S. Department of Agriculture, for appropriate groupings of residents, discounted for any savings which might result from institutional procurement of such food.

b. Provisions shall be made for special therapeutic diets and for substitutes at the request of the resident or his guardian or next of kin, in accordance with the religious requirements of any resident's faith.

c. Denial of a nutritionally adequate diet shall not be

used as punishment.

   d. Residents, except for the non-mobile, shall eat or be fed in dining rooms.

35. Each resident shall have an adequate allowance of neat, clean, suitably fitting and seasonable clothing.

   a. Each resident shall have his own clothing, which is properly and inconspicuously marked with his name, and he shall be kept dressed in this clothing. The institution has an obligation to supply an adequate allowance of clothing to any residents who do not have suitable clothing of their own. Residents shall have the opportunity to select from various sorts of neat, clean, and seasonable clothing. Such clothing shall be considered the resident's throughout his stay in the institution.

   b. Such clothing shall make it possible for residents to go out of doors in inclement weather, to go for trips or visits appropriately dressed, and to make a normal appearance in the community.

   c. Non-ambulatory residents shall be dressed daily in their own clothing, including shoes, unless contraindicated in written medical orders.

   d. Washable clothing shall be designed for multiply handicapped residents being trained in self-help skills, in accordance with individual needs.

   e. Clothing for incontinent residents shall be designed to foster comfortable sitting, crawling and/or walking, and toilet training.

   f. A current inventory shall be kept of each resident's personal and clothing items.

   g. The institution shall make provision for the adequate and regular laundering of the resident's clothing.

36. Each resident shall have the right to keep and use his own personal possessions except insofar as such clothes or personal possessions may be determined to be dangerous by a Qualified Mental Retardation Professional.

37. a. Each resident shall be assisted in learning normal

grooming practices with individual toilet articles, including soap and toothpaste, that are available to each resident.

b. Teeth shall be brushed daily, with an effective dentrifice. Individual brushes shall be properly marked, used, and stored.

c. Each resident shall have a shower or tub bath at least daily, unless medically contraindicated.

d. Residents shall be regularly scheduled for hair cutting and styling, in an individualized manner, by trained personnel.

e. For residents who require such assistance, cutting of toe nails and fingernails shall be scheduled at regular intervals.

38. *Physical Facilities.* A resident has a right to a humane physical environment within the institutional facilities. These facilities shall be designed to make a positive contribution to the efficient attainment of the habilitation goals of the institution.

a. *Resident Unit.* All ambulatory residents shall sleep in single rooms or in multi-resident rooms of no more than six persons. The number of non-ambulatory residents in a multi-resident room shall not exceed ten persons. There shall be allocated a minimum of 80 square feet of floor space per resident in a multi-resident room. Screens or curtains shall be provided to ensure privacy. Single rooms shall have a minimum of 100 square feet of floor space. Each resident shall be furnished with a comfortable bed with adequate changes of linen, a closet or locker for his personal belongings, and appropriate furniture such as a chair and a bedside table, unless contraindicated by a Qualified Mental Retardation Professional who shall state the reasons for any such restriction.

b. *Toilets and Lavatories.* There shall be one toilet and one lavatory for each six residents. A lavatory shall be provided with each toilet facility. The toilets shall be installed in separate stalls for ambulatory residents, or in curtained areas for non-ambulatory residents, to ensure privacy, shall be clean and free of odor, and shall be equipped with appropriate safety devices for the physically handicapped. Soap and towels and/or drying mechanisms shall be available in each lavatory. Toilet paper shall be available in each toilet facility.

c. *Showers.* There shall be one tub or shower for each eight residents. If a central bathing area is provided, each tub or shower shall be divided by curtains to ensure privacy. Showers and tubs shall be equipped with adequate safety accessories.

d. *Day Room.* The minimum day room area shall be 50 square feet per resident. Day rooms shall be attractive and adequately furnished with reading lamps, tables, chairs, television, radio and other recreational facilities. They shall be conveniently located to resident bedrooms and shall have outside windows. There shall be at least one day room area on each bedroom floor in a multi-story facility. Areas used for corridor traffic shall not be counted as day room space, nor shall a chapel with fixed pews be counted as a day room area.

e. *Dining Facilities.* The minimum dining room area shall be 10 square feet per resident. The dining room shall be separate from the kitchen and shall be furnished with tables with hard, washable surfaces and comfortable chairs.

f. *Linen Servicing and Handling.* The institution shall provide adequate facilities and equipment for handling clean and soiled bedding and other linen. There must be frequent changes of bedding and other linen, but in any event no less than every 7 days, to assure resident comfort. After soiling by an incontinent resident, bedding and linen must be immediately changed and removed from the living unit. Dirty linen and laundry shall be removed from the living unit daily.

g. *Housekeeping.* Regular housekeeping and maintenance procedures shall be developed and implemented which will ensure that the institution is maintained in a safe, clean, and attractive condition.

h. *Non-Ambulatory Residents.* There must be special facilities for non-ambulatory residents to assure their safety and comfort, including special fittings on toilets and wheelchairs. Appropriate provision shall be made to permit non-ambulatory residents to communicate their needs to staff.

i. *Physical Plant*

(1) Pursuant to an established routine maintenance and repair program, the physical plant shall be kept in a continuous state of good repair and operation so as to ensure the health, comfort, safety and well being of the residents.

(2) Adequate heating, air conditioning and ventilation systems and equipment shall be afforded to maintain temperatures and air changes which are required for the comfort of residents at all times. Ventilation systems shall be adequate to remove steam and offensive odors or to mask such odors.

(3) Thermostatically controlled hot water shall be provided in adequate quantities and maintained at the required temperature for resident use (110 degrees F. at the fixture) and for mechanical dish washing and laundry use (180 degrees F. at the equipment). Thermostatic controlled hot water valves shall be equipped with a double valve system that provides both auditory and visual signals of valve failures.

(4) Adequate refuse facilities shall be provided so that solid waste, rubbish and other refuse will be collected and disposed of in a manner which will prohibit transmission of disease and not create a nuisance or fire hazard or provide a breeding place for rodents and insects.

V. *Qualified Staff in Numbers Sufficient to Provide Adequate Habilitation.*

39. Each Qualified Mental Retardation Professional and

each physician shall meet all licensing and certification requirements promulgated by the State of Alabama for persons engaged in private practice of the same profession elsewhere in Alabama. Other staff members shall meet the same licensing and certification requirements as persons who engage in private practice of their specialty elsewhere in Alabama.

    a. All Resident Care Workers who have not had prior clinical experience in a mental retardation institution shall have suitable orientation training.

    b. Staff members on all levels shall have suitable regularly scheduled in-service training.

40. Each Resident Care Worker shall be under the direct professional supervision of a Qualified Mental Retardation Professional.

41. The guardian or next of kin of each resident shall promptly upon resident's admission receive a written copy of all the above standards for adequate habilitation. Each resident, if the resident is able to comprehend, shall promptly upon his admission be orally informed in clear language of the above standards, and where appropriate be provided with a written copy.

42. The superintendent shall report in writing to the next of kin or guardian of the resident at least every six months on the resident's educational, vocational and living skills progress, and medical condition. Such report shall also state what habilitation program, if any, is appropriate to the resident but has not been afforded because of inadequate habilitation resources.

43. a. No resident shall be subjected to a behavior modification program designed to eliminate a particular pattern of behavior without prior certification by a physician that he has examined the patient in regard to behavior to be extinguished and finds that such behavior is not caused by a physical condition which could be corrected by appropriate medical procedures.

b. In no case shall a resident be subjected to a behavior modification program to try to extinguish socially appropriate behavior or to develop new behavior patterns when such behavior modifications serve only institutional convenience.

44. No resident shall have any of his organs removed for the purpose of transplantation without compliance with the procedures set forth in Standard 30 and after a court hearing on such transplantation in which the resident is represented by a guardian *ad litem.* This standard shall apply to any other surgical procedure which is undertaken for reasons other than therapeutic benefit to the resident.

45. Each resident of the institution shall be evaluated or re-evaluated as to his mental, emotional, social, and physical condition within 90 days of the date of the stipulation. Such evaluation or re-evaluation shall be conducted by an interdisciplinary team or Qualified Mental Retardation Professionals who shall use recognized tests and examination procedures. Each resident's guardian, next of kin, or legal representative shall be contacted and their readiness to make provisions for the resident's care in the community shall be ascertained.

46. No person shall be admitted to any public-supported residential institution caring for mentally retarded persons unless such institution meets the above standards.

47. Each resident discharged to the community shall have a program of transitional habilitation assistance.

(signed) _____

JAMES JERRY WOOD, SR.
ASSISTANT ATTORNEY GENERAL
502 Washington Avenue
Montgomery, Alabama 36104

_____
GEORGE DEAN
Post Office Box 248
Destin, Florida

_____ATTORNEYS FOR PLAINTIFFS

JOHN J. COLEMAN
SPECIAL ASSISTANT ATTORNEY GENERAL
1500 Brown Marx Building
Birmingham, Alabama 35203

ATTORNEYS FOR DEFENDANTS
     (signed) _____

STANLEY HERR
NLADA NATIONAL LAW OFFICE
1601 Connecticut Avenue, N.W.
Washington, D.C. 20009

     (signed) _____

CHARLES R. HALPERN
CENTER FOR LAW AND SOCIAL POLICY
1600 20th Street, N.W.
Washington, D.C. 20009

ATTORNEYS FOR AMICI CURIAE
AMERICAN PSYCHOLOGICAL ASSOCIATION
AMERICAN ORTHOPSYCHIATRIC ASSOCIATION
AMERICAN CIVIL LIBERTIES UNION, and
AMERICAN ASSOCIATION ON MENTAL DEFICIENCY

United States District Court for the Eastern District of Wisconsin

LESSARD v. SCHMIDT: ORDER OF JUDGMENT

The opinion in this case was released October 18, 1972, and appears at 349 F. Supp. 1078. Nine months later this court ordered "that judgment be and hereby is entered in accordance with the Opinion heretofore entered." Defendants appealed to the Supreme Court. On January 14, 1974, the Supreme Court remanded the case because the judgment did not meet the specificity requirements for injunctive orders of Fed. R. Civ. P. 65(d).

Pursuant to remand, this court set a briefing schedule and heard arguments on plaintiffs' proposed judgment order on May 9. The following order is hereby entered to provide the declaratory and injunctive relief to which the court in its original opinion held plaintiffs were entitled:

IT IS ORDERED that final judgment in favor of plaintiff ALBERTA LESSARD, and the class she represents, and against defendants WILBUR J. SCHMIDT, as Secretary of the Wisconsin Department of Health and Social Services; LEONARD GANSER, as Director of the Wisconsin State Division of Mental Hygiene; DR. GEORGE CURRIER, as Director of the Milwaukee County Mental Health Center; BERT W. PYLE, JR., as Administrator of the Milwaukee County Mental Health Center; DR. KEVIN KENNEDY, as a psychiatrist employed by the Milwaukee County Mental Health Center; JUDGE CHRIST T. SERAPHIM, as Judge for Milwaukee County, Wisconsin, and their officers, agents, employees, servants and their successors and those persons acting in active concert or participation with them, is hereby granted and ordered entered as the judgment in this action as follows:

Class Action

This action is properly maintained as a class action under Fed. R. Civ. P. 23(b) (2). The class represented by plaintiff ALBERTA LESSARD includes all persons 18 years of age or older who are being held or will be held involuntarily pursuant to any emergency, temporary or permanent commitment provision of the Wisconsin involuntray commitment statute.

Declaratory Judgment

1. The Wisconsin civil commitment procedures contained in the State Mental Health Act, Chapter 51, WISCONSIN STATUTES (1971), are declared to be unconstitutional under the Due Process Clause of the Fourteenth Amendment to the United States Constitution in the following respects:

Written and Oral Notice of Rights

a. Section 51.02(1), WISCONSIN STATUTES (1971), is declared invalid in that it fails to require that all persons undergoing mental commitment procedures under Section 51.01, WISCONSIN STATUTES (1971), be provided with a written and oral notice informing them of (1) the factual basis for their detention; (2) their right to a jury trial; (3) the standards upon which they may be detailed; (4) the names of the examining physicians and all other persons who may testify in favor of their continued detention; and (5) a summary of the proposed testimony of those who may testify in favor of their commitment.

Omission of Written Notice

B. Section 51.02, WISCONSIN STATUTES (1971), is further declared invalid in that it authorizes the omission of the service of the required notice;

Probable Cause Hearing

C. Sections 51.04(1), (2) and (3), WISCONSIN STATUTES

(1971), are declared invalid in that they permit detention of persons for periods in excess of 48 hours without a judicial hearing to determine whether or not probable cause exists to believe such persons are both mentally ill and dangerous to themselves or others, and in that they fail to require (1) that counsel be appointed sufficiently in advance of said hearing adequately to prepare a defense; (2) that the persons detained and members of their families be given notice of the probable cause hearing where with reasonable diligence the families can be located prior to the hearing; and (3) that the persons subject to the proceedings have the unwaivable right to be present and an opportunity to be heard at said probable cause hearing.

Privilege Against Self-Incrimination

D. Chapter 51, WISCONSIN STATUTES (1971), is declared invalid in that it fails to provide that persons involuntarily detained pursuant to its provision be informed of their due process right against self-incrimination.

Detention Pending Commitment Hearing

E. Sections 51.04(1), (2), and (3) and 51.03, WISCONSIN STATUTES (1971), are declared invalid in that they permit the detention of those awaiting involuntary commitment proceedings for periods in excess of fourteen (14) days without a full hearing on the necessity for commitment.

Commitment Hearing

F. Sections 51.02(2) and 51.02(4), WISCONSIN STATUTES (1971), are declared invalid in that they authorize a hearing procedure for the commitment of the allegedly mentally ill which (1) fails to guarantee to persons subject to the proceedings the right to be represented by adversary counsel and to be appointed said counsel if indigent; (2) fails to require the application of the rules of evidence including the hearsay rule; (3) permits the introduction of psychiatric and other expert evidence without the persons having been given the benefit of the privilege against self-incrimination; and (4) permits involuntary civil commitment without proof beyond a reasonable doubt that the persons are both mentally ill and dangerous.

Standards for Commitment

G. Sections 51.02 (5) and 51.05, WISCONSIN STATUTES (1971), are hereby declared valid insofar as they require that prior to a judicial order for commitment there must be a finding beyond reasonable doubt that (a) the subjects of the hearing are mentally ill; (b) the subjects of the hearing are dangerous to themselves or others based at minimum upon a recent act, attempt or threat to do substantial harm; (c) all available less drastic alternatives to commitment to a mental hospital or institution have been investigated; and (d) all available less drastic alternatives to commitment to a mental hospital or institution are unsuitable.

2. It is hereby declared that the order adjudging the named plaintiff, ALBERTA LESSARD, mentally ill and in need of commitment is unconstitutional and invalid.

3. It is hereby declared that the unnamed plaintiffs, all persons 18 years of age or older who are being held or will be held involuntarily pursuant to any emergency, temporary or permanent commitment procedure which does not comply with the declarations of paragraphs one and four of this Order are unconstitutionally held.

4. It is hereby declared that all persons who are or will become the subjects of a commitment proceeding pursuant to Chapter 51, WISCONSIN STATUTES (1971), are entitled to:

Written and Oral Notice of Rights

A. Written and oral notice of (1) the right not to converse with the examining physicians; (2) the fact that anything said to the examining physician may be used as evidence against them at the commitment hearing; (3) the right to consult with counsel, retained or appointed, before requests are made that they sign a voluntary commitment form; (4) the right to access to counsel sufficiently in advance of any hearing adequately to prepare a defense, and to appointment of counsel, if indigent; (5) the right to refuse medication which renders persons unable to adequately prepare to defend themselves; (6) the exact time and place of the probable cause hearing, and the factual basis for detention. The notice specified in (6) shall be provided to the persons and, if they can be located, to immediate families.

Probable Cause Hearing

B. A judicial hearing within forty-eight (48) hours (Saturdays, Sundays and holidays excluded) of detention to determine whether or not probable cause exists to believe persons are both mentally ill and dangerous to themselves or others at which hearing the persons shall have (1) the unwaivable right to be present and to be heard and (2) to be represented by adversary counsel, appointed sufficiently in advance of said hearing adequately to prepare a defense.

Written Notice of the Final Hearing

C. Notice of (1) the date, time and place of the scheduled final hearing; (2) the factual basis for detention; (3) the right to jury trial and the necessity of finding of both mental illness and dangerousness before commitment may be ordered; and (4) the names of examining physicians and all other persons who may testify in favor of continued detention and a summary of their proposed testimony, all to be given sufficiently in advance of scheduled court proceedings so that reasonable opportunity to prepare will be afforded, and in no case to be given less than 96 hours prior to the final hearing.

Commitment Hearing

D. A full hearing within fourteen (14) days of the original detention wherein: (1) persons alleged to be mentally ill are present and are represented by adversary counsel; (2) the rules of evidence, including hearsay rules, are properly applied; (3) the findings and standard of proof necessary for an order of commitment are "mental illness and imminent dangerousness to self or others beyond a reasonable doubt" based at minimum upon a recent act, attempt or threat to do substantial harm; and (4) a showing to the court by evidence "beyond a reasonable doubt" that all less drastic alternatives to commitment to a state or county mental health hospital or institution have been investigated and are unsuitable or unavailable before said commitment can be ordered. Less drastic alternatives shall include but shall not be limited to out-patient treatment, day or night treatment in a hospital, placement in the custody of a friend or relative, placement in a nursing home or other community based facility, referral to a community mental health clinic and home health aide services.

Injunctive Relief

IT IS FURTHER ORDERED that defendant SERAPHIM and his officers, agents, servants, employees, successors and those persons in active concert or participation with him who receive actual notice of this Order are hereby enjoined to ensure that prior to the issuance of an order of commitment under Chapter 51, WISCONSIN STATUTES (1971), in all future commitment proceedings the persons subject to the proceedings are provided:

Written and Oral Notice of Rights

5. Written and oral notice of (A) the right not to converse with the examining physicians; (B) the fact that anything said to the examining physicians may be used as evidence against them at the commitment hearing; (C) the right to consult with counsel, retained or appointed, before requests are made that they sign a voluntary commitment form; (D) the right to access to counsel sufficiently in advance of any hearing adequately to prepare a defense, and to appointment of counsel, if indigent; (E) the right to refuse medication which renders persons unable adequately to

prepare to defend themselves; (F) the exact time and place of the probable cause hearing, and the factual basis for detention. The notice specified in (F) shall be provided to the persons and, if they can be located, to their immediate families.

Probable Cause Hearing

6. A probable cause hearing within forty-eight (48) hours (Saturdays, Sundays and holidays excluded) of their apprehension to determine whether probable cause exists that they are both mentally ill and dangerous to themselves or others at which hearing the persons shall have: (A) the unwaivable right to be present and to be heard and (B) to be represented by adversary counsel, appointed sufficiently in advance of said hearing adequately to prepare a defense.

Written Notice of the Final Hearing

7. Notice of (A) the date, time and place of the scheduled final hearing; (B) the factual basis for detention; (C) the right to jury trial and the necessity of finding of both mental illness and dangerousness before commitment may be ordered; and (D) the names of examining physicians and all other persons who may testify in favor of continued detention, and a summary of their proposed testimony, all to be given sufficiently in advance of scheduled court proceedings so that reasonable opportunity to prepare will be afforded, and in no case to be given less than 96 hours prior to the final hearing.

Commitment Hearing

8. A full hearing within fourteen (14) days of the original detention wherein: (A) persons alleged to be mentally ill are present and are represented by adversary counsel; (B) the rules of evidence, including hearsay rules, are properly applied; (C) the findings and standard of proof necessary for an order of commitment are "mental illness and imminent dangerousness to self or others beyond a reasonable doubt" based at minimum upon a recent act,

attempt or threat to do substantial harm; and (D) those attempting to commit any persons must show the court by evidence beyond a reasonable doubt that all less drastic alternatives to commitment to a state or county mental health hospital or institution have been investigated and are unsuitable or unavailable before said commitment can be ordered. Less drastic alternatives shall include but shall not be limited to out-patient treatment, day or night treatment in a hospital, placement in the custody of a friend or relative, placement in a nursing home or other community based facility, referral to a community mental health clinic and home health aide services.

IT IS FURTHER ORDERED that defendants CURRIER, SCHMIDT and GANSER and their officers, agents, employees, servants and their successors and those persons in active concert or participation with them, who receive actual notice of this Order are hereby enjoined to provide:

9. Reasonable access by attorneys for plaintiffs to the grounds and facilities of all mental hospitals and institutions, to their individual clients and to the institutional and hospital records pertaining to the clients' involuntary commitments; and

IT IS FURTHER ORDERED that defendant SERAPHIM and his officers, agents, servants, employees, successors and those persons in active concert or participation with him who receive actual notice of this Order are hereby enjoined to provide:

10. Reasonable access by the plaintiffs and their attorneys to court records pertaining to their past or present involuntary commitments; and

IT IS FURTHER ORDERED that defendants SCHMIDT, GANSER, CURRIER and SERAPHIM and their officers, agents, servants, employees, successors and those persons acting in active concert or participation with them who receive actual notice of this Order are hereby enjoined to provide:

11. Notation upon all medical and court records of any person involuntarily committed pursuant to Chapter 51 prior to October 18, 1972, that such person was either discharged or released prusuant to the *Lessard* opinion or was recommitted according to the procedures required by the *Lessard* opinion; such notation to be entered upon written demand of the person or his attorney.

Dated this 15th day of August, 1974.

(signed) _____

The Honorable Robert A. Sprecher
United States Circuit Judge

(signed) _____

The Honorable John W. Reynolds
United States District Judge

(signed) _____

The Honorable Myron L. Gordon
United States District Judge

Appendix III

United States District Court for
the District of Columbia

SOUDER v. BRENNAN: DECLARATORY JUDGMENT
AND INJUNCTION ORDER

This cause came before this Court upon plaintiffs' motion for summary judgment and defendants' combined motion to dismiss and for summary judgment. Upon the entire record before this Court including the pleadings, interrogatories and affidavits, and upon the Memorandum Opinion of the Court dated November 14, 1973, it is hereby ORDERED that plaintiffs' motion for summary judgment is granted, and defendants' motions are denied. The Court having ruled that the Secretary of Labor has a duty to implement reasonable enforcement efforts applying the minimum wage and overtime compensation provisions of the Fair Labor Standards Act to patient-workers at non-Federal institutions for the residential care of the mentally ill and/or mentally retarded, it is further ordered, adjudged and declared:

A. NOTIFICATION TO THE CLASS. That the Secretary of Labor, his officers, agents, servants, and all persons acting or claiming to act in his behalf and interest (hereinafter, the "Secretary"), undertake the following notification activities:

(1) Within 120 days from the date of the Order, notify the Superintendent of each non-Federal facility for the residential care of the mentally ill and/or mentally retarded, and the chief executive officer or officers of the supervising state agency for mental health and/or mental retardation, that they have the same statutory responsibility to compensate patient-workers as non-patient workers, and that defendants intend to enforce the minimum wage and overtime compensation provisions of the Fair Labor Standards Act on behalf of patient-workers.

(2) Within 120 days from the date of the Order, inform the Superintendent of each non-Federal facility for the residential

248

care of the mentally ill and/or mentally retarded, and the chief executive officer or officers of the supervising state agency for mental health and/or mental retardation of their obligation to maintain records of hours worked and other conditions of employment under 29 U.S.C. 211(c) and 29 C.F.R. Part 516 for patient-workers, just as is required for non-patient employees at the same facilities.

(3) Within 120 days from the date of this Order, contact the Superintendent of each non-Federal facility for the residential care of the mentally ill and/or mentally retarded and request that he inform patient-workers at his facility of their rights under the Fair Labor Standards Act. Indications that proper attention has been given to informing the patient-workers of their rights will be:

a. That the Superintendent has notified *in writing* every resident and his guardian of his rights under the Fair Labor Standards Act, as declared in this decision;

b. That copies of such written notifications have been posted on every living unit of residential facilities for the mentally ill and/or mentally retarded;

c. That efforts have also been made to notify all residents *orally* of their rights — e.g., by holding group meetings for present residents and by establishing procedures under which each new resident will be notified of his rights within one week of his admission. In order to increase the chances that plaintiffs will fully comprehend such oral presentations, defendants may suggest to the Superintendents and to the chief executive officers of the supervising state agencies that representatives of concerned organizations be invited to observe and perhaps to participate at such meetings;

d. That non-patient employees of all non-Federal facilities for the residential care of the mentally ill and/or mentally retarded and their collective bargaining representatives or other representatives who deal with the employer on their behalf with respect to wages, hours, or other terms and conditions of employment, have been notified of this decision.

B.   REASONABLE ENFORCEMENT ACTIVITIES. Within one year from the date of this Order, defendants shall contact every institution to which the Order applies so as to establish and implement the necessary procedures (including any special certifications under 29 U.S.C. 214) whereby every patient-worker in such institutions will be paid the wages due him. After the Department of Labor has made its initial efforts to aid the institutions in establishing their procedures for paying wages, it shall continue in the second year to give attention to investigation and enforcement of employment situations affecting the patient-workers. Thereafter, "reasonable" enforcement shall be defined to include those activities which are necessary to ensure the benefits of 29 U.S.C. 206, and 207, to which patient-workers are entitled.

C. IMPLEMENTATION REPORTS. That the Secretary shall keep written records of his enforcement activities, which shall be available to the public through the Labor Department's Advisory Committee on Sheltered Workshops as six-month intervals. These reports should include a description of the activities taken to comply with the Order; the number of investigations of alleged violations of rights of patient-workers under the Fair Labor Standards Act (including a breakdown at each such establishment), and the reason for such investigations; and the disposition of each investigation confirming statutory violations, including lawsuits, settlements, and other enforcement activities.

D. COSTS. That Court costs be taxed to defendants.

(signed) _____

Aubrey E. Robinson, Jr.
Judge

December 7, 1973

AUTHOR INDEX

251

SUBJECT INDEX

A

Abendberg, 61
Accreditation (see also: Joint Commission on Accreditation of Hospitals), 75, 76-78, 82
Adaptive behavior, 6-10
Advocacy, 105, 150-160, 199-200
  Advocate, duties of, 153-154
  Citizen, 152, 157-158
  Legal, 112-113, 121, 158-160
  State, 154-157
Allis Training Center, 211
American Academy of Pediatrics, 73
American Association on Mental Deficiency, 4, 6, 8, 61, 66-67, 70, 76, 152, 166-167
Anna State Hospital, 212
Attitudes,
  Europe, 164
  Parent, 167-178
  Public, 161-167
  School, 164-166
Austin State School, 212

B

Beatrice State Home, 120
Burnham v. *Department of Public Health of the State of Georgia*, 100

C

Cambridge State School, 109
Central points of referral, 144-145
Central Wisconsin Colony, 211
Children's rights, 118-122
Citizens Advocacy Council for the Developmentally Disabled, Inc., 105
Cloverbottom Developmental Center, 211
Coastal Center, 211

Community services, 129-148, 160-161
Continuum of care, 143-145
Conway Center, 211
Corpus Christi State School, 211
Council for Exceptional Children, 152
County responsibilities, 117

D

Deinstitutionalization, 125-186
  Advocacy, 151-160
  As an attitude, 125-126
  As a principle, 126-128
  As a process, 128-129
  Back-up services, 151
  Community placement, 171-180
  Current status and trend, 168-180
  Definitions of, 125-129
  Goal of, 177
  Local authority, 148-149
  Standard setting and monitoring, 149-151
Dixon State School, 211

E

Educational achievement, 33, 43-44
ENCORE, 178
  Developmental model, 68, 71
Elizabeth Ludeman Center, 211
Expeditor, 144-145

F

Fair Labor Standards Act, 107, 113, 114, 122
Fernald,Walter, 62
Florida
  "Bill of Rights", 180
  Human Rights Advocacy Committees, 199
Florida State Hospital, 100

255